GENESIS

Putting the Pieces Together

An Examination of the Chronological Events
in the Book of Genesis

john † barr

Jn. 3:30

Unless otherwise indicated, all Scripture quotations are taken from the King James Version of the Bible.

Verse marked NAB is taken from the New American Bible, revised edition © 2010, 1991, 1986, 1970 Confraternity of Christian Doctrine, Washington, D.C. All Rights Reserved.

All emphasis added to Scripture quotations are the author's.

All entries indicated by a "#" are firm and scripturally verifiable.
All entries indicated by a "?" are accompanied by supporting evidence of high probability *.

* Probable - supported by evidence strong enough to establish presumption but not proof.
(Merriam-Webster's 11th Collegiate Dictionary)

Questions or comments – email: genesispieces@att.net

DEDICATION

I wish to dedicate this book to my Father in heaven. He continually revealed insight into questions I have pondered and others have posed for many years. Often I encountered investigative obstacles that caused me to entertain the thought that I was treading uncharted territory into which I should not enter. No sooner did I consider abandoning the project, than a revelation would overwhelm me that I knew was beyond my human logic. The assurance that it was from my Father in heaven was the clear supporting scriptural evidence that would flood into my mind and compel me to forge ahead. Thank you Father for your many blessings.

To Mark & Dawn
May this book stimulate
you to dig deeper into Scripture.
John T. Bass
5/20/14

The Author – john † barr
Former State Tax Investigator, Corporate Internal Investigator and
Christian College teacher.

The Author's purpose: to emulate the Berean's commendable approach
(Acts 17:11) of searching the scriptures.

> Acts 17: ¹⁰ *And the brethren immediately sent away Paul and Silas by night
> unto Berea: who coming thither went into the synagogue of the Jews.* ¹¹ *These
> were more noble than those in Thessalonica, in that they received the word
> with all readiness of mind, and searched the scriptures daily, whether those
> things were so.*

The Author's perspective regarding the dating of ancient events:
It seems that no two chronologists agree on every date for every Biblical or
secular event of ancient eras. For that reason, the widely accepted creation
date of 4004 B.C. (established by Archbishop James Ussher) is the reference
date for this Genealogical study of the book of Genesis.

The Reader's prerogative:
If the reader prefers a reference date further back in time than 4004 B.C.,
simply subtract the 4004 B.C. date from the preferred earlier date; then add
that number to the dates listed in this study.

Example:
If an earlier date of 10000 B.C. is favored, subtract 4004 from 10000 = 5996
Then, add 5996 to the dates listed in this study.

Birth of Noah		2948 B.C.
	+	5996
		8944 B.C.

If the reader prefers a reference date further forward in time than 4004 B.C.,
simply subtract the preferred later date from 4004 B.C.; then subtract that
number from the dates listed in this study.

Example:
If a later date of 3000 B.C. is favored, subtract 3000 from 4004 = 1004
Then, subtract 1004 from the dates listed in this study.

Birth of Noah		2948 B.C.
	-	1004
		1944 B.C.

How to **READ** this book

(read an entire Chapter before studying the Chapter)

<u>First</u> - note the topic title and its associated date reference (see 1).

<u>Second</u> - read the Scripture associated with that topic title (see 2).

<u>Third</u> - read **ONLY** the **Probability Scenario** (see 3).
       (information below the **Probability Scenario** is study material)

1. **The Pre-Existent Christ –**   [Undated]
2.   Jn.1:1-2 [1] In the beginning was the Word, and the Word was with God, and the Word was God. [2] The same was in the beginning with God.

3.

> **Probability Scenario**
> It appears that Christ existed before creation and "*… was in the beginning with God*" (v.2 & see 1, 2 & 3).

How to **STUDY** this book

(read an entire Chapter before studying the Chapter)

<u>First</u> - repeat the steps above.

<u>Second</u> - consider the **Probability Scenario** in conjunction with a careful study of the **Supporting Evidence** and associated information provided (see below).

> **Probability Scenario**
> It appears that Christ existed before creation and "*… was in the beginning with God*" (v.2 & see 1, 2 & 3).
> **Supporting Evidence**
> 1. "Word" beginning with a capital "W" indicates it is a proper noun. A proper noun is a specific name of a person, place or thing.
> 2. It appears that this proper noun "Word" indicates a person. "*… his name is called The Word of God*" (Rev.19:13).
> 3. "*… his name*" (Rev.19:13) refers to Jesus Christ according to the context of Revelation 19.
> **Note**
> "*And the Word was made flesh, and dwelt among us …*" (Jn.1:14)

CONTENTS

Chapter 1

Eternity Past

The Pre-Existence of Deity –   [Undated]

Psa.90:2 - 2 Before the mountains were brought forth, or ever thou hadst formed the earth and the world, even from everlasting to everlasting, thou *art* God.

The Pre-Existent Christ –   [Undated]

Jn.1:1-2 - 1 In the beginning was the Word, and the Word was with God, and the Word was God. 2 The same was in the beginning with God.

Probability Scenario

It appears that Christ existed before creation and "*… was in the beginning with God*" (v.2 & see 1, 2 & 3).

Supporting Evidence

1. "Word" beginning with a capital "W" indicates it is a proper noun. A proper noun is a specific name of a person, place or thing.
2. It appears that this proper noun "Word" indicates a person. "*… his name is called The Word of God*" (Rev.19:13).
3. "*… his name*" (Rev.19:13), refers to Jesus Christ according to the context of Revelation 19.

Note

"*And the Word was made flesh, and dwelt among us …*" (Jn.1:14)

Chapter 2

Creation

The Origin of Creation - (heaven/angels/earth)   [First Day – 4004 B.C.#]
Gen.1:1 - [1] In the beginning God created the heaven and the earth.

Probability Scenario
It would seem that satan and all the angelic host appears to have been created *"In the beginning* [after] *God created the heaven and* [before] *the earth"* (v.1 & see 1).
Supporting Evidence
1. Angels are destined to shout for joy at the laying of *"… the corner stone"* of the earth (Job 38:6). (see **The Angels Rejoiced** – [p.4])

Creation Intended for Habitation –
Isa.45:18 - [18] For thus saith the LORD that created the heavens; God himself that formed the earth and made it; he hath established it, he created it not in vain, he formed it to be inhabited: I *am* the LORD; and *there is* none else.

Probability Scenario		
God seems to prepare the habitat first then the inhabitants (see below).		
Supporting Evidence		
Habitat	**Inhabitants**	
Day 1 Heaven & Earth (Gen.1:1)	Day 1 Angels (Job 38:7)	
	Day 4 Sun, Moon & Stars (Gen.1:14-19)	
Day 2 Sky & Water (Gen.1:6-8)	Day 5 Fowl & Fish (Gen.1:20-23)	
Day 3 Land & Seas (Gen.1:9-10)	Day 3 Vegetation (Gen.1:11-12)	
	Day 6 Animals & Humans (Gen.1:24-27)	

Description of Pre-Formed Creation –

Gen.1:2 - ² And the earth was without form, and void; and darkness was on the face of the deep. And the Spirit of God moved upon the face of the waters.

Probability Scenario

At this point in time, it is apparently still in the darkness of the first day (v.2). satan would have been in existence less than 12 hours (see 1). It will be at least another 12 hours before the first day of creation ends; and even before the first day ends, all the angels (including satan) will be shouting for joy (see 2).

Supporting Evidence

1 **Sabbath Established** – (literal 24-hour days) [p.9]
2 **The Angels Rejoiced** – [p.4]

Points to Ponder

A. It has been said that Lucifer (satan) incited an angelic rebellion against God in Genesis 1 between verses 1 & 2, resulting in satan's fall /exile from heaven (see a & b).
B. There are some who say that the words "… *was without form, and void*" (v.1) would be better rendered became without form, and void as a result of satan's rebellion (see c & d).

Considerations

a. It appears that satan did not fall (exile from heaven) between verses 1 & 2 (Job 38:4-7). (see **The Angels Rejoiced** – [p.4])
b. It would seem that within the context of v.2 "*And the Spirit of God moved upon the face of the waters*", that God maintained complete control over His creation.
c. The words "… *was without form, and void*" clearly describe the <u>actual</u> condition of the earth in its pre-formed state. The words <u>became without form, and void</u> would imply an <u>altered</u> condition of the earth from its original state due to some catastrophic event such as an angelic rebellion incited by satan which apparently did not occur (see a & b).
d. It would seem that the words "… *without form, and void*" clearly indicate "unformed and unfilled". It appears that God initially put all the elements in place and then formed His creation in preparation to fill His creation (see **Creation Intended for Habitation** – [p.3])

The Angels Rejoiced –   [First Day – 4004 B.C.#]

Job.38:7 - ⁷ When the morning stars sang together, and all the sons of God shouted for joy?

Probability Scenario

Apparently, there was no rebellion in heaven, only total agreement (see 1 & 2). It is likely that the angels were created immediately after their habitation was spoken into existence (see 3) and before "… *God said, Let there be light*" (Gen.1:3 & see 4). One can only imagine the joy the angels must have experienced when God lit up His magnificanct creation.

1. It would appear that God dispelled the question of rebellion in His discourse with Job.

   Job 38:4-7 [4] Where were you when I laid the foundations of the earth? declare, if you have understanding. [5] Who has laid the measures thereof, if you know? or who has stretched the line on it? [6] Whereupon are the foundations thereof fastened? or who laid the corner stone thereof; [7] When the morning stars sang together, and all the sons of God shouted for joy?

2. It would seem that if "... **all** *the sons of God shouted for joy*" (v.7), that "**all**" would include Lucifer and his <u>future</u> cohorts.

3. **Creation Intended for Habitation** – [p.3]

4. **Light** – (darkness/light) [p.5]

Description of the Forming of Creation –

Gen.2:4 - [4] These *are* the generations of the heavens and of the earth when they were created, in the day that the LORD God made the earth and the heavens,

Light – (darkness/light)   [First Day – 4004 B.C.#]

Gen.1:3-5 – [3] And God said, Let there be light: and there was light. [4] And God saw the light, that *it was* good: and God divided the light from the darkness. [5] And God called the light Day, and the darkness he called Night. And the evening and the morning were the first day.

Sky / Water -   [Second Day – 4004 B.C.#]

Gen.1:6-8 – [6] And God said, Let there be a firmament in the midst of the waters, and let it divide the waters from the waters. [7] And God made the firmament, and divided the waters which *were* under the firmament from the waters which *were* above the firmament: and it was so. [8] And God called the firmament Heaven. And the evening and the morning were the second day.

Land / Seas / Vegetation -   [Third Day – 4004 B.C.#]

Gen.1:9-13 – [9] And God said, Let the waters under the heaven be gathered together unto one place, and let the dry *land* appear: and it was so. [10] And God called the dry *land* Earth; and the gathering together of the waters called he Seas: and God saw that *it was* good. [11] And God said, Let the earth bring forth grass, the herb yielding seed, *and* the fruit tree yielding fruit after his kind, whose seed *is* in itself, upon the earth: and it was so. [12] And the earth brought forth grass, *and* herb yielding seed after his kind, and the tree yielding fruit, whose seed *was* in itself, after his kind: and God saw that *it was* good. [13] And the evening and the morning were the third day.

Gen.2:5-6 – ⁵ And every plant of the field before it was in the earth, and every herb of the field before it grew: for the LORD God had not caused it to rain upon the earth, and *there was* not a man to till the ground. ⁶ But there went up a mist from the earth, and watered the whole face of the ground.

Sun / Moon / Stars -   Fourth Day – 4004 B.C.#]
Gen.1:14-19 – ¹⁴ And God said, Let there be lights in the firmament of the heaven to divide the day from the night; and let them be for signs, and for seasons, and for days, and years: ¹⁵ And let them be for lights in the firmament of the heaven to give light upon the earth: and it was so. ¹⁶ And God made two great lights; the greater light to rule the day, and the lesser light to rule the night: *he made* the stars also. ¹⁷ And God set them in the firmament of the heaven to give light upon the earth, ¹⁸ And to rule over the day and over the night, and to divide the light from the darkness: and God saw that *it was* good. ¹⁹ And the evening and the morning were the fourth day.

Fish / Fowl -   [Fifth Day – 4004 B.C.#]
Gen.1:20-23 – ²⁰ And God said, Let the waters bring forth abundantly the moving creature that has life, and fowl that may fly above the earth in the open firmament of heaven. ²¹ And God created great whales, and every living creature that moves, which the waters brought forth abundantly, after their kind, and every winged fowl after his kind: and God saw that it was good. ²² And God blessed them, saying, Be fruitful, and multiply, and fill the waters in the seas, and let fowl multiply in the earth. ²³ And the evening and the morning were the fifth day.

Animals / Man ("Adam") -   [Sixth Day – 4004 B.C.#]
Gen.1:24-26 – ²⁴ And God said, Let the earth bring forth the living creature after his kind, cattle, and creeping thing, and beast of the earth after his kind: and it was so. ²⁵ And God made the beast of the earth after his kind, and cattle after their kind, and every thing that creepeth upon the earth after his kind: and God saw that *it was* good.

²⁶ And God said, Let us make man in our image, after our likeness: and let them have dominion over the fish of the sea, and over the fowl of the air, and over the cattle, and over all the earth, and over every creeping thing that creepeth upon the earth.

Gen.2:7 – ⁷ And the LORD God formed man *of* the dust of the ground, and breathed into his nostrils the breath of life; and man became a living soul.

Probability Scenario

It would seem that prior to this point in time there would be no logical reason for satan to incite rebellion against God (see 1). God Himself declared at various stages of His creation that "... *it was good*" (see 2). It is very likely that even a superior being such as satan would require a little time to compare himself with other angels and the creatures of the earth in order to become aware of his superiority (see 3). It seems that by the sixth day satan might be very aware of what a magnificent creation he was. It is possible that at this point in time he might also be entertaining prideful thoughts – is not the seed of pride (see 4) planted in the soil of evil?

Supporting Evidence

1. satan is destined to incite rebellion in the form of disobedience/sin among mankind (see **Deception of Humankind** – [p.11]).
2. God Himself, speaking of His creation, declared "... *it was good*" (Gen.1:4, 10, 12, 18, 21, 25).
3. God's word makes it very clear that satan's pride caused him to fall into condemnation (1Tim.3:6).
4. God declared His intention to create man and give them dominion over everything on the earth (v.26).

Point to Ponder

Do we get **evil** from the D**evil** or do we get the D**evil** from **evil**?

Garden of Eden -   [Sixth Day – 4004 B.C.#]

Gen.2:8-14 – 8 And the LORD God planted a garden eastward in Eden; and there he put the man whom he had formed. 9 And out of the ground made the LORD God to grow every tree that is pleasant to the sight, and good for food; the tree of life also in the midst of the garden, and the tree of knowledge of good and evil. 10 And a river went out of Eden to water the garden; and from thence it was parted, and became into four heads. 11 The name of the first *is* Pison: that *is* it which compasseth the whole land of Havilah, where *there is* gold; 12 And the gold of that land *is* good: there *is* bdellium and the onyx stone. 13 And the name of the second river *is* Gihon: the same *is* it that compasseth the whole land of Ethiopia. 14 And the name of the third river *is* Hiddekel: that *is* it which goeth toward the east of Assyria. And the fourth river *is* Euphrates.

Adam's Residence - (God assigns conditions)   [Sixth Day – 4004 B.C.#]

Gen.2:15-17 – 15 And the LORD God took the man, and put him into the garden of Eden to dress it and to keep it.

16 And the LORD God commanded the man, saying, Of every tree of the garden thou mayest freely eat: 17 But of the tree of the knowledge of good and evil, thou shalt not eat of it: for in the day that thou eatest thereof thou shalt surely die.

Adam's Responsibility and Revelation –   [Sixth Day – 4004 B.C.#]
   Gen.2:18-20 – [18] And the LORD God said, *It is* not good that the man should be alone; I will make him an help meet for him. [19] And out of the ground the LORD God formed every beast of the field, and every fowl of the air; and brought *them* unto Adam to see what he would call them: and whatsoever Adam called every living creature, that *was* the name thereof. [20] And Adam gave names to all cattle, and to the fowl of the air, and to every beast of the field; but for Adam there was not found an help meet for him.

God Creates Woman ("Eve") -   [Sixth Day – 4004 B.C.#]
   Gen.2:21-23 – [21] And the LORD God caused a deep sleep to fall upon Adam, and he slept: and he took one of his ribs, and closed up the flesh instead thereof; [22] And the rib, which the LORD God had taken from man, made he a woman, and brought her unto the man. [23] And Adam said, This *is* now bone of my bones, and flesh of my flesh: she shall be called Woman, because she was taken out of Man.

God Establishes Marriage –   [Sixth Day – 4004 B.C.#]
   Gen.2:24 – [24] Therefore shall a man leave his father and his mother, and shall cleave unto his wife: and they shall be one flesh.

Adam and Eve – (in innocence of sin)   [Sixth Day – 4004 B.C.#]
   Gen.2:25 – [25] And they were both naked, the man and his wife, and were not ashamed.

Creation of Mankind Concludes –   [Sixth Day – 4004 B.C.#]
   Gen.1:27 – [27] So God created man in his *own* image, in the image of God created he him; male and female created he them.

   Gen.5:2 – [2] Male and female created he them; and blessed them, and called their name Adam, in the day when they were created.

God Appoints His Co-Regents - (with responsibilities) [Sixth Day – 4004 B.C.#]
   Gen.1:28-30 – [28] And God blessed them, and God said unto them, Be fruitful, and multiply, and replenish the earth, and subdue it: and have dominion over the fish of the sea, and over the fowl of the air, and over every living thing that moveth upon the earth.
   [29] And God said, Behold, I have given you every herb bearing seed, which is on the face of all the earth, and every tree, in the which is the fruit of a tree yielding seed; to you it shall be for meat. [30] And to every beast of the earth, and to every fowl of the air, and to every thing that creepeth on

the earth, wherein there is life, I have given every green herb for meat: and it was so.

Probability Scenario

It would seem that prior to this point in time there would be no logical reason for satan to incite rebellion against God (see 1). By this time it is probable that satan has indeed become fully aware of his exalted position in heaven and his superiority over other angels and the creatures of the earth (see 2). That seed of pride (see 3), likely planted earlier this same day could now be germinating in the soil of evil (see 4). satan's pride could be in the process of blooming into the fulfillment of satan's destined rebellion (see 1).

Supporting Evidence

1. satan is destined to incite rebellion among mankind in the form of disobedience/sin. (see **Deception of Humankind** – [p.11])
2. God's word makes it very clear that satan's pride caused him to fall into condemnation (1Tim.3:6).
3. God declared His intention to create man and give them dominion over everything on the earth. (see **Animals / Man** ("Adam") - [p.6]).
4. God has created man and actually given them dominion over everything on the earth (v.28).

Creation Completed – "by him" (Jesus)   [Sixth Day – 4004 B.C.#]

Gen.1:31 – [31] And God saw every thing that he had made, and, behold, *it was* very good. And the evening and the morning were the sixth day.

Gen.2:1 – [1] Thus the heavens and the earth were finished, and all the host of them.

Jn.1:3 – [3] All things were made <u>by him</u>; and without him was not any thing made that was made.

Sabbath Established - (literal 24 hour days)   Seventh Day – 4004 B.C.#]

Gen.2:2-3 – [2] And on the seventh day God ended his work which he had made; and he rested on the seventh day from all his work which he had made. [3] And God blessed the seventh day, and sanctified it: because that in it he had rested from all his work which God created and made so.

Probability Scenario

There is much debate concerning the rendering of the word "*day*" associated with the days of creation. Moses clearly equates the six work days of the Israelites to the six days of God's work of creation, followed by one day of rest (see 3, 4, 5 & Note).

Supporting Evidence

1. It is clear that the word "*day*" can be used to reference different spans of time. In Genesis chapter 1 & 2, there are several different uses.

---

       a.   the hours of light exclusive of the hours of darkness
           (Gen.1:5a, 14a, 16, 18).
       b.   a 24-hour period
           (Gen.1:5b, 8, 13, 14b, 19, 23, 31, 2:2a, 2b, 3, 17).
       c.   a short or long period of time (Gen.2:4)
       d.   a lifetime (not in the context of Genesis 1 & 2)
       e.   an era (not in the context of Genesis 1 & 2)
       f.   an epoch (not in the context of Genesis 1 & 2)

2. Consider the context in which the word "day" is used and other scriptural references specifically applicable to the context (see 4 & 5 below).

3. Ex.20:8-11 *8 Remember the sabbath day, to keep it holy. 9 Six days shalt thou labour, and do all thy work: 10 But the seventh day is the sabbath of the LORD thy God: in it thou shalt not do any work, thou, nor thy son, nor thy daughter, thy manservant, nor thy maidservant, nor thy cattle, nor thy stranger that is within thy gates: 11 For <u>in six days the LORD made heaven and earth, the sea, and all that in them is, and rested the seventh day</u>: wherefore the LORD blessed the sabbath day, and hallowed it.*

4. Ex.31:15-17 *15 Six days may work be done; but in the seventh is the sabbath of rest, holy to the LORD: whosoever doeth any work in the sabbath day, he shall surely be put to death. 16 Wherefore the children of Israel shall keep the sabbath, to observe the sabbath throughout their generations, for a perpetual covenant. 17 It is a sign between me and the children of Israel for ever: for <u>in six days the LORD made heaven and earth, and on the seventh day he rested, and was refreshed</u>.*

5. In every instance where "... the evening and the morning were the __ day", the context is clearly referencing a 24-hour period and is specifically addressed by other scriptural references.

<u>Note</u>

From these passages it is difficult to imagine that God is asking man to work for six decades, generations, centuries or eons of time and then rest for one decade, generation, century or eon of time.

Chapter 3

Fall of Man

Deception of Humankind –   [4004 B.C.?]

Gen.3:1-5 – [1] Now the serpent was more subtil than any beast of the field which the LORD God had made. And he said unto the woman, Yea, hath God said, Ye shall not eat of every tree of the garden?

[2] And the woman said unto the serpent, We may eat of the fruit of the trees of the garden: [3] But of the fruit of the tree which *is* in the midst of the garden, God hath said, Ye shall not eat of it, neither shall ye touch it, lest ye die.

[4] And the serpent said unto the woman, Ye shall not surely die: [5] For God doth know that in the day ye eat thereof, then your eyes shall be opened, and ye shall be as gods, knowing good and evil.

<u>Probability Scenario</u>

satan's destiny, to incite rebellion among mankind in the form of disobedience/sin, appears to have arrived (see 1). It seems probable that deep within satan entertained evil thoughts of wickedness and pride (see 2 & 3); and he did not rule over them (see 4). Wickedness and pride seems to have found fertile ground in satan and blossomed into such a fragrant evil that satan himself became subject to its intoxicating power; and he became defiled (see 3). Evil often appears to be a more formidable force than good, but appearances are deceiving – as is satan.

<u>Supporting Evidence</u>

1. This subtle serpent (v.1) is revealed as "... *that old serpent, called the Devil, and satan, which deceives the whole world*" (Rev.12:9).

> 2. God's Word makes it very clear that satan's pride caused him to fall into condemnation (1Tim.3:6).
> 3. Jesus said "²⁰ *That which comes out of the man, that defiles the man.* ²¹*For from within, out of the heart of men, proceed evil thoughts ...* ²² *... wickedness ... pride.* ²³*All these evil things come from within and defile the man.*" (Mk.7:22 and apparently satan).
> 4. God "*... said to Cain,* ⁷ *If you do well, shall you not be accepted? And if you do not do well, sin lies at the door. And to you shall be his desire, and you shall rule over him.*" (Gen.4:7).
>
>
> **Points to Ponder**
>
>
> A. One might question whether God created evil (see a & b).
>
>
> **Considerations**
>
>
> a. God Himself declared at various stages of His creation that "*... it was good*" (Gen.1:4, 10, 12, 18, 21, 25). "*Then God saw everything that He had made, and indeed it was very good*" (Gen.1:31).
> b. It seems apparent that to "*... do well*" (Gen.4:7) equates to "*... good*" (Gen.3:5) and to "*... not do well*" (Gen.4:7) equates to "*... evil*" (Gen.3:5).

Fall of Humankind –   [4004 B.C.?]

Gen.3:6 – ⁶ And when the woman saw that the tree *was* good for food, and that it *was* pleasant to the eyes, and a tree to be desired to make *one* wise, she took of the fruit thereof, and did eat, and gave also unto her husband with her; and he did eat.

>
>
> **Probability Scenario**
>
>
> It seems probable that in the same manner satan entertained evil thoughts, in like manner Adam and Eve did also (see 1 & 2).
>
>
> **Supporting Evidence**
>
>
> 1. Jesus said "... ²⁰ *That which comes out of the man, that defiles the man.* ²¹*For from within, out of the heart of men, proceed evil thoughts ...* ²² *... wickedness ... pride.* ²³*All these evil things come from within and defile the man.*" (Mk.7:22 and apparently woman).
> 2. **Deception of Humankind – [p.11]**
>
>
> **Note**
>
>
> The good of God is so very pure that any external alteration results in contamination.

Consequence – (guilty conscience)   [4004 B.C.?]

Gen.3:7 – ⁷ And the eyes of them both were opened, and they knew that they *were* naked; and they sewed fig leaves together, and made themselves aprons.

>
>
> **Probability Scenario**
>
>
> It appears that Adam and Eve were ashamed (v.7a) of their disobedience/sin. It seems that God is prepared to look at their act of making a covering for themselves as a feeble act of repentance (v.7b), followed by an equally feeble

act of confession (see 1).
Supporting Evidence
1. **Confession –** (Adam & Eve pass the blame) [p.13]

Confession – (Adam & Eve pass the blame)   [4004 B.C.?]

Gen.3:8-13 – 8 And they heard the voice of the LORD God walking in the garden in the cool of the day: and Adam and his wife hid themselves from the presence of the LORD God amongst the trees of the garden.

9 And the LORD God called unto Adam, and said unto him, Where *art* thou? 10 And he said, I heard thy voice in the garden, and I was afraid, because I *was* naked; and I hid myself.

11 And he said, Who told thee that thou *wast* naked? Hast thou eaten of the tree, whereof I commanded thee that thou shouldest not eat? 12 And the man said, The woman whom thou gavest *to be* with me, she gave me of the tree, and I did eat. 13 And the LORD God said unto the woman, What *is* this *that* thou hast done? And the woman said, The serpent beguiled me, and I did eat.

Judgment & Curse – (serpent/Eve/ground)   [4004 B.C.?]

Gen.3:14-19 – 14 And the LORD God said unto the serpent, Because thou hast done this, thou *art* cursed above all cattle, and above every beast of the field; upon thy belly shalt thou go, and dust shalt thou eat all the days of thy life: 15 And I will put enmity between thee and the woman, and between thy seed and her seed; it shall bruise thy head, and thou shalt bruise his heel.

16 Unto the woman he said, I will greatly multiply thy sorrow and thy conception; in sorrow thou shalt bring forth children; and thy desire *shall be* to thy husband, and he shall rule over thee.

17 And unto Adam he said, Because thou hast hearkened unto the voice of thy wife, and hast eaten of the tree, of which I commanded thee, saying, Thou shalt not eat of it: cursed *is* the ground for thy sake; in sorrow shalt thou eat *of* it all the days of thy life; 18 Thorns also and thistles shall it bring forth to thee; and thou shalt eat the herb of the field; 19 In the sweat of thy face shalt thou eat bread, till thou return unto the ground; for out of it wast thou taken: for dust thou *art*, and unto dust shalt thou return.

Probability Scenario
It seems that satan's fall into condemnation has come to fruition. He is here being judged; and a punishment of chastisement is dispensed (see 1). At this point in time, it does not appear that satan is being sentenced to his final punishment of exile from heaven, and will not be until after war breaks out in heaven with Michael and his angels (see 2, 3 & 4).
Supporting Evidence
1. God's word makes it very clear that satan's pride caused him to fall into

condemnation (1Tim.3:6 & Note).

2. Job 1:6-12; 2:1-7 states that satan, possibly two thousand years after creation, was allowed in God's presence with God even initiating what appears to be cordial conversation.

3. Possibly four thousand years after creation, Jesus' disciples, upon returning from their missionary assignment, were told by the Lord – "… I beheld satan as lightning fall from heaven" (Lk.10:18).

4. Many years after Jesus's words to His disciples (Lk.10:18), the apostle John, wrote of a vision of what appears to be satan's still future fall (exile from heaven – Rev.12:7-9).

Note

satan appears to be guilty of condemnation for succumbing to the temptation of wickedness and pride and then inciting rebellion among mankind in the form of disobedience/sin. As for Adam, God gave him the whole world and only one restriction. (see **Adam's Residence** – [p.7])

Adam Names His Wife Eve – ("… mother of all living")   [4004 B.C.?]

Gen.3:20 – ²⁰ And Adam called his wife's name Eve; because she was the mother of all living.

Probability Scenario

It is likely that at this point in time Eve has not yet brought forth children. This statement appears to indicate that Adam believes that it is God's will that they fulfill His command (see 1 & Gen.1:28), and that they will have children. It seems that Adam, in his naming of Eve (mother of all living), is making a profession of faith / belief in God (see 2 & Gen.15:6).

Supporting Evidence

1. **God Appoints His Co-Regents** – (with responsibilities) [p.8]
   "… God said unto them, Be fruitful, and multiply, and replenish the earth," (Gen.1:28)

2. **Abram Believed God** - (God counts belief as righteousness) [p.71]
   "And he believed in the LORD; and he counted it to him for righteousness." (Gen.15:6)

God Bestows Mercy – (atonement/animal sacrificed)   [4004 B.C.?]

Gen.3:21 – ²¹ Unto Adam also and to his wife did the LORD God make coats of skins, and clothed them.

Probability Scenario

It appears that God has graciously acknowledged that Adam was ashamed of his disobedience/sin (see 1 & 2) and is prepared to accept his confession (see 3 & Gen.3:12; 1Jn.1:9) and act of faith (see 4 & Note).

Supporting Evidence

1. "… the eyes of them both were opened, and they knew that they were naked; and they sewed fig leaves together" (Gen.3:7 – see **Consequence** – [p.12])

2. They "… made themselves aprons." (Gen.3:7 – see **Consequence** – [p.12])

> 3. **Confession** – (Adam & Eve pass the blame) [p.13])
> 4. **Adam Names His Wife Eve** – ("… mother of all living") [p.14]
> <u>Note</u>
> Might this be "…*faith* [tiny] *as a grain of mustard seed*" (Mat.17:20; Lk.17:6)?

Expulsion from Eden –   [4004 B.C.?]

Gen.3:22-24 – 22 And the LORD God said, Behold, the man is become as one of us, to know good and evil: and now, lest he put forth his hand, and take also of the tree of life, and eat, and live for ever: 23 Therefore the LORD God sent him forth from the garden of Eden, to till the ground from whence he was taken. 24 So he drove out the man; …

God Bestows Grace – (prevents eternal suffering)   [4004 B.C.?]

Gen.3:24 – 24 … and he placed at the east of the garden of Eden Cherubims, and a flaming sword which turned every way, to keep the way of the tree of life.

Chapter 4

The First Society

The Generations of Adam –
    Gen.5:1 – [1] This *is* the book of the generations of Adam. In the day that God created man, in the likeness of God made he him;

Cain and Able

Birth of Cain – son of Adam   [4003 B.C.?]
    Gen.4:1 – [1] And Adam knew Eve his wife; and she conceived, and bare Cain, and said, I have gotten a man from the LORD.

Probability Scenario

One might imagine that Adam and Eve may have abstained from intimacy for a short time to reflect on their act of disobedience to God's one and only restriction concerning *"… the tree of the knowledge of good and evil"* (Gen.2:17 & see 1). In time, they may have then sought to be obedient to God's command to *"Be fruitful and multiply; fill the earth and subdue it …"* (Gen.1:28 & see 2). It is probable that the normal time from conception to birth (9 months) would then take place. This event likely occurred approximately one year after creation – 4003 B.C.?.

Supporting Evidence

1. **Adam's Residence –** [p.7]
2. **God Appoints His Co-Regents –** (with responsibilities) [p.8]

Factors involved in the calculation
x = 4004 B.C.# – Creation of Adam
y = 1 ? – year between Creation of Adam and birth of Cain
z = 4003 B.C.? – Birth of Cain

Formula

(x) + (y) = z

(4004 B.C.#) - (1 ?) = 4003 B.C.?

Probable age of contemporaries

Adam 1 – Eve 1

Birth of Abel – son of Adam   [4002 B.C.?]

Gen.4:2 – ² And she again bare his brother Abel. And Abel was a keeper of sheep, but Cain was a tiller of the ground.

Probability Scenario

One might imagine after the birth of Cain, that Adam and Eve may have continued in their attempt to remain obedient to God's command to *"Be fruitful and multiply; fill the earth and subdue it …"* (Gen.1:28 & see 1). It is probable that the normal time from conception to birth (9 months) would then take place. This event very likely occurred approximately one year after the birth of Cain – 4002 B.C.?.

Supporting Evidence

1. **Birth of Cain** – son of Adam [p.17]
2. **God Appoints His Co-regents** – (with responsibilities) [p.8]

Points to Ponder

A. There are some who say that Cain and Able were twins (see a & b).

Considerations

a. It is possible that Cain and Able may have, in fact, been twins. However, scripture, neither here (v.2) nor elsewhere, provides unquestionable validity for this assumption.
b. Whether Cain and Able were twins or not will have no bearing on future events.

Factors involved in the calculation

x = 4003 B.C.? – Birth of Cain

y = 1 ? – year between Birth of Cain and birth of Abel

z = 4002 B.C.? – Birth of Abel

Formula

(x) + (y) = z

(4003 B.C.?) - (1 ?) = 4002 B.C.?

Probable age of contemporaries

Adam 2 – Eve 2 – Cain 1

Offerings to the LORD – (Abel's accepted/Cain's rejected)   [3875 B.C.?]

Gen.4:3-5 – ³ And in process of time it came to pass, that Cain brought of the fruit of the ground an offering unto the LORD. ⁴ And Abel, he also brought of the firstlings of his flock and of the fat thereof. And the LORD

18

had respect unto Abel and to his offering: 5 But unto Cain and to his offering he had not respect. And Cain was very wroth, and his countenance fell.

Probability Scenario

It seems that the "... *process of time*" (v.3) may have been a long period of time and this was the first offering to the LORD. It is probable that this event and the ensuing events immediately preceded and led up to the birth of Seth. This event very likely occurred approximately one year before the birth of Seth (see 1).

Supporting Evidence

1. **Birth of Seth** – son of Adam [p.21]

Factors involved in the calculation

x = 3874 B.C.# – Birth of Seth

y = 1 ? – year before birth of Seth

z = 3875 B.C.? – year of the offerings of Cain and Able

Formula

$$(x) \leftrightarrow (y) = z$$

$$(3874 \text{ B.C.\#}) + (1 \text{ ?}) = 3875 \text{ B.C.?}$$

Probable age of contemporaries

Adam 129 – Eve 129 – Cain 128 – Abel 127

God Offers Grace – (Cain offered repentance/warning)   [3875 B.C.?]

Gen.4:6-7 – 6 And the LORD said unto Cain, Why art thou wroth? and why is thy countenance fallen? 7 If thou doest well, shalt thou not be accepted? and if thou doest not well, sin lieth at the door. And unto thee *shall be* his desire, and thou shalt rule over him.

Cain Murders Abel

Cain's Anger Escalates –   [3875 B.C.?]

Gen.4:8-9 – 8 And Cain talked with Abel his brother: and it came to pass, when they were in the field, that Cain rose up against Abel his brother, and slew him.

9 And the LORD said unto Cain, Where *is* Abel thy brother? And he said, I know not: *Am* I my brother's keeper?

Cain Judged and Cursed –   [3875 B.C.?]

Gen.4:10-12 – 10 And he said, What hast thou done? the voice of thy brother's blood crieth unto me from the ground. 11 And now *art* thou cursed from the earth, which hath opened her mouth to receive thy brother's blood from thy hand; 12 When thou tillest the ground, it shall not henceforth yield unto thee her strength; a fugitive and a vagabond shalt thou be in the earth.

Cain Appeals to God –   [3875 B.C.?]

Gen.4:13-14 – [13] And Cain said unto the LORD, My punishment *is* greater than I can bear. [14] Behold, thou hast driven me out this day from the face of the earth; and from thy face shall I be hid; and I shall be a fugitive and a vagabond in the earth; and it shall come to pass, *that* every one that findeth me shall slay me.

Probability Scenario

Adam and Eve had other "*… sons and daughters*" (Gen.5:4 & see 1). It seems that Cain is fearful that one of his own relatives; brothers, sisters, nephews, nieces, etc., may find him and kill him (v.14). This event very likely occurred approximately one year before the birth of Seth (see 2).

Supporting Evidence

1. **Death of Adam** (at age 930) [p.24]
2. **Birth of Seth** – son of Adam [p.21]

Note

It is likely that, pre-flood, with their extensive life spans, Adam and Eve could have easily had thirty or more sons and daughters considering that post-flood Jair had 30 sons (Judg.10:3-4), Ibzan had 30 sons and 30 daughters (Judg.12:8-9) and Abdon had 40 sons (Judg.12:13-14). Some have estimated that at this time, approximately 129 years after the birth of Cain, that Adam and Eve's descendants could conservatively be well into the thousands.

God Bestows Grace – (Cain is marked/sign of God's protection)   [3875 B.C.?]

Gen.4:15-16 – [15] And the LORD said unto him, Therefore whosoever slayeth Cain, vengeance shall be taken on him sevenfold. And the LORD set a mark upon Cain, lest any finding him should kill him. [16] And Cain went out from the presence of the LORD, and dwelt in the land of Nod, on the east of Eden.

* * * * * * * BEGIN PARALLEL NATIONS * * * * * * *

THE GODLY LINE OF SETH	THE UNGODLY LINE OF CAIN

Birth of Seth –   [3874 B.C.#]
(son of Adam)
Gen.4:25 – 25 And Adam knew his wife again; and she bare a son, and called his name Seth: For God, *said she*, hath appointed me another seed instead of Abel, whom Cain slew.

Gen.5:3 – 3 And Adam lived an hundred and thirty years, and begat *a son* in his own likeness, after his image; and called his name Seth:

1Chron.1:1 - 1 Adam, Sheth, Enosh,

Year is Calculated from Scripture References
see "Genesis Genealogical Chart" [pp.218 & 219]
Age of contemporaries
Adam 130

Birth of Enos –   [3769 B.C.#]
(son of Seth)
Gen.4:26 – 26 And to Seth, to him also there was born a son; and he called his name Enos: then began men to call upon the name of the LORD.

Gen.5:6 – 6 And Seth lived an hundred and five years, and begat Enos:

Year is Calculated from Scripture References
see "Genesis Genealogical Chart" [pp.218 & 219]
Age of contemporaries
Adam 235 – Seth 105

Birth of Enoch –   [3874 B.C.?]
(son of Cain)
Gen.4:17 – 17 And Cain knew his wife; and she conceived, and bare Enoch: and he builded a city, and called the name of the city, after the name of his son, Enoch.

Probability Scenario
Cain may have immediately begun to father children to establish his own protection (see 1).
Supporting Evidence
1. Cain feared for his life from his own relatives (brothers, sisters, nephews, nieces – Gen.4:14).

Birth of Irad –   [?]
(son of Enoch)
Gen.4:18 – 18 And unto Enoch was born Irad: …

Birth of Mehujael –   [?]
(son of Irad)
Gen.4:18 – 18 … and Irad begat Mehujael: …

Birth of Methusael –   [?]
(son of Mehujael)
Gen.4:18 – 18 … and Mehujael begat Methusael, …

Birth of Cainan – [3679 B.C.#]
(son of Enos)
Gen.5:9 – ⁹ And Enos lived ninety years, and begat Cainan:

> **Year is Calculated from Scripture References**
> see "Genesis Genealogical Chart"
> [pp.218 & 219]
> **Age of contemporaries**
> Adam 325 – Enos 90

Birth of Mahalaleel – [3609 B.C.#]
(son of Cainan)
Gen.5:12 – ¹² And Cainan lived seventy years, and begat Mahalaleel:

1Chron.1:2 – ² Kenan, Mahalaleel, Jered,

> **Year is Calculated from Scripture References**
> see "Genesis Genealogical Chart"
> [pp.218 & 219]
> **Age of contemporaries**
> Adam 395 – Cainan 70

Birth of Jared – [3544 B.C.#]
(son of Mahalaleel)
Gen.5:15 – ¹⁵ And Mahalaleel lived sixty and five years, and begat Jared:

> **Year is Calculated from Scripture References**
> see "Genesis Genealogical Chart"
> [pp.218 & 219]
> **Age of contemporaries**
> Adam 460 – Mahalalel 65

Birth of Enoch – [3382 B.C.#]
(son of Jared)

Birth of Lamech – [?]
(son of Methusael)
Gen.4:18-19 – ¹⁸ … and Methusael begat Lamech. ¹⁹ And Lamech took unto him two wives: the name of the one *was* Adah, and the name of the other Zillah.

Birth of Jabal and Jubal – [?]
(sons of Lamech and Adah)
Gen.4:20-21 – ²⁰ And Adah bare Jabal: he was the father of such as dwell in tents, and *of such as have* cattle. ²¹ And his brother's name *was* Jubal: he was the father of all such as handle the harp and organ.

Birth of Tubalcain and Naamah – [?]
(children of Lamech and Zillah)
Gen.4:22 – ²² And Zillah, she also bare Tubalcain, an instructer of every artificer in brass and iron: and the sister of Tubalcain *was* Naamah.

Lamech Acts in Self-Defense – [?]
Gen.4:23-24 – ²³ And Lamech said unto his wives, Adah and Zillah, Hear my voice; ye wives of Lamech, hearken unto my speech: for I have slain a man to my wounding, and a young man to my hurt. ²⁴ If Cain shall be avenged sevenfold, truly Lamech seventy and sevenfold.

Gen.5:18 – ¹⁸ And Jared lived an hundred sixty and two years, and he begat Enoch:

> **Year is Calculated from Scripture References**
> see "Genesis Genealogical Chart"
> [pp.218 & 219]
> **Age of contemporaries**
> Adam 622 – Jared 162

Birth of Methuselah –   [3317 B.C.#]
(son of Enoch)
Gen.5:21 – ²¹ And Enoch lived sixty and five years, and begat Methuselah:

1Chron.1:3 – ³ Henoch, Methuselah, Lamech,

> **Year is Calculated from Scripture References**
> see "Genesis Genealogical Chart"
> [pp.218 & 219]
> **Age of contemporaries**
> Adam 687 – Enoch 65

Enoch Walks with God –[3317 B.C.#]
Gen.5:22 – ²² And Enoch walked with God after he begat Methuselah three hundred years, and begat sons and daughters:

> **Probability Scenario**
> It seems that Enoch may have had an eye-opening encounter with God. God may have inspired Enoch to name his son Methuselah (man of the javelin – see 1). One might wonder if God may have revealed to Enoch that his son's passage through time would be like a javelin passing through the sky and that the end of his passage would mark the end of time for unrighteous mankind (see 1).

Supporting Evidence
1. **Death of Methuselah [p.32]**
**Factors involved in calculating the
year**
x = 3017 B.C.# Enoch taken by God
y = 300 years Enoch walked w/God
z = 3317 B.C.# Enoch began to walk
with God
Formula
(x) - (y) = z
(3017 B.C.#) + (300) = 3317 B.C.#
Age of contemporaries
Adam 687

Birth of Lamech –   [3130 B.C.#]
(son of Methuselah)
Gen.5:25 – 25 And Methuselah lived an hundred eighty and seven years, and begat Lamech:

**Year is Calculated from Scripture
References**
see "Genesis Genealogical Chart"
[pp.218 & 219]
Age of contemporaries
Adam 874 – Methuselah 187

Death of Adam –   [3074 B.C.#]
(at age 930)
Gen.5:4-5 – 4 And the days of Adam after he had begotten Seth were eight hundred years: and he begat sons and daughters: 5 And all the days that Adam lived were nine hundred and thirty years: and he died.

**Years are Calculated from Scripture
References**
see "Genesis Genealogical Chart"
[pp.218 & 219]
Age of contemporaries
Seth 800

Enoch Taken by God –   [3017 B.C.#]
(at age 365)

Gen.5:23-24 – 23 And all the days of Enoch were three hundred sixty and five years: 24 And Enoch walked with God: and he *was* not; for God took him.

Years are Calculated from Scripture References
see "Genesis Genealogical Chart" [pp.218 & 219]
Age of contemporaries
Seth 857 – Methuselah 300

Death of Seth –   [2962 B.C.#]
        (at age 912)

Gen.5:7-8 – 7 And Seth lived after he begat Enos eight hundred and seven years, and begat sons and daughters: 8 And all the days of Seth were nine hundred and twelve years: and he died.

Years are Calculated from Scripture References
see "Genesis Genealogical Chart" [pp.218 & 219]
Age of contemporaries
Enosh 717 – Methuselah 355

Birth of Noah –   [2948 B.C.#]
      (son of Lamech)

Gen.5:28-29 – 28 And Lamech lived an hundred eighty and two years, and begat a son: 29 And he called his name Noah saying, This *same* shall comfort us concerning our work and toil of our hands, because of the ground which the LORD hath cursed.

Year is Calculated from Scripture References
see "Genesis Genealogical Chart" [pp.218 & 219]
Age of contemporaries
Lamech 182 – Methuselah 369

Death of Enos –   [2864 B.C.#]

(at age 905)

Gen.5:10-11 – [10] And Enos lived after he begat Cainan eight hundred and fifteen years, and begat sons and daughters: [11] And all the days of Enos were nine hundred and five years: and he died.

Years are Calculated from Scripture References
"Genesis Genealogical Chart" [pp.218 & 219]
Age of contemporaries
Cainan 815 – Methuselah 453

Death of Cainan –   [2769 B.C.#]

(at age 910)

Gen.5:13-14 – [13] And Cainan lived after he begat Mahalaleel eight hundred and forty years, and begat sons and daughters: [14] And all the days of Cainan were nine hundred and ten years: and he died.

Years are Calculated from Scripture References
see "Genesis Genealogical Chart" [pp.218 & 219]
Age of contemporaries
Mahalalel 840 – Methuselah 548

Death of Mahalaleel –   [2714 B.C.#]

(at age 895)

Gen.5:16-17 – [16] And Mahalaleel lived after he begat Jared eight hundred and thirty years, and begat sons and daughters: [17] And all the days of Mahalaleel were eight hundred ninety and five years: and he died.

Years are Calculated from Scripture References
see "Genesis Genealogical Chart"

[pp.218 & 219] **Age of contemporaries** Jared 830 – Methuselah 603 **Death of Jared –** **[2582 B.C.#]** (at age 962) Gen.5:19-20 – ¹⁹ And Jared lived after he begat Enoch eight hundred years, and begat sons and daughters: ²⁰ And all the days of Jared were nine hundred sixty and two years: and he died. **Years are Calculated from Scripture** **References** see "Genesis Genealogical Chart" **[pp.218 & 219]** **Age of contemporaries** Enoch 800 – Methuselah 735	

* * * * * * PAUSE PARALLEL NATIONS * * * * * * *

Events Preceding the Flood

God Grieved Because of Man's Wickedness –   [2468 B.C.?]

Gen.6:1-2 – ¹ And it came to pass, when men began to multiply on the face of the earth, and daughters were born unto them, ² That the sons of God saw the daughters of men that they *were* fair; and they took them wives of all which they chose.

Gen.6:4-7 – ⁴ There were giants in the earth in those days; and also after that, when the sons of God came in unto the daughters of men, and they bare *children* to them, the same *became* mighty men which *were* of old, men of renown. ⁵ And GOD saw that the wickedness of man *was* great in the earth, and *that* every imagination of the thoughts of his heart *was* only evil continually.

⁶ And it repented the LORD that he had made man on the earth, and it grieved him at his heart. ⁷ And the LORD said, I will destroy man whom I have created from the face of the earth; both man, and beast, and the creeping thing, and the fowls of the air; for it repenteth me that I have made them.

Gen.6:11-12 – [11] The earth also was corrupt before God, and the earth was filled with violence. [12] And God looked upon the earth, and, behold, it was corrupt; for all flesh had corrupted his way upon the earth.

Flood "WARNING" – (120 years to repent)   [2468 B.C.#]
Gen.6:3 – [3] And the LORD said, My spirit shall not always strive with man, for that he also *is* flesh: yet his days shall be an hundred and twenty years.

Probability Scenario
God declared 120 years before Noah entered the ark in 2348 B.C.#, that He would strive with man only 120 more years (v.3 & see 1)
Supporting Evidence
1. Genesis Genealogical Chart – see "WARNING" at 2468 B.C. [pp.218 & 219]
Note
There are some who say that God is declaring His intent to limit man to live only to 120 years of age. Scripture makes it very clear that following the warning there were eleven successive generations in which men lived to be more than 120 years of age. (see "Genesis Genealogical Chart" – Arphaxad thru Jacob - also see **Death of Levi** [p.183]).
Factors involved in the calculation
w = 2948 B.C.# – Noah's year of birth (see "Genesis Genealogical Chart")
x = 600 – Noah's age upon entering the ark (Gen.7:11) in 2348 B.C.#
y = 120 – years before entering the ark the Warning was given (Gen.6:3)
z = 2468 B.C.# – year God issued the Warning
Formula
(w + x) - (y) = z
(2948 B.C.# - 600) + (120) = 2468 B.C.#
(2348 B.C.#) + (120) = 2468 B.C.#
Probable age of contemporaries
Noah 480 – Methuselah 849 – Lamech 662

Noah Began Having Children –   [2448 B.C.#]
Gen.6:9-10 – [9] These *are* the generations of Noah: Noah was a just man *and* perfect in his generations, *and* Noah walked with God. [10] And Noah begat three sons, Shem, Ham, and Japheth.

Gen.5:32 – [32] And Noah was five hundred years old: and Noah begat Shem, Ham, and Japheth.

1Chron.1:4 – [4] Noah, Shem, Ham, and Japheth.

Year is Calculated from Scripture References
see "Genesis Genealogical Chart"
Probable age of contemporaries
Noah 500 – Methuselah 869 – Lamech 682

Birth of Japheth – son of Noah   [2448 B.C.#]

Probability Scenario
It seems that a "precedence format" (see 1) is most often used when recording the names of the sons of Noah ("Shem, Ham and Japheth" Gen.5:32; 6:10; 7:13; 9:18; 10:1). However, in Genesis 10:2, 6, 21 and 1 Chronicles 1:5, 8, 17, the names appear to be listed in "birth order format" (see 1) offering significant evidence that Japheth was born before Ham and Shem (also see 2).
Supporting Evidence
1. Scholars generally agree that scripture predominantly records names in birth order format, but this pattern is altered in precedence format, thus giving priority to the name of a direct descendant of the Messiah.
2. Japheth is referenced as the eldest son of Noah (Gen.10:21).
Factors involved in the calculation
x = 2948 B.C.# – Noah's year of birth (see "Genesis Genealogical Chart")
y = 500 – age Noah began having children (Gen.5:32)
z = 2448 B.C.# – Noah fathered Japheth the elder (Gen.10:21)
Formula
$(x) + (y) = z$
(2948 B.C.#) - (500) = 2448 B.C.#
Probable age of contemporaries
Noah 500 – Methuselah 869 – Lamech 682

Birth of Ham – son of Noah   [2447 B.C.?]

Probability Scenario
It seems that a "precedence format" (see 1) is most often used when recording of the names of the sons of Noah ("Shem, Ham and Japheth" Gen.5:32; 6:10; 7:13; 9:18; 10:1). However, in Genesis 10:2, 6, 21 and 1 Chronicles 1:5, 8, 17, the names appear to be listed in "birth order format" (see 1) offering significant evidence that Ham was born after Japheth (see 2), and before Shem (see 3).
Supporting Evidence
1. Scholars generally agree that scripture predominantly records names in birth order format, but this pattern is altered in precedence format, thus giving priority to the name of a direct descendant of the Messiah.
2. It is clear that Japheth is the eldest son of Noah (see **Birth of Japheth** – son of Noah [p.29])
3. It is clear that Shem was born two years after Japheth (see **Birth of Shem** – son of Noah [p.30])
Note
Ham could have been born in the same year as either Japheth [2448 B.C.#] or Shem [2446 B.C.#], the mid point [2447 B.C.?] should provide a suitable approximation.
Probable age of contemporaries
Noah 501 – Methuselah 870 – Lamech 683

Birth of Shem – son of Noah   [2446 B.C.#]

Probability Scenario

Genesis 9:28 states, "… *Noah lived after the flood **three hundred and fifty years**.*" The next verse states "*And all the days of Noah were **nine hundred and fifty years:** and he died.*" Clearly, the words "… *after the flood*" (Gen.9:28) mean "… *after the flood*" <u>began</u> (see 1) and does not mean "… *after the flood*" <u>ended</u> (see 2). With the establishment of this point of reference Shem's year of birth is apparently 2446 B.C.#.

Supporting Evidence

1. Genesis 9:28 states that "… *Noah lived after the flood **three hundred and fifty years**.*" The next verse states "*So all the days of Noah were **nine hundred and fifty years**; and he died.*" Genesis 7:6-7 states that Noah entered the ark at age 600, adding 350 years "*after the flood*" <u>began</u>, gives the correct age of 950 years of age at death (Gen.9:29).
2. Genesis 8:13-16 states that Noah was 601 (v.13) one month and twenty-seven days old (v.14) when God told him to go out of the ark (v.16). If the words "… *after the flood*" meant "… *after the flood*" <u>ended</u>, adding 350 years would render an incorrect age of 951 years of age at death (Gen. 9:29).

Factors involved in the calculation

x = 2948 B.C.# – Noah's year of birth (see "Genesis Genealogical Chart")
y1 = 600 – Noah's age when entering the ark (Gen.7:6)
y2 = 602 – Noah's age two years after the flood began = (y1 +2 years)
y3 = 100 – Shem's age two years after the flood began (Gen.11:10)
y4 = 502 – Noah's age when Shem was born = (y2 – y3)
z = 2446 B.C.# – Noah fathered Shem (Gen.10:21)

Formula

(x) + (y4) = z
(2948 B.C.#) - (502) = 2446 B.C.#

Probable age of contemporaries

Noah 502 – Methuselah 871 – Lamech 684

Shem Marries - (approximate age 20)   [2426 B.C.?]

Probability Scenario

It is apparent that Shem was the youngest son of Noah (see 1, 2 & 3) and his possible year of marriage would seem to provide the most suitable reference point from which to estimate the earliest probable year that God may have instructed Noah to build the ark. It is likely that Shem might have reached a marriageable age around 20 years of age – 2426 B.C.?.

Supporting Evidence

1. **Birth of Shem** – son of Noah [p.30]
2. **Birth of Japheth** – son of Noah [p.29]
3. **Birth of Ham** – son of Noah [p.29]

Factors involved in the calculation

x = 2446 B.C.# – Shem's year of birth (see "Genesis Genealogical Chart")
y = 20 ? – Shem's probable age upon taking a wife (Gen.7:11) in 2348 B.C.#

Noah Instructed to Build an Ark – [2426 B.C.?]

Gen.6:8 – ⁸ But Noah found grace in the eyes of the LORD.

Gen.6:13-21 – ¹³ And God said unto Noah, The end of all flesh is come before me; for the earth is filled with violence through them; and, behold, I will destroy them with the earth. ¹⁴ Make thee an ark of gopher wood; rooms shalt thou make in the ark, and shalt pitch it within and without with pitch. ¹⁵ And this *is the fashion* which thou shalt make it *of*: The length of the ark *shall be* three hundred cubits, the breadth of it fifty cubits, and the height of it thirty cubits. ¹⁶ A window shalt thou make to the ark, and in a cubit shalt thou finish it above; and the door of the ark shalt thou set in the side thereof; *with* lower, second, and third *stories* shalt thou make it. ¹⁷ And, behold, I, even I, do bring a flood of waters upon the earth, to destroy all flesh, wherein *is* the breath of life, from under heaven; *and* every thing that *is* in the earth shall die. ¹⁸ But with thee will I establish my covenant; and thou shalt come into the ark, thou, and thy sons, and thy wife, and thy sons' wives with thee. ¹⁹ And of every living thing of all flesh, two of every *sort* shalt thou bring into the ark, to keep *them* alive with thee; they shall be male and female. ²⁰ Of fowls after their kind, and of cattle after their kind, of every creeping thing of the earth after his kind, two of every *sort* shall come unto thee, to keep *them* alive. ²¹ And take thou unto thee of all food that is eaten, and thou shalt gather *it* to thee; and it shall be for food for thee, and for them.

Probability Scenario

It seems likely that this event may have taken place after the birth of Noah's sons and after they reached a marriageable age (see 1) but before they had children (see 2). It is apparent that Shem was the youngest son of Noah (see 3, 4 & 5) and his possible year of marriage would seem to provide the most suitable reference point from which to estimate the earliest probable year that God may have instructed Noah to build the ark. It is likely that Shem might have reached a marriageable age, at the earliest, around 20 years of age –2426 B.C.?. This date would be, maximum, 78 years before the flood began.

Supporting Evidence

1. It appears that God is speaking of Noah's living sons and their present wives (v.18; Gen.7:7).
2. Gen.10:1; 7:7; 2Pet.2:5
3. **Birth of Shem** – son of Noah [p.30]

> 4. **Birth of Japheth** – son of Noah [p.29]
> 5. **Birth of Ham** – son of Noah [p.29]
> ### Note
> This occasion may be similar to the occasions when God observed the sinfulness of mankind over a period of time before meting out His judgment (Gen.11:5; 18:19-21). One might also consider God is "… *longsuffering … not willing that any should perish*" (2Pet.3:9).
> ### Factors involved in the calculation
> x = 2446 B.C.# – Shem's year of birth (see "Genesis Genealogical Chart")
> y = 20 ? – Shem's earliest probable marriageable age (Gen.7:11) in 2348 B.C.#
> z = 2426 B.C.? – probable year Noah instructed to build the Ark
> ### Formula
> $$(x) + (y) = z$$
> $$(2446 \text{ B.C.\#}) - (20\ ?) = 2426 \text{ B.C.?}$$
> ### Probable age of contemporaries
> Noah 522 – Methuselah 891 – Lamech 704 – Japheth 22 – Ham 21 – Shem 20

Noah Preaches Righteousness – [2426–2348 B.C.?]

2Pet.2:5 – ⁵ and [God] did not spare the ancient world, but saved Noah, *one of* eight *people,* a preacher of righteousness, bringing in the flood on the world of the ungodly;

> ### Probability Scenario
> It seems probable that Noah preached righteousness for a period of approximately 78 years. Noah likely began preaching immediately following the time God instructed him to build the ark (see 1) and concluded the day God told Noah to enter the ark (see 2).
> ### Supporting Evidence
> 1. **Noah Instructed to Build an Ark** – [p.31]
> 2. **Noah Enters the Ark** – [p.33]
> ### Note
> Noah's building of the ark was a vivid sermon illustration.

Death of Lamech - (at age 777) [2353 B.C.#]

Gen.5:30-31 – ³⁰ And Lamech lived after he begat Noah five hundred ninety and five years, and begat sons and daughters: ³¹ And all the days of Lamech were seven hundred seventy and seven years: and he died.

> ### Years are Calculated from Scripture References
> see "Genesis Genealogical Chart"
> ### Probable age of contemporaries
> Noah 595 – Methuselah 964 – Japheth 95 – Ham 94 – Shem 93

Death of Methuselah - (at age 969) [2348 B.C.#]

Gen.5:26-27 – ²⁶ And Methuselah lived after he begat Lamech seven hundred eighty and two years, and begat sons and daughters: ²⁷ And all the days of Methuselah were nine hundred sixty and nine years: and he died.

Probability Scenario

It appears that Methuselah (the man of a javelin[1] – see 1) has completed his passage through time (see 2), likely signifying the end of time for unrighteous mankind (see 3).

Supporting Evidence
1. **Enoch Walks with God** – [p.23]
2. See "Genesis Genealogical Chart"
3. **Flood "WARNING" Expires** – [p.33]

Probable age of contemporaries
Noah 600 – Japheth 100 – Ham 99 – Shem 98

Events of the Flood

Flood "WARNING" Expires –   [2348 B.C.#]

Year is Calculated from Scripture References
Factors involved in the calculation

x = 2468 B.C.# – year flood warning issued (see **Flood "WARNING"** – [p.28])
y = 120 – years before entering the ark the Warning was given (Gen.6:3)
z = 2348 B.C.# – year warning expires

Formula
(x) + (y) = z
(2468 B.C.#) – (120) = 2348 B.C.#

Probable age of contemporaries
Noah 600 – Japheth 100 – Shem 98

Noah Enters the Ark –   [2348 B.C.#]

Gen.6:22 – 22 Thus did Noah; according to all that God commanded him, so did he.

Gen.7:1-9 – 1 And the LORD said unto Noah, Come thou and all thy house into the ark; for thee have I seen righteous before me in this generation. 2 Of every clean beast thou shalt take to thee by sevens, the male and his female: and of beasts that *are* not clean by two, the male and his female. 3 Of fowls also of the air by sevens, the male and the female; to keep seed alive upon the face of all the earth. 4 For yet seven days, and I will cause it to rain upon the earth forty days and forty nights; and every

---

[1]Thomas Nelson Publishers: *Nelson's Quick Reference Topical Bible Index*. Nashville, Tenn. : Thomas Nelson Publishers, 1995 (Nelson's Quick Reference), S. 414

living substance that I have made will I destroy from off the face of the earth.

⁵ And Noah did according unto all that the LORD commanded him. ⁶ And Noah *was* six hundred years old when the flood of waters was upon the earth. ⁷ And Noah went in, and his sons, and his wife, and his sons' wives with him, into the ark, because of the waters of the flood. ⁸ Of clean beasts, and of beasts that *are* not clean, and of fowls, and of every thing that creepeth upon the earth, ⁹ There went in two and two unto Noah into the ark, the male and the female, as God had commanded Noah.

Year is Calculated from Scripture References
Factors involved in the calculation
x = 2948 B.C.# = Noah's year of birth (see "Genesis Genealogical Chart")
y = 600 = Noah's age upon entering the ark (v.6)
z = 2348 B.C.# = year Noah entered the ark
Formula
(x) + (y) = z
(2948B.C.#) - (600) = 2348B.C.#
Probable age of contemporaries
Noah 600 – Japheth 100 – Shem 98

The Rains Begin and Prevail –   [2348 B.C.#]

Gen.7:10-24 – ¹⁰ And it came to pass after seven days, that the waters of the flood were upon the earth.

¹¹ In the six hundredth year of Noah's life, in the second month, the seventeenth day of the month, the same day were all the fountains of the great deep broken up, and the windows of heaven were opened. ¹² And the rain was upon the earth forty days and forty nights.

¹³ In the selfsame day entered Noah, and Shem, and Ham, and Japheth, the sons of Noah, and Noah's wife, and the three wives of his sons with them, into the ark; ¹⁴ They, and every beast after his kind, and all the cattle after their kind, and every creeping thing that creepeth upon the earth after his kind, and every fowl after his kind, every bird of every sort. ¹⁵ And they went in unto Noah into the ark, two and two of all flesh, wherein *is* the breath of life. ¹⁶ And they that went in, went in male and female of all flesh, as God had commanded him: and the LORD shut him in.

¹⁷ And the flood was forty days upon the earth; and the waters increased, and bare up the ark, and it was lift up above the earth. ¹⁸ And the waters prevailed, and were increased greatly upon the earth; and the ark went upon the face of the waters. ¹⁹ And the waters prevailed exceedingly upon the earth; and all the high hills, that *were* under the whole heaven, were covered. ²⁰ Fifteen cubits upward did the waters prevail; and the mountains were covered.

21 And all flesh died that moved upon the earth, both of fowl, and of cattle, and of beast, and of every creeping thing that creepeth upon the earth, and every man: 22 All in whose nostrils *was* the breath of life, of all that *was* in the dry *land*, died. 23 And every living substance was destroyed which was upon the face of the ground, both man, and cattle, and the creeping things, and the fowl of the heaven; and they were destroyed from the earth: and Noah only remained *alive*, and they that *were* with him in the ark. 24 And the waters prevailed upon the earth an hundred and fifty days.

Gen.8:1-2 – 1 And God remembered Noah, and every living thing, and all the cattle that *was* with him in the ark: and God made a wind to pass over the earth, and the waters asswaged; 2 The fountains also of the deep and the windows of heaven were stopped, and the rain from heaven was restrained;

Year is Calculated from Scripture References
Factors involved in the calculation
x = 2948 B.C.# – Noah's year of birth (see "Genesis Genealogical Chart")
y = 600 – Noah's age upon entering the ark (v.11)
z = 2348 B.C.# – year ~~Noah entered the ark~~ *rains began*
Formula
(x) + (y) = z
(2948B.C.#) - (600) = 2348B.C.#
Probable age of contemporaries
Noah 600 – Japheth 100 – Shem 98

* * * * * * RESUME PARALLEL NATIONS * * * * * *

THE GODLY LINE OF SETH (continued through Noah)	THE UNGODLY LINE OF CAIN (imprisoned in Hades)
Heb 11:7 – 7 By faith Noah, being warned of God of things not seen as yet, moved with fear, prepared an ark to the saving of his house; by the which he condemned the world, and became heir of the righteousness which is by faith.	1Pet.3:19-20 – 19 By which [Spirit] also he [Christ] went and preached unto the spirits in prison [Hades]; 20 Which sometime were disobedient, when once the longsuffering of God waited in the days of Noah, while the ark was a preparing, wherein few, that is, eight souls were saved by water.

* * * * * * * END PARALLEL NATIONS * * * * * * *

Conclusion of the Flood

The Waters Recede –   [2348 B.C.#]

    Gen.8:3-12 – ³ And the waters returned from off the earth continually: and after the end of the hundred and fifty days the waters were abated.

    ⁴ And the ark rested in the seventh month, on the seventeenth day of the month, upon the mountains of Ararat. ⁵ And the waters decreased continually until the tenth month: in the tenth *month*, on the first *day* of the month, were the tops of the mountains seen.

    ⁶ And it came to pass at the end of forty days, that Noah opened the window of the ark which he had made: ⁷ And he sent forth a raven, which went forth to and fro, until the waters were dried up from off the earth. ⁸ Also he sent forth a dove from him, to see if the waters were abated from off the face of the ground; ⁹ But the dove found no rest for the sole of her foot, and she returned unto him into the ark, for the waters *were* on the face of the whole earth: then he put forth his hand, and took her, and pulled her in unto him into the ark. ¹⁰ And he stayed yet other seven days; and again he sent forth the dove out of the ark; ¹¹ And the dove came in to him in the evening; and, lo, in her mouth *was* an olive leaf pluckt off: so Noah knew that the waters were abated from off the earth. ¹² And he stayed yet other seven days; and sent forth the dove; which returned not again unto him any more.

Year is Calculated from Scripture References
Factors involved in the calculation
x = 2948 B.C.# – Noah's year of birth (see "Genesis Genealogical Chart")
y = 600 – Noah's age when waters receded (Gen.8:3-4)
z = 2348 B.C.# – year ark rested on mountains of Ararat
Formula
(x) + (y) = z
(2948B.C.#) - (600) = 2348B.C.#
Probable age of contemporaries
Noah 600 – Japheth 100 – Shem 98

The Ground Dries – (God commands Noah to leave the Ark)   [2347 B.C.#]

    Gen.8:13-19 – ¹³ And it came to pass in the six hundredth and first year, in the first *month*, the first *day* of the month, the waters were dried up from off the earth: and Noah removed the covering of the ark, and looked, and, behold, the face of the ground was dry. ¹⁴ And in the second month, on the seven and twentieth day of the month, was the earth dried.

    ¹⁵ And God spake unto Noah, saying, ¹⁶ Go forth of the ark, thou, and thy wife, and thy sons, and thy sons' wives with thee. ¹⁷ Bring forth with thee every living thing that *is* with thee, of all flesh, *both* of fowl, and of

cattle, and of every creeping thing that creepeth upon the earth; that they may breed abundantly in the earth, and be fruitful, and multiply upon the earth. [18] And Noah went forth, and his sons, and his wife, and his sons' wives with him: [19] Every beast, every creeping thing, and every fowl, *and* whatsoever creepeth upon the earth, after their kinds, went forth out of the ark.

Year is Calculated from Scripture References
Factors involved in the calculation

x = 2948 B.C.# – Noah's year of birth (see "Genesis Genealogical Chart")
y = 601 – Noah's age upon exiting the ark – 601 years (v.13)
z = 2347 B.C.# – year Noah exited the ark

Formula

$$(x) + (y) = z$$
$$(2948 B.C.\#) - (601) = 2347 B.C.\#$$

Note

Noah was in the ark 377 days total.
Noah exited the Ark at age 601 years (v.13) 1 month and 27 days (vv.14, 18).
The rains began in the 600th year 1st month and 17th day (Gen.7:11).
Noah entered the ark 7 days before the rains began (Gen.7:1, 4, 5, 10).

Calculation: 601 years 1 month and 27 days (date ark exited – vv.13,14,18)
        - 600 years 1 month and 17 days (date rains began – Gen.7:11)
          1 year (360 days*) + 10 days = 370 days
                        + 7 days = 377 days (Gen.7:1, 4, 5, 10)

Probable age of contemporaries
Noah 601 – Japheth 101 – Shem 99

---

* Jewish calendar

Chapter 5

Flood to Patriarchs

Events Following the Flood

Noah Prepares an Altar and a Burnt Offering –   [2347 B.C.#]

Gen.8:20 – [20] And Noah builded an altar unto the LORD; and took of every clean beast, and of every clean fowl, and offered burnt offerings on the altar.

Year is Calculated from Scripture References
Factors involved in the calculation
x = 2948 B.C.# – Noah's year of birth (see "Genesis Genealogical Chart")
y = 601 – Noah's age upon exiting the ark (Gen.8:13-15)
z = 2347 B.C.# – year Noah offered a burnt offering
Formula
(x) + (y) = z
(2948B.C.#) - (601) = 2347B.C.#
Probable age of contemporaries
Noah 601 – Japheth 101 – Shem 99

The LORD is Pleased –   [2347 B.C.#]

Gen.8:21-22 – [21] And the LORD smelled a sweet savour; and the LORD said in his heart, I will not again curse the ground any more for man's sake; for the imagination of man's heart *is* evil from his youth; neither will I again smite any more every thing living, as I have done. [22] While the earth remaineth, seedtime and harvest, and cold and heat, and summer and winter, and day and night shall not cease.

God Blesses Noah and His Sons –   [2347 B.C.#]

Gen.9:1-2 – [1] And God blessed Noah and his sons, and said unto them, Be fruitful, and multiply, and replenish the earth. [2] And the fear of you and the dread of you shall be upon every beast of the earth, and upon every fowl of the air, upon all that moveth *upon* the earth, and upon all the fishes of the sea; into your hand are they delivered.

God Permits Man to be Both Herbivorous and Carnivorous –   [2347 B.C.#]

Gen.9:3-4 – [3] Every moving thing that liveth shall be meat for you; even as the green herb have I given you all things. [4] But flesh with the life thereof, *which is* the blood thereof, shall ye not eat.

God Permits Man to Have Judicial Authority on Earth –   [2347 B.C.#]

Gen.9:5-7 – [5] And surely your blood of your lives will I require; at the hand of every beast will I require it, and at the hand of man; at the hand of every man's brother will I require the life of man. [6] Whoso sheddeth man's blood, by man shall his blood be shed: for in the image of God made he man. [7] And you, be ye fruitful, and multiply; bring forth abundantly in the earth, and multiply therein.

God Gives a Sign of His Covenant – (the rainbow)   [2347 B.C.#]

Gen.9:8-17 – [8] And God spake unto Noah, and to his sons with him, saying, [9] And I, behold, I establish my covenant with you, and with your seed after you; [10] And with every living creature that *is* with you, of the fowl, of the cattle, and of every beast of the earth with you; from all that go out of the ark, to every beast of the earth. [11] And I will establish my covenant with you; neither shall all flesh be cut off any more by the waters of a flood; neither shall there any more be a flood to destroy the earth.

[12] And God said, This *is* the token of the covenant which I make between me and you and every living creature that *is* with you, for perpetual generations: [13] I do set my bow in the cloud, and it shall be for a token of a covenant between me and the earth. [14] And it shall come to pass, when I bring a cloud over the earth, that the bow shall be seen in the cloud: [15] And I will remember my covenant, which *is* between me and you and every living creature of all flesh; and the waters shall no more become a flood to destroy all flesh. [16] And the bow shall be in the cloud; and I will look upon it, that I may remember the everlasting covenant between God and every living creature of all flesh that *is* upon the earth. [17] And God said unto Noah, This *is* the token of the covenant, which I have established between me and all flesh that *is* upon the earth.

Noah's descendants

Noah's Sons to Replenish the Earth –   [2347 B.C.#]

Gen.9:18-19 – ¹⁸ And the sons of Noah, that went forth of the ark, were Shem, and Ham, and Japheth: and Ham *is* the father of Canaan. ¹⁹ These *are* the three sons of Noah: and of them was the whole earth overspread.

Future Descendants of Noah's Sons –

Gen.10:1 – ¹ Now these *are* the generations of the sons of Noah, Shem, Ham, and Japheth: and unto them were sons born after the flood.

Gen.10:32 – ³² These *are* the families of the sons of Noah, after their generations, in their nations: and by these were the nations divided in the earth after the flood.

Sons of Japheth –

Gen.10:2-5 – ² The sons of Japheth; Gomer, and Magog, and Madai, and Javan, and Tubal, and Meshech, and Tiras. ³ And the sons of Gomer; Ashkenaz, and Riphath, and Togarmah. ⁴ And the sons of Javan; Elishah, and Tarshish, Kittim, and Dodanim. ⁵ By these were the isles of the Gentiles divided in their lands; every one after his tongue, after their families, in their nations.

1Chron.1:5-7 – ⁵ The sons of Japheth; Gomer, and Magog, and Madai, and Javan, and Tubal, and Meshech, and Tiras. ⁶ And the sons of Gomer; Ashchenaz, and Riphath, and Togarmah. ⁷ And the sons of Javan; Elishah, and Tarshish, Kittim, and Dodanim.

Sons of Ham –

Gen.10:6-20 – ⁶ And the sons of Ham; Cush, and Mizraim, and Phut, and Canaan. ⁷ And the sons of Cush; Seba, and Havilah, and Sabtah, and Raamah, and Sabtecha: and the sons of Raamah; Sheba, and Dedan. ⁸ And Cush begat Nimrod: he began to be a mighty one in the earth. ⁹ He was a mighty hunter before the LORD: wherefore it is said, Even as Nimrod the mighty hunter before the LORD. ¹⁰ And the beginning of his kingdom was Babel, and Erech, and Accad, and Calneh, in the land of Shinar. ¹¹ Out of that land went forth Asshur, and builded Nineveh, and the city Rehoboth, and Calah, ¹² And Resen between Nineveh and Calah: the same *is* a great city. ¹³ And Mizraim begat Ludim, and Anamim, and Lehabim, and Naphtuhim, ¹⁴ And Pathrusim, and Casluhim, (out of whom came Philistim,) and Caphtorim.

¹⁵ And Canaan begat Sidon his firstborn, and Heth, ¹⁶ And the Jebusite,

and the Amorite, and the Girgasite, 17 And the Hivite, and the Arkite, and the Sinite, 18 And the Arvadite, and the Zemarite, and the Hamathite: and afterward were the families of the Canaanites spread abroad. 19 And the border of the Canaanites was from Sidon, as thou comest to Gerar, unto Gaza; as thou goest, unto Sodom, and Gomorrah, and Admah, and Zeboim, even unto Lasha. 20 These *are* the sons of Ham, after their families, after their tongues, in their countries, *and* in their nations.

1Chron.1:8-16 – 8 The sons of Ham; Cush, and Mizraim, Put, and Canaan. 9 And the sons of Cush; Seba, and Havilah, and Sabta, and Raamah, and Sabtecha. And the sons of Raamah; Sheba, and Dedan. 10 And Cush begat Nimrod: he began to be mighty upon the earth. 11 And Mizraim begat Ludim, and Anamim, and Lehabim, and Naphtuhim, 12 And Pathrusim, and Casluhim, (of whom came the Philistines,) and Caphthorim. 13 And Canaan begat Zidon his firstborn, and Heth, 14 The Jebusite also, and the Amorite, and the Girgashite, 15 And the Hivite, and the Arkite, and the Sinite, 16 And the Arvadite, and the Zemarite, and the Hamathite.

Sons of Shem –
Gen.10:21-23 – 21 Unto Shem also, the father of all the children of Eber, the brother of Japheth the elder, even to him were *children* born. 22 The children of Shem; Elam, and Asshur, and Arphaxad, and Lud, and Aram. 23 And the children of Aram; Uz, and Hul, and Gether, and Mash.

Gen.10:31 – 31 These *are* the sons of Shem, after their families, after their tongues, in their lands, after their nations.

1Chron.1:17 – 17 The sons of Shem; Elam, and Asshur, and Arphaxad, and Lud, and Aram, and Uz, and Hul, and Gether, and Meshech.

Birth of Canaan – son of Ham   [2346 B.C.?]
Gen.10:6 – 6 And the sons of Ham; Cush, and Mizraim, and Phut, and Canaan

1Chron.1:8 – 8 The sons of Ham; Cush, and Mizraim, Put, and Canaan.

Probability Scenario
Canaan has the dubious honor of being the first grandson of Noah mentioned in scripture (see 1). Even though Canaan is recorded in genealogical records as the fourth son of Ham (vv.6, 8), it is possible that Canaan may have been Ham's firstborn. Canaan is destined to receive a curse from his grandfather, Noah (see 2). It would seem probable that along with the curse might be

eviction from the esteemed position of firstborn, hence the dubious honor of first mention. It is likely that Canaan may have been born several weeks earlier than Arphaxad (see 3) and in the same year.

<u>**Supporting Evidence**</u>

1. Ham is the first of Noah's sons mentioned as having fathered a son, Canaan (Gen.9:18). (see **Noah's Sons to Replenish the Earth** – [p.41])
2. **Noah's Nakedness Seen by His Son Ham** – (Canaan cursed) [p.44]
3. **Birth of Arphaxad** – son of Shem [p.43]

<u>**Probable age of contemporaries**</u>

Noah 602 – Japheth 102 – Ham 101 – Shem 100

Birth of Arphaxad – son of Shem   [2346 B.C.#]

Gen.11:10 – ¹⁰ These *are* the generations of Shem: Shem *was* an hundred years old, and begat Arphaxad two years after the flood:

1Chron.1:24 – ²⁴ Shem, Arphaxad, Shelah,

<u>**Year is Calculated from Scripture References**</u>
<u>**Factors involved in the calculation**</u>

x = 2446 B.C.# – Shem's year of birth (see "Genesis Genealogical Chart")
y = 100 – Shem's age when Arphaxad was born (v.10)
z = 2346 B.C.# – Shem fathered Arphaxad

<u>**Formula**</u>

$(x) + (y) = z$
$(2446 \text{ B.C.\#}) - (100) = 2346 \text{ B.C.\#}$

<u>**Note**</u>

The words *"after the flood"* (v.10) indicate *"after the flood"* **began** (and not after it ended). They are similar to those in Genesis 9:28-29 - ²⁸ *And Noah lived <u>after the flood</u> three hundred and fifty years.* ²⁹*So all the days of Noah were nine hundred and fifty years; and he died"* (See **Birth of Shem** – son of Noah [p.30])

<u>**Probable age of contemporaries**</u>

Noah 602 – Japheth 102 – Ham 101 – Shem 100

Birth of Cush – son of Ham   [2344 B.C.?]

Gen.10:6 – ⁶ And the sons of Ham; Cush, and Mizraim, and Phut, and Canaan

1Chron.1:8 – ⁸ The sons of Ham; Cush, and Mizraim, Put, and Canaan.

<u>**Probability Scenario**</u>

Cush appears first in the genealogical line of Ham (v.6, 8), however Canaan has first mention (Gen.9:18) and therefore may possibly be the actual firstborn (see 1). In keeping with God's command to Noah's sons to *"Be fruitful, and multiply, and replenish the earth"* (Gen.9:1), it is probable that Cush was born within a few years after exiting the ark (see 2). Cush is destined to be the father of Nimrod a mighty hunter before the LORD (see 3).

<u>Supporting Evidence</u>
1. **Birth of Canaan** – son of Ham [p.42]
2. **The Ground Dries** – (God commands Noah to leave the Ark) [p.36]
3. **Birth of Nimrod** – son of Cush & grandson of Ham [p.45]

<u>Probable age of contemporaries</u>
Noah 604 – Japheth 104 – Ham 103 – Shem 102

Noah's Vineyard Invites Sin

Noah's Nakedness Seen by His Son Ham – (Canaan cursed)   [2335 B.C.?]

Gen.9:20-27 – ²⁰ And Noah began *to be* an husbandman, and he planted a vineyard: ²¹ And he drank of the wine, and was drunken; and he was uncovered within his tent. ²² And Ham, the father of Canaan, saw the nakedness of his father, and told his two brethren without. ²³ And Shem and Japheth took a garment, and laid *it* upon both their shoulders, and went backward, and covered the nakedness of their father; and their faces *were* backward, and they saw not their father's nakedness.

²⁴ And Noah awoke from his wine, and knew what his younger son had done unto him. ²⁵ And he said, Cursed *be* Canaan; a servant of servants shall he be unto his brethren. ²⁶ And he said, Blessed *be* the LORD God of Shem; and Canaan shall be his servant. ²⁷ God shall enlarge Japheth, and he shall dwell in the tents of Shem; and Canaan shall be his servant.

<u>Probability Scenario</u>
It seems probable that Canaan, Noah's grand-son (see 1 & 2) may have sinned against Noah. Canaan would then be the primary bearer of guilt (*The son shall not bear the iniquity of the father, neither shall the father bear the iniquity of the son:* - Ezek.18:20). Canaan may have been young enough to not be held accountable for his actions but old enough to know right from wrong. Ham may have been held responsible for Canaan's conduct and therefore guilty by omission of his parental responsibilities, reminiscent of Eli the priest regarding his sons Hophni and Phinehas (1Sam.2:22-25; 27-30).

<u>Supporting Evidence</u>
1. It seems that Ham was not the "… *younger son*" (Gen.9:24) considering that order of the genealogies first lists the sons of Japheth, second the sons of Ham and lastly sons of Shem. (Gen.10:1-32; 1Chron.1:5-17)
2. The term "*son*" can also refer to grand-children or descendants (Gen.46:15, 18, 22; Mat.1:1, 20; Mk.10:47; Lk.18:38)

<u>Note</u>
It is not scripturally discernable what the sin against Canaan was, however, it is note worthy that the land settled by Canaan (Canaanites) included Sodom and Gomorrah, infamous for their decadent life style.

Factors involved in the calculation
x = 2346 B.C.? – Birth of Canaan – son of Ham
y = 11 ? – age of Canaan at the time of this event
z = 2335 B.C.? – year of this event
Formula
(x) + (y) = z
(2346B.C.?) - (11 ?) = 2335B.C.?
Probable age of contemporaries
Noah 613 – Japheth 113 – Ham 112 – Shem 111 – Canaan 11

Godly Line of Seth (continued through Shem)

Birth of Salah – son of Arphaxad   [2311 B.C.#]
    Gen.10:24 – 24 And Arphaxad begat Salah; and Salah begat Eber.

    Gen.11:12 – 12 And Arphaxad lived five and thirty years, and begat Salah:

    1Chron.1:18 – 18 And Arphaxad begat Shelah, and Shelah begat Eber.

Year is Calculated from Scripture References
see "Genesis Genealogical Chart"
Age of contemporaries
Noah 637 – Shem 135 – Arphaxad – 35

Birth of Nimrod – son of Cush & grandson of Ham   [2295 B.C.?]
    Gen.10:8-10 – 8 And Cush begat Nimrod: he began to be a mighty one in the earth. 9 He was a mighty hunter before the LORD: wherefore it is said, Even as Nimrod the mighty hunter before the LORD. 10 And the beginning of his kingdom was Babel, and Erech, and Accad, and Calneh, in the land of Shinar.

Probability Scenario
It is reckoned that Nimrod's father, Cush, was born around 2344 B.C.? (see 1). If Cush began having children approximately 31 years later (see Note) around 2313 B.C.?, and if each of his sons were born approximately 3 years apart, Nimrod (see 2) may have been born around 18 years later in 2295 B.C.?.
Supporting Evidence
1. **Birth of Cush** – son of Ham [p.43]
2. It appears that Nimrod was the 6th son of Cush (Gen.10:6-8).
Note
After the flood new generations were born approximately every 31 years. Shem's son, Arphaxad, fathered Salah at age 35, who fathered Eber at 30, who fathered Peleg at 34, who fathered Reu at 30, who fathered Serug at 32, who fathered Nahor I at 30, who fathered Terah at 29.

> Formula: (35 + 30 + 34 + 30 + 32 + 30 + 29) = 220 years
> (220) / (7) = 31.43 years (see "Genesis Genealogical Chart")
> **Probable age of contemporaries**
> Noah 653 – Japheth 153 – Ham 152 – Shem 151

Birth of Eber – son of Salah   [2281 B.C.#]

Gen.11:14 – 14 And Salah lived thirty years, and begat Eber:

> **Year is Calculated from Scripture References**
> see "Genesis Genealogical Chart"
> **Age of contemporaries**
> Noah 667 – Shem 165 – Salah 30

Birth of Peleg and Joktan – sons of Eber   [2247 B.C.#]

Gen.10:25 – 25 And unto Eber were born two sons: the name of one *was* Peleg; for in his days was the earth divided; and his brother's name *was* Joktan.

Gen.11:16 – 16 And Eber lived four and thirty years, and begat Peleg:

1Chron.1:19 – 19 And unto Eber were born two sons: the name of the one *was* Peleg; because in his days the earth was divided: and his brother's name *was* Joktan.

1Chron.1:25 – 25 Eber, Peleg, Reu,

> **Year is Calculated from Scripture References**
> see "Genesis Genealogical Chart"
> **Age of contemporaries**
> Noah 701 – Shem 199 – Eber 34

* * * * * BEGIN PARALLEL GENEALOGIES * * * * *

LINEAGE OF PELEG	LINEAGE OF JOKTAN
Birth of Reu – [2217 B.C.#] (son of Peleg) Gen.11:18 – 18 And Peleg lived thirty years, and begat Reu: **Year is Calculated from Scripture References** see "Genesis Genealogical Chart" **Age of contemporaries** Noah 731 – Shem 229 – Peleg 30	**Future Descendants of Joktan –** Gen.10:26-30 – 26 And Joktan begat Almodad, and Sheleph, and Hazarmaveth, and Jerah, 27 And Hadoram, and Uzal, and Diklah, 28 And Obal, and Abimael, and Sheba, 29 And Ophir, and Havilah, and Jobab: all these *were* the sons of Joktan. 30 And their dwelling was from Mesha, as thou goest unto

Birth of Serug – [2185 B.C.#]	Sephar a mount of the east.
(son of Reu)	
Gen.11:20 - 20 And Reu lived two and thirty years, and begat Serug:	1Chron.1:20-23 – 20 And Joktan begat Almodad, and Sheleph, and Hazarmaveth, and Jerah, 21 Hadoram also, and Uzal, and Diklah, 22 And Ebal, and Abimael, and Sheba, 23 And Ophir, and Havilah, and Jobab. All these *were* the sons of Joktan.

Inside the left cell box:

Year is Calculated from Scripture References
see "Genesis Genealogical Chart"
Age of contemporaries
Noah 763 – Shem 261 – Reu 32

* * * * * END PARALLEL GENEALOGIES * * * * *

Tower of Babel

Man Seeks to Enthrone Self and Dethrone God – [2247 B.C. – 2008 B.C.?]

Gen.11:1-4 – 1 And the whole earth was of one language, and of one speech. 2 And it came to pass, as they journeyed from the east, that they found a plain in the land of Shinar; and they dwelt there. 3 And they said one to another, Go to, let us make brick, and burn them throughly. And they had brick for stone, and slime had they for morter. 4 And they said, Go to, let us build us a city and a tower, whose top *may reach* unto heaven; and let us make us a name, lest we be scattered abroad upon the face of the whole earth.

Probability Scenario

It is appears that Nimrod was the founder of Babel (see 1 & Gen.10:10) where this infamous tower was built. Man's intent in building a tower was to avoid being "… *scattered abroad upon the face of the whole earth*" (v.4) in direct opposition to God's intent to *"Be fruitful and multiply, and replenish the earth"* (Gen.9:1 & see 2). This event occurred during the lifetime of Peleg (see 3 & 4)

Supporting Evidence

1. **Birth of Nimrod** – son of Cush & grandson of Ham [p.45]
2. **Noah's Sons to Replenish the Earth** – [p.41]
3. **Birth of Peleg and Joktan** – sons of Eber [p.46]
4. **Death of Peleg** - (at age 239) [p.50]

Probable age of contemporaries

Noah 701–940 – Shem 199–438 – Nimrod 48–274 – Peleg 0–239

God Observes Man's Disobedience – [2165 B.C.?]

Gen.11:5 – 5 And the LORD came down to see the city and the tower, which the children of men builded.

(continued – next page)

Probability Scenario
It appears that Nimrod was responsible for building at least nine cities (see 1 & Gen.10:10-12). It is possible that Nimrod named the cities after his sons and placed them in authority to establish "... *his kingdom*" (Gen.10:10 & see 1). It would seem that Babel may have been the first city Nimrod established and may have been his base of operations. It is likely that after going to Assyria and establishing cities (see 1), he returned to Babel to build the tower of Babel (see 2) in his later years. It is reckoned that if Nimrod fathered his first son around age 30 and spent as little as ten years to build each city, he would have been at least 120 years old before beginning to build the tower. If the tower could be built is as little as ten years Nimrod could then be at least 130 years of age in 2165 B.C.?.
<u>Supporting Evidence</u>
1. **Birth of Nimrod** – son of Cush & grandson of Ham [p.45]
2. **God's Passes Judgment and Administers Justice** – [p.48]
<u>Factors involved in the calculation</u>
x = 2295 B.C.? – Birth of Nimrod
y = 130 ? – age of Nimrod at the time of this event
z = 2165 B.C.? – year of this event
<u>Formula</u>
(x) + (y) = z
(2295B.C.?) - (130 ?) = 2165B.C.?
Probable age of contemporaries
Noah 783 – Shem 281 – Nimrod 130? – Peleg 82

God Passes Judgment and Administers Justice –   [2165 B.C.?]

Gen.11:6-9 – [6] And the LORD said, Behold, the people *is* one, and they have all one language; and this they begin to do: and now nothing will be restrained from them, which they have imagined to do. [7] Go to, let us go down, and there confound their language, that they may not understand one another's speech. [8] So the LORD scattered them abroad from thence upon the face of all the earth: and they left off to build the city. [9] Therefore is the name of it called Babel; because the LORD did there confound the language of all the earth: and from thence did the LORD scatter them abroad upon the face of all the earth.

* * * * * * * BEGINNING OF NATIONS * * * * * * *

Godly Line of Seth (continued through Nahor I)

Birth of Nahor I – son of Serug   [2155 B.C.#]

Gen.11:22 – [22] And Serug lived thirty years, and begat Nahor:

1Chron.1:26 – ²⁶ Serug, Nahor, Terah,

> **Year is Calculated from Scripture References**
> see "Genesis Genealogical Chart"
> **Probable age of contemporaries**
> Noah 793 – Shem 291 – Nimrod 140? – Peleg 92 – Serug 30

Birth of Terah – son of Nahor I   [2126 B.C.#]
Gen.11:24 – ²⁴ And Nahor lived nine and twenty years, and begat Terah:

> **Year is Calculated from Scripture References**
> see "Genesis Genealogical Chart"
> **Probable age of contemporaries**
> Noah 822 – Shem 320 – Nimrod 169? – Peleg 121 – Nahor I 29

Formation of the Patriarchal Period
- see Map 1(1) p.211 -

Terah Began Having Children – (in Ur of the Chaldees)   [2056 B.C.#]
      Gen.11:26 – ²⁶ And Terah lived seventy years, and begat Abram, Nahor, and Haran.

> **Year is Calculated from Scripture References**
> see "Genesis Genealogical Chart"
> **Probable age of contemporaries**
> Noah 892 – Shem 390 – Nimrod 239? – Peleg 191 – Terah 70

Birth of Haran – son of Terah   [2056 B.C.#]
      Gen.11:26 – ²⁶ And Terah lived seventy years, and begat Abram, Nahor, and Haran.

> **Probability Scenario**
> It is probable that Haran was the eldest son of Terah. It is unlikely that Haran's brother, Nahor II, was the eldest as it was seemingly uncommon, at this time and before, for two people to have the same name in the same family while both were still living (see 1). Abram is clearly the younger brother of the three sons named (see 2). Abram is named first here in "precedence format" as opposed to "birth order format" (see 3).
> **Supporting Evidence**
> 1. **Death of Nahor I** - (at age 148) [p.50]
>   Terah's father, Nahor I, was still living at this time.
> 2. **Birth of Abram / Abraham** – son of Terah [p.53]
> 3. **Birth of Ham** – son of Noah [p.29]
>   (under **Supporting Evidence**)

Factors involved in the calculation
x = 2126 B.C.# – Terah's year of birth (see "Genesis Genealogical Chart")
y = 70 – Terah's age when Haran was born (v.26)
z = 2056 B.C.# – Terah fathered Haran
Formula
(x) + (y) = z
(2126 B.C.#) - (70) = 2056 B.C.#
Probable age of contemporaries
Noah 892 – Shem 390 – Nimrod 239? – Peleg 191 – Terah 70

Death of Nimrod - (at age 274 ?)   [2021 B.C.?]

Probability Scenario
It is possible that Nimrod may have lived approximately 274 years, the average life span of post-flood people (see 1 & note).
Supporting Evidence
1. Nimrod's year of birth, reckoned at 2295 B.C.?.
(see **Birth of Nimrod** – son of Cush & grandson of Ham [p.45])
Note
After the flood the average life span was approximately 274 years.
Shem's son, Arphaxad, died at age 438, Salah at age 433, Eber at age 464, Peleg at age 239, Reu at age 239, Serug at age 230, Nahor I at age 148, Terah at age 205.
Formula: (438 + 433 + 464 + 239 + 239 + 230 + 148 + 205) = 2191 years
(2191) / (8) = 273.88 years (see "Genesis Genealogical Chart")
Factors involved in the calculation
x = 2295 B.C.? – Nimrod's year of birth
y = 274 ? – Nimrod's age at death (see **Note** above)
z= 2021 B.C.? – Nimrod's year of death
Formula
(x) + (y) = z
(2295 B.C.?) - (274 ?) = 2021 B.C.?
Probable age of contemporaries
Noah 927 – Shem 425 – Peleg 226 – Terah 105

Death of Peleg - (at age 239)   [2008 B.C.#]
     Gen.11:19 – [19] And Peleg lived after he begat Reu two hundred and nine years, and begat sons and daughters.

Years are Calculated from Scripture References
see "Genesis Genealogical Chart"
Probable age of contemporaries
Noah 940 – Shem 93 – Terah 118

Death of Nahor I - (at age 148)   [2007 B.C.#]
     Gen.11:25 – [25] And Nahor lived after he begat Terah an hundred and nineteen years, and begat sons and daughters.

Years are Calculated from Scripture References
see "Genesis Genealogical Chart"
Probable age of contemporaries
Noah 941 – Shem 439 – Terah 119

Birth of Nahor II – son of Terah   [2005 B.C.?]

Gen.11:26 – 26 And Terah lived seventy years, and begat Abram, Nahor, and Haran.

Probability Scenario

It seems that after the death of Nahor I (see 1), Terah honored his father's memory by naming his next son after his father. It was seemingly uncommon, at this time and before, for two people to have the same name in the same family while both were still living. Abram is clearly the younger brother of the three sons named (see 2). Nahor II was likely born between 2007 B.C. – 1997 B.C.? (see 1 & 2).

Supporting Evidence

1. **Death of Nahor I -** (at age 148) [p.50]
2. **Birth of Abram / Abraham –** son of Terah [p.53]

Probable age of contemporaries
Noah 943 – Shem 441 – Terah 121

Birth of Lot – son of Haran & nephew of Abram   [2005 B.C.?]

Gen.11:27 – 27 Now these *are* the generations of Terah: Terah begat Abram, Nahor, and Haran; and Haran begat Lot.

Probability Scenario

After the flood new generations were born approximately every 31 years (see 1). It seems likely that the example of his father Terah, fathering children at the later age of 70 (see 2), could have influenced Haran to also father children a bit later in life. Considering an approximate age between 31 and 70, it is possible that Haran may have begun fathering children around 2005 B.C. at age 51. It appears that Lot was the eldest child of Haran considering "birth order format" (see 3) and first mention (see 4). It is probable that Lot may have been born before his uncle Abram (see 5).

Supporting Evidence

1. Compare with similar data at **Birth of Nimrod –** son of Cush [p.45].
2. **Terah Began Having Children –** (in Ur of the Chaldees) [p.49]
3. See **Supporting Evidence** #1 at **Birth of Ham –** son of Noah [p.29]
4. Lot is the first of Haran's children mentioned (Gen.11:27, 29).
   Compare with similar data at **Noah's Sons to Replenish the Earth –** [p.41]
5. **Birth of Abram / Abraham –** son of Terah [p.53]

Factors involved in the calculation

x = 2056 B.C.? – Birth of Haran – son of Terah
y = 51 ? – Haran's age when Lot was born
z = 2005 B.C.? – Haran fathered Lot

```
                              Formula
                            (x) + (y) = z
                    (2056 B.C.?) - (51 ?) = 2005 B.C.?
                    Probable age of contemporaries
         Noah 943 – Shem 441 – Terah 121 – Haran 51 – Nahor II 0
```

Birth of Milcah – daughter of Haran (Abram's brother)   [2002 B.C.?]

Gen.11:29 – 29 … Milcah, the daughter of Haran, the father of Milcah, and the father of Iscah.

```
                        Probability Scenario
    It seems that Milcah may have been the 2nd child and eldest daughter fathered
    by Haran considering "birth order format" (see Gen.11:29). It appears that Lot
    was Milcah's older brother (see 1). Reckoning approximately 3 years between
    the births of Haran's children could place Milcah's birth around 2002 B.C.?, 3
    years after her brother Lot (see 2). It is probable that Milcah may have been
    born before her aunt Sarai (see 3).
                        Supporting Evidence
    1.  Birth of Lot – son of Haran & nephew of Abram [p.51]
    2.  Compare with similar data at Birth of Nimrod – son of Cush [p.45]
    3.  Birth of Sarai / Sarah – daughter of Terah & half-sister of Abram [p.55]
                    Factors involved in the calculation
    x = 2005 B.C.? – Birth of Lot
    y = 3 ? – probable time between birth of Lot and birth of Milcah
    z = 2002 B.C.? – Haran fathered Milcah
                              Formula
                            (x) + (y) = z
                    (2005 B.C.?) - (3 ?) = 2002 B.C.?
                    Probable age of contemporaries
     Noah 946 – Shem 444 – Terah 124 – Haran 54 – Nahor II 3 – Lot 3
```

Birth of Iscah – daughter of Haran (Abram's brother)   [1999 B.C.?]

Gen.11:29 – 29 … Milcah, the daughter of Haran, the father of Milcah, and the father of Iscah.

```
                        Probability Scenario
    It seems that Iscah may have been the 3rd child and youngest daughter
    fathered by Haran considering "birth order format" (see Gen.11:29). It appears
    that Lot was Iscah's older brother (see 1). Reckoning approximately 3 years
    between the births of Haran's children could place Iscah's birth around 1999
    B.C.?, 6 years after her brother Lot and 3 years after her sister Milcah (see 2). It
    is probable that Iscah may have been born before her aunt Sarai (see 3).
                        Supporting Evidence
    1.  Birth of Lot – son of Haran & nephew of Abram [p.51]
    2.  Compare with similar data at Birth of Nimrod – son of Cush [p.45]
    3.  Birth of Sarai / Sarah – daughter of Terah & half-sister of Abram [p.55]
```

Factors involved in the calculation
x = 2005 B.C.? – Birth of Lot
y = 6 ? – probable time between birth of Lot and birth of Iscah
z = 1999 B.C.? – Haran fathered Iscah
Formula
(x) + (y) = z
(2005 B.C.?) - (6 ?) = 1999 B.C.?
Probable age of contemporaries
Noah 949 – Shem 447 – Terah 127 – Haran 57 – Nahor II 6 – Lot 6

Death of Noah - (at age 950)   [1998 B.C.#]

    Gen.9:28-29 – [28] And Noah lived after the flood three hundred and fifty years. [29] And all the days of Noah were nine hundred and fifty years: and he died.

Years are Calculated from Scripture References
see "Genesis Genealogical Chart"
Probable age of contemporaries
Shem 448 – Terah 128 – Haran 58 – Nahor II 7 – Lot 7

Godly Line of Seth (continued through Abram)
- see Map 1(1) p.211 -

Birth of Abram / Abraham – son of Terah   [1996 B.C.#]

    1Chron.1:26-27 – [26] ... Nahor, Terah, [27] Abram; the same *is* Abraham.

Year is Calculated from Scripture References
To determine Abram's year of birth requires two calculations: first, Terah's age when Abram was born, second, Abram's year of birth.
- - - - - - - Calculation #1 - - - - - - -
Factors involved in the calculation
x = 205 – age Terah died in Haran (Gen.11:32)
y = 75 – Abram appears to have left Haran at age 75 (Gen.12:4) the same year Terah died.
z = 130 – age Terah fathered Abram
Formula
(x) - (y) = z
(205) - (75) = 130
- - - - - - - Calculation #2 - - - - - - -
Factors involved in the calculation
x = 2126 B.C.# – Terah's year of birth (see "Genesis Genealogical Chart")
y = 130 – Terah's age when Abram was born (see **Calculation #1** above)
z = 1996 B.C.# – Terah fathered Abram
Formula
(x) + (y) = z
(2126 B.C.#) - (130) = 1996 B.C.#
Probable age of contemporaries
Shem 450 – Terah 130 – Haran 60 – Nahor II 9 – Lot 9

Chapter 6

Abraham to Isaac

The Era of the Patriarchs

Birth of Sarai / Sarah – daughter of Terah & half-sister of Abram [1986 B.C.#]
Gen.20:12 – [12] And yet indeed *she is* my sister; she *is* the daughter of my father, but not the daughter of my mother; and she became my wife.

Year is Calculated from Scripture References
Sarai was 10 years younger than Abram (Gen.17:17)
Factors involved in the calculation
x = 1996 B.C.# – Birth of Abram / Abraham – son of Terah
y = 10 – years between birth of Abram and birth of Sarai (Gen.17:17)
z = 1986 B.C.# – Terah fathered Sarai
Formula
(x) + (y) = z
(1996 B.C.#) - (10) = 1986 B.C.#
Probable age of contemporaries
Shem 460 – Terah 140 – Haran 70 – Nahor II 19 – Lot 19 – Abram 10

Death of Reu - (at age 239)   [1978 B.C.#]
Gen.11:21 – [21] And Reu lived after he begat Serug two hundred and seven years, and begat sons and daughters.

Years are Calculated from Scripture References
see "Genesis Genealogical Chart"
Probable age of contemporaries
Shem 468 – Terah 148 – Haran 78 – Lot 27 – Abram 18 – Sarai 8

Abram's Call to Walk With God

God Calls Abram at Ur of the Chaldees –   [1966 B.C.?]

Acts 7:2 – 2 And he said, Men, brethren, and fathers, hearken; The God of glory appeared unto our father Abraham, when he was in Mesopotamia, before he dwelt in Charran,

---

Probability Scenario

It seems that many of God's servants were called / designated for service long before they officially began their service (see 1, 2, 3 & 4). It is probable that Abram may have been officially called by God around 30 years of age (see 2).

Supporting Evidence

1. Joseph (Gen.41:46) seems to have been designated in his youth, but officially began his service to God when he stood before pharaoh at age 30.
2. The son's of Kohath (Num.4:3), Gershon (Num.4:23) and Merari (Num.4:29) were designated as a result of being descendants of Levi, but officially began their tabernacle service at age 30 - 50.
3. David (2Sam.5:4) was designated in his youth, but officially began his service to God when he began to reign as king at age 30.
4. Jesus (Lk.3:23) was designated before the foundation of the world (1Pet.1:20), but began His ministry "… *at about thirty years of age*" (Lk.3:23).

Factors involved in the calculation

x = 1996 B.C.# – Birth of Abram / Abraham – son of Terah
y = 30 ? – years between birth of Abram and God's call
z = 1966 B.C.? – God's call of Abram

Formula

(x) + (y) = z
(1996 B.C.#) - (30 ?) = 1966 B.C.?

Probable age of contemporaries

Shem 480 – Terah 160 – Haran 90 – Lot 39 – Abram 30 – Sarai 20

Death of Haran – brother of Abram   [1956 B.C.?]

Gen.11:28 – 28 And Haran died before his father Terah in the land of his nativity, in Ur of the Chaldees.

Probability Scenario

It seems that the death of Haran might be setting the stage for Abram to begin to fulfill God's call to leave Ur of the Chaldeans (see 1). It is possible that Haran may have had some sort of debilitating illness (v.28) that required Terah, Nahor II and Abram to look after him and which caused a seemingly premature death. It is estimated that Haran may have lived to be around 100 years of age.

Supporting Evidence

1. **God Calls Abram at Ur of the Chaldees –** [p.56]

Factors involved in the calculation

x = 2056 B.C.? – Birth of Haran – son of Terah
y = 100 ? – age at death

```
z = 1996 B.C.? – year of death
                        Formula
                      (x) + (y) = z
              (2056 B.C.?) - (100 ?) = 1956 B.C.?
              Probable age of contemporaries
        Shem 490 – Terah 170 – Lot 49 – Abram 40 – Sarai 30
```

Marriage of Abram and Sarai – (half-sister of Abram)   [1956 B.C.?]

Gen.11:29-30 – ²⁹ And Abram and Nahor took them wives: the name of Abram's wife *was* Sarai; and the name of Nahor's wife, Milcah, the daughter of Haran, the father of Milcah, and the father of Iscah. ³⁰ But Sarai was barren; she *had* no child.

Gen.20:12 – ¹² But indeed *she is* truly my sister. She *is* the daughter of my father, but not the daughter of my mother; and she became my wife.

```
                    Probability Scenario
It is probable that Nahor II, the older brother of Abram (see 1 & 2), may have
been betrothed to his niece, Milcah, the eldest daughter of Haran (see 3 &
Note) well in advance of this date. It is likely that just prior to his death, Lot's
father, Haran, may have instructed to Lot to take his younger sister Iscah (v.29
& see 4) as wife. It seems that Terah may have then instructed Abram to
marry his half-sister Sarai (v.12). Now with all the children and grand-
children established in acceptable marriage relationships, they would not be
corrupting the family line by marrying foreigners. It is probable that the
marriages of Abram and Nahor II took place within the same year as Haran's
death (around the time Abram was 40 years of age in 1956 B.C.?).
                    Supporting Evidence
1.  Birth of Nahor II – son of Terah [p.51]
2.  Birth of Abram / Abraham – son of Terah [p.53]
3.  Birth of Milcah – daughter of Haran (Abram's brother) [p.52]
4.  Birth of Iscah – daughter of Haran (Abram's brother) [p.52]
                         Note
Looking forward in time (approximately 250 years) it is interesting to note
that upon the death of Er, Judah's eldest son, Judah instructed his next older
son, Onan, to marry his brothers wife and raise up an heir to his brother
(Gen.38:8). This seems to indicate that the practice of the next closest relative
marrying the widow of the deceased brother was at least a custom at that
point in time - although not yet a law (Levirate law, Deut.25:5-10). If this
practice was also a custom when Haran died, Nahor II would not have been
responsible to marry Haran's widow since a son, Lot, had already been born.
               Factors involved in the calculation
x = 1996 B.C.# – Abram's year of birth (see "Genesis Genealogical Chart")
y = 40 ? – Abram's estimated age upon marrying Sarai
z = 1956 B.C.? – year of Abram's marriage
```

Formula
(x) + (y) = z
(1996 B.C.#) - (40 ?) = 1956 B.C.?
Probable age of contemporaries
Shem 490 – Terah 170 – Nahor II 49 – Lot 49 – Milcah 46 – Iscah 43
Abram 40 – Sarai 30

Abram Journeys from Ur of the Chaldees to Haran
- see Map 1(2) p.211 -

Terah and His Family Leave Ur of the Chaldees – [1956 B.C.?]

Gen.11:31 – [31] And Terah took Abram his son, and Lot the son of Haran his son's son, and Sarai his daughter in law, his son Abram's wife; and they went forth with them from Ur of the Chaldees, to go into the land of Canaan; and they came unto Haran, and dwelt there.

Probability Scenario
The loss of Terah's father, Nahor I, may have hurt Terah very deeply (see 1). It appears that Terah may have named his next son, Nahor II, to honor the memory of his father (see 2). Now, with the death of Terah's eldest son Haran (see 3), it is possible that Terah wanted to remove himself from any reminders of those unpleasant memories. This event very likely occurred shortly after the preceding events and likely within the same year - 1956 B.C.?.
Supporting Evidence
1. **Death of Nahor I** – at age 148 [p.50]
2. **Birth of Nahor II** – son of Terah [p.51]
3. **Death of Haran** – brother of Abram [p.56]
Note
It is interesting that Iscah, Lot's youngest sister, is not mentioned either as staying in Ur or going to Haran (v.31). One might wonder if Iscah is not mentioned because she may be the infamous wife of Lot whose disobedience caused her to be turned to a pillar of salt. (see **Lot's Wife is Turned to a Pillar of Salt** - [p.81], also see **Lot Began Having Children** – in Haran [p.59]).
Probable age of contemporaries
Shem 490 – Terah 170 – Nahor II 49 – Lot 49 – Milcah 46 – Iscah 43 – Abram 40
Sarai 30

Death of Serug (at age 230) [1955 B.C.#]

Gen.11:23 – [23] And Serug lived after he begat Nahor two hundred years, and begat sons and daughters.

Years are Calculated from Scripture References
see "Genesis Genealogical Chart"
Probable age of contemporaries
Shem 491 – Terah 171 – Lot 50 – Abram 41 – Sarai 31

Lot Began Having Children – in Haran   [1946 B.C.?]

Probability Scenario
Approximately thirty-two years in the future, Lot and "… *the women*" (Gen.14:12, 16 & see 1) are destined to become prisoners of war. Approximately fifty years in the future, Lot's daughters are destined to be concerned about their future security, their prospects of marrying, having children and the "… *old*" age of their father (Gen.19:31 & see 2). It would seem that a couple of years after arriving in Haran (see 3) might be the appropriate point in time for these future events to be set in motion around 1946 B.C.?.
<u>Supporting Evidence</u>
1. **Lot, His Women, People and Goods are Regained** – [p.69]
2. **Lot's Daughters Devise a Plan to Have Children by their Father** – [p.85]
3. **Terah and His Family Leave Ur of the Chaldees** – [p.58]
<u>Probable age of contemporaries</u>
Shem 500 – Terah 180 – Lot 59 – Abram 50 – Sarai 40

King Chedorlaomer Becomes Ruler of Southern Canaan –   [1928 B.C.?]

Gen.14:1-3 – [1] And it came to pass in the days of Amraphel king of Shinar, Arioch king of Ellasar, Chedorlaomer king of Elam, and Tidal king of nations; [2] *That these* made war with Bera king of Sodom, and with Birsha king of Gomorrah, Shinab king of Admah, and Shemeber king of Zeboiim, and the king of Bela, which is Zoar. [3] All these were joined together in the vale of Siddim, which is the salt sea.

Probability Scenario
This event occurred 14 years prior to Lot being taken as a prisoner of war (see 1). The date for this event is reckoned using several steps, beginning with the year Abram and Lot left Haran in 1921 B.C.# (see 2) following the death of Terah (see 3). Upon entering Canaan, they encountered famine and passed through Canaan to Egypt (Gen.12:4-10) in 1921 B.C.#. Abram and Lot stayed in Egypt for several months, but returned to Canaan in 1920 B.C.# where Abram remained ten years (Gen.16:3) before Abram's son Ishmael was born in 1910 B.C.# (see 4). Abram and Lot separated approximately three years after arriving in Canaan around 1917 B.C.? (see 5). Lot became a prisoner of war approximately three years later around 1914 B.C.? (see 1 & Gen.14:12).
<u>Supporting Evidence</u>
1. **Lot is Taken Captive by Chedorlaomer** – [p.69]
2. **Abram and His Family Leave Haran** – [p.61]
3. **Death of Terah** (at age 205) [p.60]
4. **Birth of Ishmael** – son of Abram (at age 86) [p.73]
5. **Abram and Lot Dwell Together then Separate** – [p.66]
<u>Factors involved in the calculation</u>
x = 1914 B.C.? – Lot taken captive
y = 14 ? – years between the beginning of Chedorlaomer's rule and Lot's captivity
z = 1928 B.C.? – year Chedorlaomer became ruler of Southern Canaan

Formula
(x) - (y) = z
(1914 B.C.?) + (14 ?) = 1928 B.C.?
Probable age of contemporaries
Shem 518 – Terah 198 – Lot 77 – Abram 68 – Sarai 58

Death of Terah (at age 205)   [1921 B.C.#]

Gen.11:32 – 32 And the days of Terah were two hundred and five years: and Terah died in Haran.

Years are Calculated from Scripture References
see "Genesis Genealogical Chart"
Probable age of contemporaries
Shem 525 – Lot 84 – Abram 75 – Sarai 65

Death of Terah to Abram's Entry into Egypt

Abram Remembers God's Call and Promise –   [1921 B.C.#]

Gen.12:1-3 – 1 Now the LORD had said unto Abram, Get thee out of thy country, and from thy kindred, and from thy father's house, unto a land that I will shew thee: 2 And I will make of thee a great nation, and I will bless thee, and make thy name great; and thou shalt be a blessing: 3 And I will bless them that bless thee, and curse him that curseth thee: and in thee shall all families of the earth be blessed.

Probability Scenario
Abram had initially been called of God in Ur of the Chaldeans (see 1). It seems that Abram may have been reluctant to leave his family in Ur to answer God's call (see 2). Now, following the death of his father (see 3), it is very likely that his older brother Nahor II will receive his fathers inheritance and move to Haran. Abram is no longer entwined with family responsibilities and is free to answer God's call. This event very likely occurred shortly after the preceding event, likely within the same year - 1921 B.C.#.
Supporting Evidence
1. **God Calls Abram at Ur of the Chaldees** – [p.56]
2. **Death of Haran** – brother of Abram [p.56]
3. **Death of Terah** (at age 205) [p.60]
Probable age of contemporaries
Shem 525 – Lot 84 – Abram 75 – Sarai 65

—

60

Abram Journeys from Haran to Sichem in Canaan
- see Map 1(3) p.211 -

Abram and His Family Leave Haran – [1921 B.C.#]

Gen.12:4-6 – ⁴ So Abram departed, as the LORD had spoken unto him; and Lot went with him: and Abram *was* seventy and five years old when he departed out of Haran. ⁵ And Abram took Sarai his wife, and Lot his brother's son, and all their substance that they had gathered, and the souls that they had gotten in Haran; and they went forth to go into the land of Canaan; and into the land of Canaan they came. ⁶ And Abram passed through the land unto the place of Sichem …

Year is Calculated from Scripture References
Factors involved in the calculation
x = 1996 B.C.# – Abram's year of birth (see "Genesis Genealogical Chart")
y = 75 – Abram's age upon leaving Haran (v.4)
z = 1921 B.C.# – year Abram departed from Haran
Formula
$$(x) + (y) = z$$
(1996 B.C.#) - (75) = 1921 B.C.#
Probable age of contemporaries
Shem 525 – Lot 84 – Abram 75 – Sarai 65

Abram Journeys toward Bethel
- see Map 1(4) p.211 -

Abram Passes through Sichem – [1921 B.C.#]

Gen.12:6-8 – ⁶ … unto the plain of Moreh. And the Canaanite *was* then in the land. ⁷ And the LORD appeared unto Abram, and said, Unto thy seed will I give this land: and there builded he an altar unto the LORD, who appeared unto him. ⁸ And he removed from thence unto a mountain on the east of Bethel, and pitched his tent, *having* Bethel on the west, and Hai on the east: and there he builded an altar unto the LORD, and called upon the name of the LORD.

Probability Scenario
From this point in time (v.5) there are eleven years before Ishmael, the son of Abram, will be born (see 1). Abram is destined to spend ten of those years in Canaan (Gen.16:3) after a brief sojourn in Egypt (see 2). This leaves only one year in which Abram could have journeyed from Haran through Sichem, Bethel, the Negev and stay for a short time in Egypt (see 3). This event likely occurred shortly after the preceding event, likely within the same year - 1921 B.C.#.

Abram Journeys toward the South Country / Negev
- see Map 1(5) p.211 -

Abram Continues to Journey South –   [1921 B.C.#]

Gen.12:9 – 9 And Abram journeyed, going on still toward the south.

Probability Scenario
It seems that Abram did not remain in Bethel very long after being informed that the land would not belong to him, but to his descendants (see 1 & Gen.12:7). It is possible that Abram decided to move further to the south, still looking for a land of his own. This event likely occurred shortly after the preceding event, likely within the same year - 1921 B.C.#.
Supporting Evidence
1. **Abram passes through Sichem** – [p.61]
Probable age of contemporaries
Shem 525 – Lot 84 – Abram 75 – Sarai 65

Abram Journeys to Egypt
- see Map 1(6) p.211 -

Abram Encounters Famine –   [1921 B.C.#]

Gen.12:10 – 10 And there was a famine in the land: and Abram went down into Egypt to sojourn there; for the famine *was* grievous in the land.

Probability Scenario
Scripture is very clear that due to the "*... famine in the land*" (v.10), Abram passed through the land and went directly to Egypt. This event likely occurred shortly after the preceding event, likely within the same year - 1921 B.C.#.
Probable age of contemporaries
Shem 525 – Lot 84 – Abram 75 – Sarai 65

Events During Abram's Stay in Egypt

Abram Obscures His Full Relationship with His Wife –   [1921 B.C.#]

Gen.12:11-13 – 11 And it came to pass, when he was come near to enter into Egypt, that he said unto Sarai his wife, Behold now, I know that thou *art* a fair woman to look upon: 12 Therefore it shall come to pass, when the Egyptians shall see thee, that they shall say, This *is* his wife: and they will kill me, but they will save thee alive. 13 Say, I pray thee, thou *art* my sister: that it may be well with me for thy sake; and my soul shall live because of thee.

Probability Scenario

One might wonder if Abram might be questioning his interpretation of God's statement concerning "… *a land that I will shew thee*" (Gen.12:1 & see 1). Abram may have initially thought he would receive land (Gen.12:1 & Gen.15:8), but then may have become a little discouraged upon learning that he would not receive the land in Canaan (Acts 7:5) but his descendants would (Gen.12:7). Finding famine in the South may have added to Abram's discouragement. At this point he may have begun to think that he was responsible for his own safety (v.13) and the wellbeing of his family. This event likely occurred shortly after the preceding event, likely within the same year - 1921 B.C.#.

Supporting Evidence

1. **Abram Passes through Sichem** – [p.61]

Probable age of contemporaries

Shem 525 – Lot 84 – Abram 75 – Sarai 65

Sarai is Taken into Pharaoh's House –   [1920 B.C.?]

Gen.12:14-16 – 14 And it came to pass, that, when Abram was come into Egypt, the Egyptians beheld the woman that she *was* very fair. 15 The princes also of Pharaoh saw her, and commended her before Pharaoh: and the woman was taken into Pharaoh's house. 16 And he entreated Abram well for her sake: and he had sheep, and oxen, and he asses, and menservants, and maidservants, and she asses, and camels.

Probability Scenario

It appears that the Egyptians noticed Sarai's beauty immediately upon entering Egypt (v.14), and quickly commended Sarai to the princes who then commended her to Pharaoh (v.15). Abram may have felt Pharaoh would not be intimate with Sarai for at least a year, as it may have been customary among kings, even at this time, for a woman to complete "…*twelve months, according to the manner of the women, (for so were the days of their purifications accomplished, to wit, six months with oil of myrrh, and six months with sweet odours, and with other things for the purifying of the women;)*" (Ester 2:12). Sarai may have been "… *taken into Pharaoh's house*" (v.15) very early in 1920 B.C.?.

Probable age of contemporaries

Shem 526 – Lot 85 – Abram 76 – Sarai 66

Abram is Rebuked by Pharaoh –   [1920 B.C.?]
Gen.12:17-20 – [17] And the LORD plagued Pharaoh and his house with great plagues because of Sarai Abram's wife. [18] And Pharaoh called Abram, and said, What *is* this *that* thou hast done unto me? why didst thou not tell me that she *was* thy wife? [19] Why saidst thou, She *is* my sister? so I might have taken her to me to wife: now therefore behold thy wife, take *her*, and go thy way. [20] And Pharaoh commanded *his* men concerning him: and they sent him away, and his wife, and all that he had.

Probability Scenario
It seems that God is again intervening in Abram's life (see 1 & 2), but this time through Pharaoh. It seems that it did not take very long for Pharaoh and his advisors to recognize that they were being plagued, and then to reach the determination that Abram was the cause. This event likely occurred shortly after the preceding event, likely within the same year - 1920 B.C.?.
Supporting Evidence
1. **Terah and His Family Leave Ur of the Chaldees** – [p.58]
2. **Abram Remembers God's Call and Promise** – [p.60]
Probable age of contemporaries
Shem 526 – Lot 85 – Abram 76 – Sarai 66

Abram Journeys toward the South Country / Negev
- see Map 1(7) p.211 -

Abram Again Journeys toward the Negev –   [1920 B.C.?]
Gen.13:1 – [1] And Abram went up out of Egypt, he, and his wife, and all that he had, and Lot with him, into the south.

Probability Scenario
It appears that this event immediately follows the preceding event. This event likely occurred shortly after the preceding event, likely within the same year - 1920 B.C.?.
Probable age of contemporaries
Shem 526 – Lot 85 – Abram 76 – Sarai 66

Abram Leaves Egypt Very Wealthy –   [1920 B.C.?]
Gen.13:2 – [2] And Abram *was* very rich in cattle, in silver, and in gold.

Nahor II Began Having Children – brother of Abram   [1920 B.C.?]
Gen.22:21-24 – [21] Huz his firstborn, and Buz his brother, and Kemuel the father of Aram, [22] And Chesed, and Hazo, and Pildash, and Jidlaph, and Bethuel. [23] … these eight Milcah did bear to Nahor, Abraham's brother.
[24] And his concubine, whose name *was* Reumah, she bare also Tebah, and Gaham, and Thahash, and Maachah.

Probability Scenario
From this point in time there are 64 years before Nahor II's yet unborn 8th son, Bethuel (see 1 & v.21), is destined to father a daughter, Rebekah (see 2), who must reach a marriageable age by the time her future husband, the yet unborn Isaac (see 3), son of Abraham, reaches 40 years of age (see 4). It is likely that both Nahor II and Abram buried their father Terah, which appears to be customary for sons to do (Isaac and Ishmael, Gen.25:7-9; Esau and Jacob, Gen.35:29). It is probable that when Terah died, Nahor II had not yet had any children since Abram was not informed about Nahor II's fathering children until many years later (see 5). It seems that Nahor II may have begun fathering children in 1920 B.C.?, the year after the death of Terah (see 6).

Supporting Evidence

1. **Birth of Bethuel** – son of Nahor II [p.74]
2. **Birth of Rebekah** – daughter of Bethuel/Abraham's nephew [p.95]
3. **Birth of Isaac** – son of Abraham (at age 100) [p.84]
4. **Isaac Takes Rebekah to be His Wife** (at age 40) [p.102]
5. **Abraham Learns His Brother Nahor II has Fathered Children** – [p.91]
6. **Death of Terah** (at age 205) [p.60]

Factors involved in the calculation

x = 1921 B.C.# – Death of Terah
y = 1 ? – year between death of Terah and birth of Nahor II's firstborn Huz
z = 1920 B.C.? – year Nahor II began having children

Formula

$(x) + (y) = z$

$(1921 \text{ B.C.\#}) - (1 ?) = 1920 \text{ B.C.?}$

Probable age of contemporaries

Shem 526 – Nahor II 85 – Lot 85 – Abram 76 – Sarai 66

Abram Journeys toward Bethel

- see Map 1(8) p.211 also Map 2(1) p.212 -

Abram Returns to Bethel –   [1920 B.C.#]

Gen.13:3-4 – 3 And he went on his journeys from the south even to Bethel, unto the place where his tent had been at the beginning, between Bethel and Hai; 4 Unto the place of the altar, which he had made there at the first: and there Abram called on the name of the LORD.

Year is Calculated from Scripture References

Factors involved in the calculation

x = 1910 B.C.# – Birth of Ishmael – son of Abram
y = 10 – years Abram dwelt in Canaan before taking Hagar as wife (Gen.16:3)
z = 1920 B.C.# – year of entry into Canaan

Formula

$(x) - (y) = z$

$(1910 \text{ B.C.\#}) + (10) = 1920 \text{ B.C.\#}$

Events During Abram's Stay in Canaan

Abram and Lot Dwell Together then Separate –   [1920–1917 B.C.?]

Gen.13:5-11 – [5] And Lot also, which went with Abram, had flocks, and herds, and tents. [6] And the land was not able to bear them, that they might dwell together: for their substance was great, so that they could not dwell together. [7] And there was a strife between the herdmen of Abram's cattle and the herdmen of Lot's cattle: and the Canaanite and the Perizzite dwelled then in the land.

[8] And Abram said unto Lot, Let there be no strife, I pray thee, between me and thee, and between my herdmen and thy herdmen; for we *be* brethren. [9] *Is* not the whole land before thee? separate thyself, I pray thee, from me: if *thou wilt take* the left hand, then I will go to the right; or if *thou depart* to the right hand, then I will go to the left.

[10] And Lot lifted up his eyes, and beheld all the plain of Jordan, that it *was* well watered every where, before the LORD destroyed Sodom and Gomorrah, *even* as the garden of the LORD, like the land of Egypt, as thou comest unto Zoar. [11] Then Lot chose him all the plain of Jordan; and Lot journeyed east: and they separated themselves the one from the other.

Probability Scenario

It would seem that it would take a year or so to get settled in the land and begin depleting the natural resources. Perhaps during the next year, Abram's and Lot's herdsmen might have begun to notice the diminishing resources. It is likely that within three years or less, the herdsmen may have become competitive and contentious enough that the issue had to be addressed

Note

It seems that the courtesy Abram was extending to Lot - first choice of the land (vv.8-9), could substantiate the premise that Lot was the elder (see 1) of his uncle Abram (see 2).

1. **Birth of Lot** – son of Haran & nephew of Abram [p.51]
2. **Birth of Abram / Abraham** – son of Terah [p.53]

Factors involved in the calculation

x = 1920 B.C.# – Abram journeys toward Bethel in Canaan –
y = 3 ? – years before separation
z = 1917 B.C.? – year of separation

Formula

$$(x) + (y) = z$$
$$(1920 \text{ B.C.\#}) - (3\ ?) = 1917 \text{ B.C.?}$$

Probable age of contemporaries

Shem 529 – Lot 88 – Abram 79 – Sarai 69

Abram Dwells Near Bethel - (Lot dwells near Sodom)   [1917–1915 B.C.?]
    Gen.13:12-13 – [12] Abram dwelled in the land of Canaan, and Lot dwelled in the cities of the plain, and pitched *his* tent toward Sodom. [13] But the men of Sodom *were* wicked and sinners before the LORD exceedingly.

Abram Journeys to Hebron (Mamre)
- see Map 2(2) p.212 -

Abram Moves His Tent to Hebron –   [1915 B.C.?]
    Gen.13:14-18 – [14] And the LORD said unto Abram, after that Lot was separated from him, Lift up now thine eyes, and look from the place where thou art northward, and southward, and eastward, and westward: [15] For all the land which thou seest, to thee will I give it, and to thy seed for ever. [16] And I will make thy seed as the dust of the earth: so that if a man can number the dust of the earth, *then* shall thy seed also be numbered. [17] Arise, walk through the land in the length of it and in the breadth of it; for I will give it unto thee.
    [18] Then Abram removed *his* tent, and came and dwelt in the plain of Mamre, which *is* in Hebron, and built there an altar unto the LORD.

Probability Scenario
It appears that Abram remained near Bethel (see 1) where the land and the wells were now sufficient to sustain his herds. It is likely that Abram may have remained near Bethel around two years after he and Lot separated. *"Then Abram removed his tent"* to Hebron (v.18) about 1915 B.C.?.
Supporting Evidence
1. **Abram Dwells Near Bethel -** (Lot dwells near Sodom) [p.67]
Factors involved in the calculation
x = 1917 B.C.? – Abram and Lot separate
y = 2 ? – years Abram continues to dwell near Bethel
z = 1915 B.C.? – year Abram journeys to Hebron (Mamre) in Canaan
Formula
(x) + (y) = z
(1917 B.C.?) - (2 ?) = 1915 B.C.?
Probable age of contemporaries
Shem 531 – Lot 90 – Abram 81 – Sarai 71

Chedorlaomer Ruler of Southern Canaan Hears of Rebellion –   [1915 B.C.?]
    Gen.14:4 – [4] Twelve years they served Chedorlaomer, and in the thirteenth year they rebelled.

Probability Scenario
It is clear that this event occurred in the thirteenth year after Chedorlaomer and his allies made war against the kings in Southern Canaan (see 1 & v.4). Lot is living among the rebels near Sodom in Southern Canaan (see 2 &

Gen.13:12). This event occurred approximately 1915 B.C.?, one year prior to Lot being taken as a prisoner of war around 1914 B.C.? (see 3 & Gen.14:1-12).

<u>Supporting Evidence</u>
1. **King Chedorlaomer Becomes Ruler of Southern Canaan** – [p.59]
2. **Abram Dwells Near Bethel** - (Lot dwells near Sodom) [p.67]
3. **Lot is Taken Captive by Chedorlaomer** – [p.69]

<u>Factors involved in the calculation</u>
x = 1928 B.C.? – year King Chedorlaomer Becomes Ruler of Southern Canaan
y = 13 ? – years Chedorlaomer ruled before the rebellion
z = 1915 B.C.? – year of the rebellion

<u>Formula</u>
(x) + (y) = z
(1928 B.C.?) - (13 ?) = 1915 B.C.?

<u>Probable age of contemporaries</u>
Shem 531 – Lot 90 – Abram 81 – Sarai 71

Chedorlaomer and His Allies Put Down the Rebellion – [1914 B.C.?]

Gen.14:5-11 – 5 And in the fourteenth year came Chedorlaomer, and the kings that *were* with him, and smote the Rephaims in Ashteroth Karnaim, and the Zuzims in Ham, and the Emims in Shaveh Kiriathaim, 6 And the Horites in their mount Seir, unto Elparan, which *is* by the wilderness. 7 And they returned, and came to Enmishpat, which *is* Kadesh, and smote all the country of the Amalekites, and also the Amorites, that dwelt in Hazezon-tamar.

8 And there went out the king of Sodom, and the king of Gomorrah, and the king of Admah, and the king of Zeboiim, and the king of Bela (the same *is* Zoar;) and they joined battle with them in the vale of Siddim; 9 With Chedorlaomer the king of Elam, and with Tidal king of nations, and Amraphel king of Shinar, and Arioch king of Ellasar; four kings with five. 10 And the vale of Siddim *was full of* slimepits; and the kings of Sodom and Gomorrah fled, and fell there; and they that remained fled to the mountain. 11 And they took all the goods of Sodom and Gomorrah, and all their victuals, and went their way.

<u>Probability Scenario</u>
It is clear that this event occurred in the fourteenth year after Chedorlaomer and his allies made war against the kings in Southern Canaan (see 1 & v.5). Lot is living among the rebels near Sodom in Southern Canaan (see 2 & Gen.13:12). This event likely occurred around 1914 B.C.?, the approximate year Lot is destined to be taken as a prisoner of war (see 3 & Gen.14:1-12).

<u>Supporting Evidence</u>
1. **King Chedorlaomer Becomes Ruler of Southern Canaan** – [p.59]
2. **Abram Dwells Near Bethel** - (Lot dwells near Sodom) [p.67]
3. **Lot is Taken Captive by Chedorlaomer** – [p.69]

Lot is Taken Captive by Chedorlaomer –   [1914 B.C.?]

Gen.14:12 – 12 And they took Lot, Abram's brother's son, who dwelt in Sodom, and his goods, and departed.

Abram is Told of Lot's Capture –   [1914 B.C.?]

Gen.14:13 – 13 And there came one that had escaped, and told Abram the Hebrew; for he dwelt in the plain of Mamre the Amorite, brother of Eshcol, and brother of Aner: and these *were* confederate with Abram.

Abram Pursues Lot's Captors to Dan
- see Map 2(3) p.212 -

Abram Arms His Trained Servants –   [1914 B.C.?]

Gen.14:14 – 14 And when Abram heard that his brother was taken captive, he armed his trained *servants*, born in his own house, three hundred and eighteen, and pursued *them* unto Dan.

Abram Pursues Lots Captors to Hobah
- see Map 2(4) p.212 -

Abram Employs Offensive Battle Tactics –   [1914 B.C.?]

Gen.14:15 – 15 And he divided himself against them, he and his servants, by night, and smote them, and pursued them unto Hobah, which *is* on the left hand of Damascus.

Lot, His Women, People and Goods are Regained –   [1914 B.C.?]

Gen.14:16 – 16 And he brought back all the goods, and also brought again his brother Lot, and his goods, and the women also, and the people.

Abram Travels to the Valley of Shaveh near Jerusalem
- see Map 2(5) p.212 -

Abram Received by Kings

Abram Meets a Ruler with No One to Rule –   [1914 B.C.?]

Gen.14:17 – 17 And the king of Sodom went out to meet him at the Valley of Shaveh (that *is,* the King's Valley), after his return from the defeat of Chedorlaomer and the kings who *were* with him.

> ### Probability Scenario
> This valley is near Salem (Jerusalem) and approximately 50 miles, as the crow flies, from Sodom. It seems that this valley was a rest stop for Abram, his allies and those he rescued (Gen.14:13, 24). It appears that this event occurred reasonably soon after the preceding event, likely within the same year - 1914 B.C.?.
> ### Probable age of contemporaries
> Shem 532 – Lot 91 – Abram 82 – Sarai 72

King of Sodom Seeks to Get His Captured People Back –   [1914 B.C.?]

Gen.14:21 – 21 And the king of Sodom said unto Abram, Give me the persons, and take the goods to thyself.

Abram Refuses King of Sodom's Reward –   [1914 B.C.?]

Gen.14:22-24 – 22 And Abram said to the king of Sodom, I have lift up mine hand unto the LORD, the most high God, the possessor of heaven and earth, 23 That I will not *take* from a thread even to a shoelatchet, and that I will not take any thing that *is* thine, lest thou shouldest say, I have made Abram rich: 24 Save only that which the young men have eaten, and the portion of the men which went with me, Aner, Eshcol, and Mamre; let them take their portion.

King of Salem Blesses Abram –   [1914 B.C.?]

Gen.14:18-20 – 18 And Melchizedek king of Salem brought forth bread and wine: and he *was* the priest of the most high God. 19 And he blessed him, and said, Blessed *be* Abram of the most high God, possessor of heaven and earth: 20 And blessed be the most high God, which hath delivered thine enemies into thy hand. And he gave him tithes of all.

God is Abram's Shield and Great Reward –   [1914 B.C.?]

Gen.15:1 – 1 After these things the word of the LORD came unto Abram in a vision, saying, Fear not, Abram: I *am* thy shield, *and* thy exceeding great reward.

Abram Concerned His Servant will be His Heir –   [1914 B.C.?]

Gen.15:2-3 – ² And Abram said, Lord GOD, what wilt thou give me, seeing I go childless, and the steward of my house *is* this Eliezer of Damascus? ³ And Abram said, Behold, to me thou hast given no seed: and, lo, one born in my house is mine heir.

God Promises Offspring More Numerous than the Stars –   [1914 B.C.?]

Gen.15:4-5 – ⁴ And, behold, the word of the LORD *came* unto him, saying, This shall not be thine heir; but he that shall come forth out of thine own bowels shall be thine heir. ⁵ And he brought him forth abroad, and said, Look now toward heaven, and tell the stars, if thou be able to number them: and he said unto him, So shall thy seed be.

Abram Believed God - (God counts belief as righteousness)   [1914 B.C.?]

Gen.15:6-7 – ⁶ And he believed in the LORD; and he counted it to him for righteousness.

⁷ And he said unto him, I *am* the LORD that brought thee out of Ur of the Chaldees, to give thee this land to inherit it.

Abram Asks God for a Sign –   [1914 B.C.?]

Gen.15:8 – ⁸ And he said, Lord GOD, whereby shall I know that I shall inherit it?

God's Unconditional Binding Agreement with Abram –   [1914 B.C.?]

Gen.15:9-21 – ⁹ And he said unto him, Take me an heifer of three years old, and a she goat of three years old, and a ram of three years old, and a turtledove, and a young pigeon. ¹⁰ And he took unto him all these, and divided them in the midst, and laid each piece one against another: but the birds divided he not. ¹¹ And when the fowls came down upon the carcases, Abram drove them away.

¹² And when the sun was going down, a deep sleep fell upon Abram; and, lo, an horror of great darkness fell upon him. ¹³ And he said unto Abram, Know of a surety that thy seed shall be a stranger in a land *that is* not theirs, and shall serve them; and they shall afflict them four hundred years; ¹⁴ And also that nation, whom they shall serve, will I judge: and afterward shall they come out with great substance. ¹⁵ And thou shalt go to thy fathers in peace; thou shalt be buried in a good old age. ¹⁶ But in the fourth generation they shall come hither again: for the iniquity of the Amorites *is* not yet full.

¹⁷ And it came to pass, that, when the sun went down, and it was dark, behold a smoking furnace, and a burning lamp that passed between those pieces. ¹⁸ In the same day the LORD made a covenant with Abram, saying,

Unto thy seed have I given this land, from the river of Egypt unto the great river, the river Euphrates: ¹⁹ The Kenites, and the Kenizzites, and the Kadmonites, ²⁰ And the Hittites, and the Perizzites, and the Rephaims, ²¹ And the Amorites, and the Canaanites, and the Girgashites, and the Jebusites.

Abram Returns to Hebron (Mamre)
- see Map 2(6) p.212 also Map 3(1) p.213 -

Abram Returns to Hebron After Rescuing Lot –   [1914 B.C.?]

Probability Scenario
It seems that Abram returned to Hebron (☺ Gen.15:22 ☺) following the events associated with Lot's rescue and his encounter with the king of Salem (Jerusalem) and the king of Sodom at the Valley of Shaveh (Gen.14:17-18). It is very likely that all of the events associated with the rescue of Lot occurred within the same approximate year previously noted - 1914 B.C.?.
Probable age of contemporaries
Shem 532 – Lot 91 – Abram 82 – Sarai 72

Abram Begins to Father Nations

Sarai Offers Her Handmaid Hagar to Abram –   [1910 B.C.#]
  Gen.16:1-3 – ¹ Now Sarai Abram's wife bare him no children: and she had an handmaid, an Egyptian, whose name *was* Hagar. ² And Sarai said unto Abram, Behold now, the LORD hath restrained me from bearing: I pray thee, go in unto my maid; it may be that I may obtain children by her. And Abram hearkened to the voice of Sarai. ³ And Sarai Abram's wife took Hagar her maid the Egyptian, after Abram had dwelt ten years in the land of Canaan, and gave her to her husband Abram to be his wife.

Year is Calculated from Scripture References
Factors involved in the calculation
x = 1920 B.C.# – year Abram entered into Canaan
y = 10 – years spent in Canaan (v.3)
z = 1910 B.C.# – year Sarai offered Hagar to Abram
Formula
(x) + (y) = z
(1920 B.C.#) - (10) = 1910 B.C.#
Probable age of contemporaries
Shem 536 – Lot 95 – Abram 86 – Sarai 76 – Hagar ?

Hagar Conceives and Despises Sarai –   [1910 B.C.#]
  Gen.16:4 – ⁴ And he went in unto Hagar, and she conceived: and when

she saw that she had conceived, her mistress was despised in her eyes.

Probability Scenario
It would seem that this event occurred reasonably soon after the preceding event, likely within a few weeks and in the same year - 1910 B.C.?.

Abram Permits Sarai to Judge the Matter –   [1910 B.C.#]
    Gen.16:5 – 5 And Sarai said unto Abram, My wrong *be* upon thee: I have given my maid into thy bosom; and when she saw that she had conceived, I was despised in her eyes: the LORD judge between me and thee.

Sarai is Harsh and Hagar Flees –   [1910 B.C.#]
    Gen.16:6 – 6 But Abram said unto Sarai, Behold, thy maid *is* in thy hand; do to her as it pleaseth thee. And when Sarai dealt hardly with her, she fled from her face.

The Angel of the LORD Comforts Hagar –   [1910 B.C.#]
    Gen.16:7-14 – 7 And the angel of the LORD found her by a fountain of water in the wilderness, by the fountain in the way to Shur. 8 And he said, Hagar, Sarai's maid, whence camest thou? and whither wilt thou go? And she said, I flee from the face of my mistress Sarai. 9 And the angel of the LORD said unto her, Return to thy mistress, and submit thyself under her hands.
    10 And the angel of the LORD said unto her, I will multiply thy seed exceedingly, that it shall not be numbered for multitude. 11 And the angel of the LORD said unto her, Behold, thou *art* with child, and shalt bear a son, and shalt call his name Ishmael; because the LORD hath heard thy affliction. 12 And he will be a wild man; his hand *will be* against every man, and every man's hand against him; and he shall dwell in the presence of all his brethren. 13 And she called the name of the LORD that spake unto her, Thou God seest me: for she said, Have I also here looked after him that seeth me? 14 Wherefore the well was called Beerlahairoi; behold, *it is* between Kadesh and Bered.

Birth of Ishmael – son of Abram (at age 86)   [1910 B.C.#]
    Gen.16:15-16 – 15 And Hagar bare Abram a son: and Abram called his son's name, which Hagar bare, Ishmael. 16 And Abram *was* fourscore and six years old, when Hagar bare Ishmael to Abram.

Year is Calculated from Scripture References
Factors involved in the calculation
x = 1996 B.C.# – Birth of Abram / Abraham – son of Terah
y = 86 – Abram's age at birth of Ishmael (v.16)
z = 1910 B.C.# – Birth of Ishmael – son of Abram

Death of Arphaxad (at age 438)   [1908 B.C.#]

Gen.11:13 – [13] And Arphaxad lived after he begat Salah four hundred and three years, and begat sons and daughters.

Years are Calculated from Scripture References
see "Genesis Genealogical Chart"
Probable age of contemporaries
Shem 538 – Lot 97 – Abram 88 – Sarai 78

Birth of Bethuel – son of Nahor II   [1899 B.C.?]

Gen.22:22 – [22] … and Bethuel.

Probability Scenario
From this point in time there are 43 years in which Bethuel must grow into a mature adult, marry and father a daughter, Rebekah (see 1), who must reach a marriageable age by the time her future husband, the yet unborn Isaac (see 2), son of Abraham, reaches 40 years of age (see 3). It seems that Bethuel, 8th son of Nahor II, was likely born approximately 21 years after Nahor II began fathering children (see 4 & 5).

Supporting Evidence
1. **Birth of Rebekah** – daughter of Bethuel/Abraham's nephew [p.95]
2. **Birth of Isaac** – son of Abraham (at age 100) [p.84]
3. **Isaac Takes Rebekah to be His Wife** (at age 40) [p.102]
4. **Nahor II Began Having Children** – brother of Abram [p.64]
5. Estimating three years between the births of Nahor II's sons (leaving time for some daughters).

Factors involved in the calculation
x = 1920 B.C.? – year Nahor II began having children
y = 21 ? – number of years before Bethuel's birth
z = 1899 B.C.? – Birth of Bethuel – son of Nahor II

Formula
(x) + (y) = z
(1920 B.C.?) - (21 ?) = 1899 B.C.?
Probable age of contemporaries
Shem 547 – Lot 108 – Nahor II 106 – Abram 97 – Sarai 87

God Changes Abram and Sarai's Names

God Renews the Covenant with Abram / Abraham (at age 99) [1897 B.C.#]
Gen.17:1-6 – ¹ And when Abram was ninety years old and nine, the LORD appeared to Abram, and said unto him, I *am* the Almighty God; walk before me, and be thou perfect. ² And I will make my covenant between me and thee, and will multiply thee exceedingly. ³ And Abram fell on his face: and God talked with him, saying,

⁴ As for me, behold, my covenant *is* with thee, and thou shalt be a father of many nations. ⁵ Neither shall thy name any more be called Abram, but thy name shall be Abraham; for a father of many nations have I made thee. ⁶ And I will make thee exceeding fruitful, and I will make nations of thee, and kings shall come out of thee.

Year is Calculated from Scripture References
Factors involved in the calculation
x = 1996 B.C.# – Birth of Abram / Abraham – son of Terah
y = 99 – Abram's age at time of this event (v.1)
z = 1897 B.C.# – year of this event
Formula
(x) + (y) = z
(1996 B.C.#) - (99) = 1897 B.C.#
Probable age of contemporaries
Shem 549 – Lot 108 – Abram 99 – Sarai 89

God Promises to Pass the Covenant through Abraham's Seed – [1897 B.C.#]
Gen.17:7-8 – ⁷ And I will establish my covenant between me and thee and thy seed after thee in their generations for an everlasting covenant, to be a God unto thee, and to thy seed after thee. ⁸ And I will give unto thee, and to thy seed after thee, the land wherein thou art a stranger, all the land of Canaan, for an everlasting possession; and I will be their God.

Circumcision to be the Mark or Sign of the Covenant – [1897 B.C.#]
Gen.17:9-14 – ⁹ And God said unto Abraham, Thou shalt keep my covenant therefore, thou, and thy seed after thee in their generations. ¹⁰ This *is* my covenant, which ye shall keep, between me and you and thy seed after thee; Every man child among you shall be circumcised. ¹¹ And ye shall circumcise the flesh of your foreskin; and it shall be a token of the covenant betwixt me and you. ¹² And he that is eight days old shall be circumcised among you, every man child in your generations, he that is born in the house, or bought with money of any stranger, which *is* not of thy seed. ¹³ He that is born in thy house, and he that is bought with thy money, must needs be circumcised: and my covenant shall be in your flesh for an everlasting covenant. ¹⁴ And the uncircumcised man child whose

flesh of his foreskin is not circumcised, that soul shall be cut off from his people; he hath broken my covenant.

Sarai Renamed Sarah –   [1897 B.C.#]
Gen.17:15-17 – ¹⁵ And God said unto Abraham, As for Sarai thy wife, thou shalt not call her name Sarai, but Sarah *shall* her name *be*. ¹⁶ And I will bless her, and give thee a son also of her: yea, I will bless her, and she shall be *a mother* of nations; kings of people shall be of her. ¹⁷ Then Abraham fell upon his face, and laughed, and said in his heart, Shall *a child* be born unto him that is an hundred years old? and shall Sarah, that is ninety years old, bear?

Abraham Requests God's Blessing on Ishmael –   [1897 B.C.#]
Gen.17:18 – ¹⁸ And Abraham said unto God, O that Ishmael might live before thee!

God Promises to Pass the Covenant through Isaac –   [1897 B.C.#]
Gen.17:19-21 – ¹⁹ And God said, Sarah thy wife shall bear thee a son indeed; and thou shalt call his name Isaac: and I will establish my covenant with him for an everlasting covenant, *and* with his seed after him. ²⁰ And as for Ishmael, I have heard thee: Behold, I have blessed him, and will make him fruitful, and will multiply him exceedingly; twelve princes shall he beget, and I will make him a great nation. ²¹ But my covenant will I establish with Isaac, which Sarah shall bear unto thee at this set time in the next year.

God Departs –   [1897 B.C.#]
Gen.17:22 – ²² And he left off talking with him, and God went up from Abraham.

Circumcision Instituted

Abraham and His Household Circumcised –   [1897 B.C.#]
Gen.17:23-24 – ²³ And Abraham took Ishmael his son, and all that were born in his house, and all that were bought with his money, every male among the men of Abraham's house; and circumcised the flesh of their foreskin in the selfsame day, as God had said unto him. ²⁴ And Abraham *was* ninety years old and nine, when he was circumcised in the flesh of his foreskin.
Gen.17:27 – ²⁷ And all the men of his house, born in the house, and bought with money of the stranger, were circumcised with him.

Year is Calculated from Scripture References
Factors involved in the calculation

x = 1996 B.C.# – Birth of Abram / Abraham – son of Terah
y = 99 – Abram's age at time of this event (v.24)
z = 1897 B.C.# – year of this event

Formula
(x) + (y) = z
(1996 B.C.#) - (99) = 1897 B.C.#

Probable age of contemporaries
Shem 549 – Lot 108 – Abraham 99 – Sarah 89

Ishmael Circumcised (at age 13)   [1897 B.C.#]
    Gen.17:25-26 – 25 And Ishmael his son *was* thirteen years old, when he was circumcised in the flesh of his foreskin. 26 In the selfsame day was Abraham circumcised, and Ishmael his son.

The Sin of Sodom and Gomorrah is Very Grievous

Abraham Entertains God and Two Angels at Mamre –   [1897 B.C.?]
    Gen.18:1-9 – 1 And the LORD appeared unto him in the plains of Mamre: and he sat in the tent door in the heat of the day; 2 And he lift up his eyes and looked, and, lo, three men stood by him: and when he saw *them*, he ran to meet them from the tent door, and bowed himself toward the ground, 3 And said, My Lord, if now I have found favour in thy sight, pass not away, I pray thee, from thy servant: 4 Let a little water, I pray you, be fetched, and wash your feet, and rest yourselves under the tree: 5 And I will fetch a morsel of bread, and comfort ye your hearts; after that ye shall pass on: for therefore are ye come to your servant. And they said, So do, as thou hast said. 6 And Abraham hastened into the tent unto Sarah, and said, Make ready quickly three measures of fine meal, knead *it*, and make cakes upon the hearth. 7 And Abraham ran unto the herd, and fetcht a calf tender and good, and gave *it* unto a young man; and he hasted to dress it. 8 And he took butter, and milk, and the calf which he had dressed, and set *it* before them; and he stood by them under the tree, and they did eat.
    9 And they said unto him, Where *is* Sarah thy wife? And he said, Behold, in the tent.

God Promises the Miraculous Birth of a Son –   [1897 B.C.?]
    Gen.18:10-15 – 10 And he said, I will certainly return unto thee according to the time of life; and, lo, Sarah thy wife shall have a son. And Sarah heard *it* in the tent door, which *was* behind him. 11 Now Abraham and Sarah *were*

old *and* well stricken in age; *and* it ceased to be with Sarah after the manner of women. 12 Therefore Sarah laughed within herself, saying, After I am waxed old shall I have pleasure, my lord being old also? 13 And the LORD said unto Abraham, Wherefore did Sarah laugh, saying, Shall I of a surety bear a child, which am old? 14 Is any thing too hard for the LORD? At the time appointed I will return unto thee, according to the time of life, and Sarah shall have a son. 15 Then Sarah denied, saying, I laughed not; for she was afraid. And he said, Nay; but thou didst laugh.

The Two Angels Rise up to Depart for Sodom – [1897 B.C.?]

Gen.18:16-19 – 16 And the men rose up from thence, and looked toward Sodom: and Abraham went with them to bring them on the way. 17 And the LORD said, Shall I hide from Abraham that thing which I do; 18 Seeing that Abraham shall surely become a great and mighty nation, and all the nations of the earth shall be blessed in him? 19 For I know him, that he will command his children and his household after him, and they shall keep the way of the LORD, to do justice and judgment; that the LORD may bring upon Abraham that which he hath spoken of him.

God Tells Abraham of Sodom and Gomorrah's Sin – [1897 B.C.?]

Gen.18:20-22 – 20 And the LORD said, Because the cry of Sodom and Gomorrah is great, and because their sin is very grievous; 21 I will go down now, and see whether they have done altogether according to the cry of it, which is come unto me; and if not, I will know. 22 And the men turned their faces from thence, and went toward Sodom: but Abraham stood yet before the LORD.

Abraham Pleads for Sodom – [1897 B.C.?]

Gen.18:23-33 – 23 And Abraham drew near, and said, Wilt thou also destroy the righteous with the wicked? 24 Peradventure there be fifty righteous within the city: wilt thou also destroy and not spare the place for the fifty righteous that *are* therein? 25 That be far from thee to do after this manner, to slay the righteous with the wicked: and that the righteous should be as the wicked, that be far from thee: Shall not the Judge of all the earth do right? 26 And the LORD said, If I find in Sodom fifty righteous within the city, then I will spare all the place for their sakes. 27 And Abraham answered and said, Behold now, I have taken upon me to speak unto the Lord, which *am but* dust and ashes: 28 Peradventure there shall lack five of the fifty righteous: wilt thou destroy all the city for *lack of* five? And he said, If I find there forty and five, I will not destroy *it*. 29 And he spake unto him yet again, and said, Peradventure there shall be forty found there. And he said, I will not do *it* for forty's sake. 30 And he said *unto him,*

Oh let not the Lord be angry, and I will speak: Peradventure there shall thirty be found there. And he said, I will not do *it*, if I find thirty there. ³¹ And he said, Behold now, I have taken upon me to speak unto the Lord: Peradventure there shall be twenty found there. And he said, I will not destroy *it* for twenty's sake. ³² And he said, Oh let not the Lord be angry, and I will speak yet but this once: Peradventure ten shall be found there. And he said, I will not destroy *it* for ten's sake. ³³ And the LORD went his way, as soon as he had left communing with Abraham: and Abraham returned unto his place.

The Two Angels Arrive to Destroy Sodom

Lot Greets the Visitors and Invites Them to His Home –   [1897 B.C.?]
     Gen.19:1-3 – ¹ And there came two angels to Sodom at even; and Lot sat in the gate of Sodom: and Lot seeing *them* rose up to meet them; and he bowed himself with his face toward the ground; ² And he said, Behold now, my lords, turn in, I pray you, into your servant's house, and tarry all night, and wash your feet, and ye shall rise up early, and go on your ways. And they said, Nay; but we will abide in the street all night. ³ And he pressed upon them greatly; and they turned in unto him, and entered into his house; and he made them a feast, and did bake unleavened bread, and they did eat.

Evil Men of the City Surround the House –   [1897 B.C.?]
     Gen.19:4-5 – ⁴ But before they lay down, the men of the city, *even* the men of Sodom, compassed the house round, both old and young, all the people from every quarter: ⁵ And they called unto Lot, and said unto him, Where *are* the men which came in to thee this night? bring them out unto us, that we may know them.

Lot Attempts to Protect the Visitors –   [1897 B.C.?]
     Gen.19:6-9 – ⁶ And Lot went out at the door unto them, and shut the door after him, ⁷ And said, I pray you, brethren, do not so wickedly. ⁸ Behold now, I have two daughters which have not known man; let me, I pray you, bring them out unto you, and do ye to them as *is* good in your eyes: only unto these men do nothing; for therefore came they under the shadow of my roof. ⁹ And they said, Stand back. And they said *again*, This one *fellow* came in to sojourn, and he will needs be a judge: now will we deal worse with thee, than with them. And they pressed sore upon the man, *even* Lot, and came near to break the door.

The Angels Rescue Lot – [1897 B.C.?]

Gen.19:10-11 – ¹⁰ But the men put forth their hand, and pulled Lot into the house to them, and shut to the door. ¹¹ And they smote the men that *were* at the door of the house with blindness, both small and great: so that they wearied themselves to find the door.

Lot Learns Sodom will be Destroyed – [1897 B.C.?]

Gen.19:12-14 – ¹² And the men said unto Lot, Hast thou here any besides? son in law, and thy sons, and thy daughters, and whatsoever thou hast in the city, bring *them* out of this place: ¹³ For we will destroy this place, because the cry of them is waxen great before the face of the LORD; and the LORD hath sent us to destroy it. ¹⁴ And Lot went out, and spake unto his sons in law, which married his daughters, and said, Up, get you out of this place; for the LORD will destroy this city. But he seemed as one that mocked unto his sons in law.

Angels Urge Lot to Hurry into the Mountains – [1897 B.C.?]

Gen.19:15-17 – ¹⁵ And when the morning arose, then the angels hastened Lot, saying, Arise, take thy wife, and thy two daughters, which are here; lest thou be consumed in the iniquity of the city. ¹⁶ And while he lingered, the men laid hold upon his hand, and upon the hand of his wife, and upon the hand of his two daughters; the LORD being merciful unto him: and they brought him forth, and set him without the city. ¹⁷ And it came to pass, when they had brought them forth abroad, that he said, Escape for thy life; look not behind thee, neither stay thou in all the plain; escape to the mountain, lest thou be consumed.

Lot Pleads to go to the City of Zoar – [1897 B.C.?]

Gen.19:18-23 – ¹⁸ And Lot said unto them, Oh, not so, my Lord: ¹⁹ Behold now, thy servant hath found grace in thy sight, and thou hast magnified thy mercy, which thou hast shewed unto me in saving my life; and I cannot escape to the mountain, lest some evil take me, and I die: ²⁰ Behold now, this city *is* near to flee unto, and it *is* a little one: Oh, let me escape thither, (*is* it not a little one?) and my soul shall live. ²¹ And he said unto him, See, I have accepted thee concerning this thing also, that I will not overthrow this city, for the which thou hast spoken. ²² Haste thee, escape thither; for I cannot do any thing till thou be come thither. Therefore the name of the city was called Zoar. ²³ The sun was risen upon the earth when Lot entered into Zoar.

Sodom and Gomorrah Destroyed

The LORD Destroys Sodom and Gomorrah –   [1897 B.C.?]

Gen.19:24-25 – 24 Then the LORD rained upon Sodom and upon Gomorrah brimstone and fire from the LORD out of heaven; 25 And he overthrew those cities, and all the plain, and all the inhabitants of the cities, and that which grew upon the ground.

Lot's Wife is Turned to a Pillar of Salt –   [1897 B.C.?]

Gen.19:26 – 26 But his wife looked back from behind him, and she became a pillar of salt.

Probability Scenario

It is possible that Lot's wife may be Iscah, his youngest sister (see 1 & 2). It is very likely that all of the events associated with the destruction of Sodom and Gomorrah occurred within the same year previously noted - 1897 B.C.?.

Supporting Evidence

1. See Probability Scenario at **Marriage of Abram and Sarai** – [p.57]
2. See Note at **Terah and his family leave Ur of the Chaldees** – [p.58]

Probable age of contemporaries

Shem 549 – Lot 108 – Iscah 102 – Abraham 99 – Sarah 89

Abraham Sees the Smoke of Sodom and Gomorrah –   [1897 B.C.?]

Gen.19:27-28 – 27 And Abraham gat up early in the morning to the place where he stood before the LORD: 28 And he looked toward Sodom and Gomorrah, and toward all the land of the plain, and beheld, and, lo, the smoke of the country went up as the smoke of a furnace.

God Sends Lot out of the Area of Destruction –   [1897 B.C.?]

Gen.19:29-30 – 29 And it came to pass, when God destroyed the cities of the plain, that God remembered Abraham, and sent Lot out of the midst of the overthrow, when he overthrew the cities in the which Lot dwelt.

30 And Lot went up out of Zoar, and dwelt in the mountain, and his two daughters with him; for he feared to dwell in Zoar: and he dwelt in a cave, he and his two daughters.

Abraham Journeys South to Gerar
- see Map 3(2) p.213 -

Abraham Dwells in Gerar –   [1897 B.C.?]

Gen.20:1 – 1 And Abraham journeyed from thence toward the south country, and dwelled between Kadesh and Shur, and sojourned in Gerar.

Abraham Obscures His Full Relationship with His Wife –   [1897 B.C.?]
   Gen.20:2 – ² And Abraham said of Sarah his wife, She *is* my sister: and Abimelech king of Gerar sent, and took Sarah.

> **Note**
> Abraham has used this same ploy previously.
> (see **Abram Obscures His Full Relationship with His Wife – [p.63]**)
> **Probable age of contemporaries**
> Shem 549 – Lot 108 – Abraham 99 – Sarah 89

God Warns Abimelech I Not to Touch Sarah –   [1897 B.C.?]
   Gen.20:3-7 – ³ But God came to Abimelech in a dream by night, and said to him, Behold, thou *art but* a dead man, for the woman which thou hast taken; for she *is* a man's wife. ⁴ But Abimelech had not come near her: and he said, Lord, wilt thou slay also a righteous nation? ⁵ Said he not unto me, She *is* my sister? and she, even she herself said, He *is* my brother: in the integrity of my heart and innocency of my hands have I done this. ⁶ And God said unto him in a dream, Yea, I know that thou didst this in the integrity of thy heart; for I also withheld thee from sinning against me: therefore suffered I thee not to touch her. ⁷ Now therefore restore the man *his* wife; for he *is* a prophet, and he shall pray for thee, and thou shalt live: and if thou restore *her* not, know thou that thou shalt surely die, thou, and all that *are* thine.

> **Probability Scenario**
> It seems that God may have withheld Abimelech from sinning against Him (v.6) because He knew that Sarah was with child. He was establishing assurance for Abraham to be confident that the child was from his own body (Gen.15:4). This event very likely occurred less than nine months prior to the birth of Isaac (see 1), still in the year 1897 B.C.?.
> **Supporting Evidence**
> 1. **Birth of Isaac** – son of Abraham (at age 100) [p.84]
> **Probable age of contemporaries**
> Shem 549 – Lot 108 – Abraham 99 – Sarah 89

Abraham is Rebuked by Abimelech I –   [1897 B.C.?]
   Gen.20:8-10 – ⁸ Therefore Abimelech rose early in the morning, and called all his servants, and told all these things in their ears: and the men were sore afraid. ⁹ Then Abimelech called Abraham, and said unto him, What hast thou done unto us? and what have I offended thee, that thou hast brought on me and on my kingdom a great sin? thou hast done deeds unto me that ought not to be done. ¹⁰ And Abimelech said unto Abraham, What sawest thou, that thou hast done this thing?

Abraham Tries to Explain His Reasoning –   [1897 B.C.?]

Gen.20:11-13 – 11 And Abraham said, Because I thought, Surely the fear of God *is* not in this place; and they will slay me for my wife's sake. <12 And yet indeed *she is* my sister; she *is* the daughter of my father, but not the daughter of my mother; and she became my wife. 13 And it came to pass, when God caused me to wander from my father's house, that I said unto her, This *is* thy kindness which thou shalt shew unto me; at every place whither we shall come, say of me, He *is* my brother.

Abraham Receives Wealth – Sarah receives vindication   [1897 B.C.?]

Gen.20:14-16 – 14 And Abimelech took sheep, and oxen, and menservants, and womenservants, and gave *them* unto Abraham, and restored him Sarah his wife. 15 And Abimelech said, Behold, my land *is* before thee: dwell where it pleaseth thee. 16 And unto Sarah he said, Behold, I have given thy brother a thousand *pieces* of silver: behold, he *is* to thee a covering of the eyes, unto all that *are* with thee, and with all *other*: thus she was reproved.

Abraham Prays that Abimelech I may again Bear Children –   [1897 B.C.?]

Gen.20:17-18 – 17 So Abraham prayed unto God: and God healed Abimelech, and his wife, and his maidservants; and they bare *children*. 18 For the LORD had fast closed up all the wombs of the house of Abimelech, because of Sarah Abraham's wife.

Abraham Departs to Beersheba

- see Map 3(3) p.213 -

Abraham Dwells in Beersheba –   [1897 B.C.?]

Probability Scenario
Abimelech was deceived by Abraham (Gen.20:2), called to account by God (v.3), learned that God restrained him from touching Sarah (v.6), and was informed that Abraham was a prophet whose prayers could spare Abimelech's life (v.7). Abimelech rebuked Abraham (Gen.20:9-10), but gave him great wealth (vv.14-16) and vindicated Sarah (v.16). It appears that God's intervention in this event caused Abimelech to offer Abraham to dwell in his

land (Gen.20:15) out of fear for both God and Abraham. It appears that Abraham had journeyed to Beersheba where he was dwelling when Abimelech came to make a covenant of peace (see 1 & Gen.21:22-23,31).

Supporting Evidence

1. **Abimelech I Seeks Abraham to Insure Safety of His Dynasty** – [p.93]

Probable age of contemporaries

Shem 549 – Lot 108 – Abraham 99 – Sarah 89 – Ishmael 13

Birth of Isaac – son of Abraham (at age 100)   [1896 B.C.#]

Gen.21:1-7 – 1 And the LORD visited Sarah as he had said, and the LORD did unto Sarah as he had spoken. 2 For Sarah conceived, and bare Abraham a son in his old age, at the set time of which God had spoken to him. 3 And Abraham called the name of his son that was born unto him, whom Sarah bare to him, Isaac. 4 And Abraham circumcised his son Isaac being eight days old, as God had commanded him. 5 And Abraham was an hundred years old, when his son Isaac was born unto him. 6 And Sarah said, God hath made me to laugh, *so that* all that hear will laugh with me. 7 And she said, Who would have said unto Abraham, that Sarah should have given children suck? for I have born *him* a son in his old age.

1Chron.1:34 – 34 And Abraham begat Isaac …

Year is Calculated from Scripture References
see "Genesis Genealogical Chart"
Probable age of contemporaries
Shem 550 – Lot 109 – Abraham 100 – Sarah 90 – Ishmael 14

Chapter 7

Isaac to Jacob

Lot's Daughters Bear Sons to Their Father

Lot's Daughters Devise a Plan to have Children by their Father - [1896 B.C.?]
    Gen.19:31-36 – 31 And the firstborn said unto the younger, Our father *is* old, and *there is* not a man in the earth to come in unto us after the manner of all the earth: 32 Come, let us make our father drink wine, and we will lie with him, that we may preserve seed of our father. 33 And they made their father drink wine that night: and the firstborn went in, and lay with her father; and he perceived not when she lay down, nor when she arose. 34 And it came to pass on the morrow, that the firstborn said unto the younger, Behold, I lay yesternight with my father: let us make him drink wine this night also; and go thou in, *and* lie with him, that we may preserve seed of our father. 35 And they made their father drink wine that night also: and the younger arose, and lay with him; and he perceived not when she lay down, nor when she arose. 36 Thus were both the daughters of Lot with child by their father.

Probability Scenario
Lot's daughters seem to have begun to anticipate a bleak future. By this time their father was probably around 109 years of age (see 1) and had seemingly lost all his wealth (see 2 & Gen.13:5-6) in the destruction of Sodom and Gomorrah (see 3). They lost their husbands in the destruction; and there were no children to provide for them in their old age (see 4). It would seem that this event occurred several months after making their residence a cave (see 5),

likely around the year 1896 B.C.?.
Supporting Evidence
1. **Birth of Lot** – son of Haran & nephew of Abram [p.51]
2. **Abram and Lot Dwell Together then Separate** – [p.66]
3. **The LORD Destroys Sodom and Gomorrah** – [p.81]
4. **Lot Learns Sodom will be Destroyed** – [p.80]
5. **God Sends Lot out of the Area of Destruction** – [p.81]
Probable age of contemporaries
Shem 550 – Lot 109 – Abraham 100 – Sarah 90 – Ishmael 14 – Isaac (months)

Birth of Moab (Moabites) – son of Lot & eldest daughter   [1895 B.C.?]
  Gen.19:37 – 37 And the firstborn bare a son, and called his name Moab: the same *is* the father of the Moabites unto this day.

Probability Scenario
If Lot's daughters devised their plan to have children by their father even one year after the destruction of Sodom and Gomorrah, another nine months (the normal time required from conception to birth) would still be required. It would seem that this event likely occurred approximately two years after the destruction of Sodom and Gomorrah, likely around the year 1895 B.C.?.
Supporting Evidence
1. **The LORD Destroys Sodom and Gomorrah** – [p.81]
Factors involved in the calculation
x = 1897 B.C.? – The LORD destroyed Sodom and Gomorrah
y = 2 ? – years between destruction of Sodom / Gomorrah and birth of child
z = 1895 B.C.? – Birth of Lot's son / grandson
Formula
(x) + (y) = z
(1897 B.C.?) - (2 ?) = 1895 B.C.?
Probable age of contemporaries
Shem 551 – Lot 110 – Abraham 101 – Sarah 91 – Ishmael 15 – Isaac 1

Birth of Benammi (Ammonites) – son of Lot & youngest daughter[1895 B.C.?]
  Gen.19:38 - 38 And the younger, she also bare a son, and called his name Benammi: the same *is* the father of the children of Ammon unto this day.

Probability Scenario
See **Birth of Moab (Moabites)** – son of Lot & eldest daughter [p.86]

Ishmael Mocks Isaac

Isaac is Weaned –   [1893 B.C.?]
  Gen.21:8 – 8 And the child grew, and was weaned: and Abraham made a great feast the *same* day that Isaac was weaned.

Probability Scenario
The weaning of a child appears to have occurred around three years of age (see 1). It would seem that this event may have likely occurred approximately three years after the birth of Isaac around the year 1893 B.C.?.

Supporting Evidence

1. 2Macc.7:27 – [27] In derision of the cruel tyrant, she leaned over close to her son and said in their native language: "Son, have pity on me, who carried you in my womb for nine months, nursed you for three years, brought you up, educated and supported you to your present age." (NAB)

Factors involved in the calculation

x = 1896 B.C.# – Birth of Isaac – son of Abraham
y = 3 ? – years between birth of Isaac and his weaning
z = 1893 B.C.? – year of Isaac's weaning

Formula

$$(x) + (y) = z$$
$$(1896 \text{ B.C.\#}) - (3 \text{ ?}) = 1893 \text{ B.C.?}$$

Probable age of contemporaries

Shem 553 – Abraham 103 – Sarah 93 – Ishmael 17 – Isaac 3

Sarah is Offended – wants Ishmael and Hagar cast out   [1893 B.C.?]

Gen.21:9-10 – [9] And Sarah saw the son of Hagar the Egyptian, which she had born unto Abraham, mocking. [10] Wherefore she said unto Abraham, Cast out this bondwoman and her son: for the son of this bondwoman shall not be heir with my son, *even* with Isaac.

Abraham is Grieved Because of Ishmael –   [1893 B.C.?]

Gen.21:11 – [11] And the thing was very grievous in Abraham's sight because of his son.

God Tells Abraham to do as Sarah Requests –   [1893 B.C.?]

Gen.21:12 – [12] And God said unto Abraham, Let it not be grievous in thy sight because of the lad, and because of thy bondwoman; in all that Sarah hath said unto thee, hearken unto her voice; for in Isaac shall thy seed be called.

God Promises Ishmael will be Blessed –   [1893 B.C.?]

Gen.21:13 – [13] And also of the son of the bondwoman will I make a nation, because he *is* thy seed.

Hagar and Ishmael Cast Out

Abraham Sends Hagar and Ishmael Away with Provisions -   [1893 B.C.?]
    Gen.21:14 – ¹⁴ And Abraham rose up early in the morning, and took bread, and a bottle of water, and gave *it* unto Hagar, putting *it* on her shoulder, and the child, and sent her away: and she departed, and wandered in the wilderness of Beersheba.

Probability Scenario
It appears that this event occurred the very next morning after the feast (v.14), and likely still in the same year previously noted - 1893 B.C.?.
Probable age of contemporaries
Shem 553 – Abraham 103 – Sarah 93 – Ishmael 17 – Isaac 3

God Speaks to Hagar when the Provisions Run Out –   [1893 B.C.?]
    Gen.21:15-17 – ¹⁵ And the water was spent in the bottle, and she cast the child under one of the shrubs. ¹⁶ And she went, and sat her down over against *him* a good way off, as it were a bowshot: for she said, Let me not see the death of the child. And she sat over against *him*, and lift up her voice, and wept. ¹⁷ And God heard the voice of the lad; and the angel of God called to Hagar out of heaven, and said unto her, What aileth thee, Hagar? fear not; for God hath heard the voice of the lad where he *is*.

God Encourages Hagar and Blesses Ishmael –   [1893 B.C.?]
    Gen.21:18-21 – ¹⁸ Arise, lift up the lad, and hold him in thine hand; for I will make him a great nation. ¹⁹ And God opened her eyes, and she saw a well of water; and she went, and filled the bottle with water, and gave the lad drink. ²⁰ And God was with the lad; and he grew, and dwelt in the wilderness, and became an archer. ²¹ And he dwelt in the wilderness of Paran: and his mother took him a wife out of the land of Egypt.

God Tests Abraham

God Tells Abraham to Sacrifice His ONLY Son Isaac –   [1879 B.C.?]
    Gen.22:1-2 – ¹ And it came to pass after these things, that God did tempt Abraham, and said unto him, Abraham: and he said, Behold, *here* I *am*. ² And he said, Take now thy son, thine only *son* Isaac, whom thou lovest, and get thee into the land of Moriah; and offer him there for a burnt offering upon one of the mountains which I will tell thee of.

Probability Scenario
One can only imagine the anguish Abraham must have felt when God approved of Sarah's demand (see 1) to send his eldest son, Ishmael, away

around the age of 17 (see 2 & 3). Now God is asking Abraham to offer his son Isaac as a burnt offering (v.2). One might wonder if Sarah might now be experiencing similar anguish at the prospect of losing Isaac, her only son, probably also around the age of 17 (see 4). It would seem that this event may have likely occurred around the year 1879 B.C.?.

<u>Supporting Evidence</u>
1. **God Tells Abraham to do as Sarah Requests** – [p.87]
2. **Birth of Ishmael** – son of Abram (at age 86) [p.73]
3. **Abraham Sends Hagar and Ishmael Away with Provisions** – [p.88]
4. **Birth of Isaac** – son of Abraham (at age 100) [p.84]

<u>Note</u>
It seems that this event may prove to be the pivotal point for surprising future events.

<u>Factors involved in the calculation</u>
x = 1896B.C.# – Isaac's year of birth (see "Genesis Genealogical Chart")
y = 17 ? – years between birth of Isaac and this event
z = 1879 B.C.? – year God tells Abraham to sacrifice Isaac

<u>Formula</u>
$$(x) + (y) = z$$
$$(1896 \text{ B.C.\#}) - (17\ ?) = 1879 \text{ B.C.?}$$

<u>Probable age of contemporaries</u>
Shem 567 – Abraham 117 – Sarah 107 – Isaac 17

Abraham Journeys to the Land of Moriah
- see Map 3(4) p.213 -

Abraham Travels Three Days to the Land of Moriah –   [1879 B.C.?]

Gen.22:3-6 – 3 And Abraham rose up early in the morning, and saddled his ass, and took two of his young men with him, and Isaac his son, and clave the wood for the burnt offering, and rose up, and went unto the place of which God had told him. 4 Then on the third day Abraham lifted up his eyes, and saw the place afar off. 5 And Abraham said unto his young men, Abide ye here with the ass; and I and the lad will go yonder and worship, and come again to you. 6 And Abraham took the wood of the burnt offering, and laid *it* upon Isaac his son; and he took the fire in his hand, and a knife; and they went both of them together.

<u>Probability Scenario</u>
Mount Moriah, in the land of Moriah (see 1 & Gen22:2), was about 24 miles from Hebron and about 50 miles from Beersheba. It would seem that if Abraham began his journey at Hebron and traveled only 2 miles per hour for 10 hours, he would have seen "... *the place afar off*" (about 2 or 3 miles) early on the second day. However if he began his journey at Beersheba and traveled only 2 miles per hour for 10 hours he would have seen "... *the place afar off*"

> (about 2 or 3 miles) around midday "... *on the third day*" (v.4). It seems that Abraham's journey began from Beersheba since no scriptural reference has been made to his leaving Beersheba and moving to another area, including Hebron. It appears that this event occurred the next morning (v.3) following the previous event in 1879 B.C.?.
> ### Supporting Evidence
> 1. **God Tells Abraham to Sacrifice His ONLY Son Isaac** – [p.88]
> #### Probable age of contemporaries
> Shem 567 – Abraham 117 – Sarah 107 – Isaac 17

Isaac Inquires about the Absence of a Sacrificial Lamb –   [1879 B.C.?]

Gen.22:7 – 7 And Isaac spake unto Abraham his father, and said, My father: and he said, Here *am* I, my son. And he said, Behold the fire and the wood: but where *is* the lamb for a burnt offering?

Abraham Tells Isaac that God will Provide the Lamb –   [1879 B.C.?]

Gen.22:8 – 8 And Abraham said, My son, God will provide himself a lamb for a burnt offering: so they went both of them together.

Abraham Prepares the Altar and the Sacrifice (Isaac)   [1879 B.C.?]

Gen.22:9-10 – 9 And they came to the place which God had told him of; and Abraham built an altar there, and laid the wood in order, and bound Isaac his son, and laid him on the altar upon the wood. 10 And Abraham stretched forth his hand, and took the knife to slay his son.

God Tells Abraham to Spare Isaac and Provides the Sacrifice –   [1879 B.C.?]

Gen.22:11-14 – 11 And the angel of the LORD called unto him out of heaven, and said, Abraham, Abraham: and he said, Here *am* I. 12 And he said, Lay not thine hand upon the lad, neither do thou any thing unto him: for now I know that thou fearest God, seeing thou hast not withheld thy son, thine only *son* from me. 13 And Abraham lifted up his eyes, and looked, and behold behind *him* a ram caught in a thicket by his horns: and Abraham went and took the ram, and offered him up for a burnt offering in the stead of his son. 14 And Abraham called the name of that place Jehovahjireh: as it is said *to* this day, In the mount of the LORD it shall be seen.

God Blesses Abraham –   [1879 B.C.?]

Gen.22:15-18 – 15 And the angel of the LORD called unto Abraham out of heaven the second time, 16 And said, By myself have I sworn, saith the LORD, for because thou hast done this thing, and hast not withheld thy son, thine only *son*: 17 That in blessing I will bless thee, and in multiplying I will multiply thy seed as the stars of the heaven, and as the sand which *is* upon the sea shore; and thy seed shall possess the gate of his enemies; ¹⁸ And in thy seed shall all the nations of the earth be blessed; because thou hast obeyed my voice.

Abraham Returns to Beersheba
- see Map 3(5) p.213 -

Abraham Dwells in Beersheba –   [1879 B.C.?]
Gen.22:19 – ¹⁹ So Abraham returned unto his young men, and they rose up and went together to Beersheba; and Abraham dwelt at Beersheba.

Probability Scenario
It is interesting that this passage states "... *and Abraham dwelt at Beersheba*" (v.19). There appears to be no further mention of Abraham being with Sarah until Sarah's death in Hebron (see 1). One might wonder if Sarah might have been so overwhelmed with the anguish surrounding Abraham's intention to sacrifice her only son Isaac that she departed from Abraham and moved back to Hebron. It is very likely that all of the events associated with the sacrifice of Isaac occurred within a very short period of time and in the same year previously noted - 1879 B.C.?.
Supporting Evidence
1. **Death of Sarah at Kirjatharba** / Hebron (at age 127) [p.96]
Note
See Note at **God Tells Abraham to Sacrifice His ONLY Son Isaac** – [p.88]
Probable age of contemporaries
Shem 567 – Abraham 117 – Sarah 107 – Isaac 17

Death of Salah (at age 433)   [1878 B.C.#]
Gen.11:15 – ¹⁵ And Salah lived after he begat Eber four hundred and three years, and begat sons and daughters.

Years are Calculated from Scripture References
see "Genesis Genealogical Chart"
Probable age of contemporaries
Shem 568 – Abraham 118 – Sarah 108 – Isaac 18

Abraham Learns His Brother Nahor II has Fathered Children –   [1876 B.C.?]
Gen.22:20 – ²⁰ And it came to pass after these things, that it was told Abraham, saying, Behold, Milcah, she hath also born children unto thy brother Nahor;

Probability Scenario
Abraham appears to have been dwelling in Beersheba (see 1), seemingly without Sarah, since the time God told Abraham to sacrifice Isaac (see 2). If

that were the case, it is likely that Abraham would have been attempting to reconcile with Sarah over the last three years. It seems probable that hearing his older brother Nahor II has fathered children may have caused Abraham to long for companionship (see 3). It is possible that this event occurred approximately three years after the sacrifice of Isaac around 1876 B.C.?.

<u>Supporting Evidence</u>
1. **Abraham Dwells in Beersheba** – [p.91]
2. **God Tells Abraham to Sacrifice His ONLY Son Isaac** – [p.88]
3. **Abraham Takes a Concubine** (Keturah) [p.92]
<u>Probable age of contemporaries</u>
Shem 570 – Abraham 120 – Sarah 110 – Isaac 20

Abraham Takes a Concubine (Keturah) [1876 B.C.?]

<u>Probability Scenario</u>
Abraham is destined to live approximately fifty-five years from this point in time (see 1) and have great-great grandchildren by Keturah. It seems that to have adequate time for even two of the three generations of children to be fathered through Abraham with his concubine, Keturah, he would have to have taken her as concubine about 1876 B.C.? (see 2).

<u>Supporting Evidence</u>
1. **Death of Abraham** (at age 175) [p.106]
2. **Keturah Begins Having Children** – Abraham's concubine [p.92]
<u>Probable age of contemporaries</u>
Shem 570 – Abraham 120 – Sarah 110 – Isaac 20

Keturah Begins Having Children – Abraham's concubine [1875 B.C.?]

Gen.25:2-4 – 2 And she bare him Zimran, and Jokshan, and Medan, and Midian, and Ishbak, and Shuah. 3 And Jokshan begat Sheba, and Dedan. And the sons of Dedan were Asshurim, and Letushim, and Leummim. 4 And the sons of Midian; Ephah, and Epher, and Hanoch, and Abida, and Eldaah. All these *were* the children of Keturah.

1Chron.1:32-33 – 32 Now the sons of Keturah, Abraham's concubine: she bare Zimran, and Jokshan, and Medan, and Midian, and Ishbak, and Shuah. And the sons of Jokshan; Sheba, and Dedan. 33 And the sons of Midian; Ephah, and Epher, and Henoch, and Abida, and Eldaah. All these *are* the sons of Keturah.

<u>Probability Scenario</u>
It appears that to have adequate time for even two of the three generations of children listed here to be fathered through Abraham with his concubine, Keturah, he would have to have taken her as concubine about 1876 B.C.?.

A probable sequence of events appears to be as follows

(a) 1876 B.C.? – Abraham Takes a Concubine (Keturah) (see 1).
(b) 1875 B.C.? – Zimran - Abraham's 1st son by Keturah, may have been born approximately one year after Keturah became Abraham's concubine (v.2).
(c) 1873 B.C.? – Jokshan - Abraham's 2nd son by Keturah, may have been born around 2 years after the birth of his brother Zimran (v.2).
(d) 1856 B.C.# – Isaac married Rebekah (see 2).
(e) 1842 B.C.? – Jokshan - may have married around age 31 (see 3).
(f) 1837 B.C.? – Dedan, 2nd son of Jokshan and grandson of Abraham, may have been born as many as five years after the marriage of his father Jokshan (v.3).
(g) 1826 B.C.? – Abraham may have made Isaac his heir around 11 years after the birth of Dedan, son of Jokshan (see 4).
(h) 1826 B.C.? – Abraham sent Keturah's children away (see 5)
(i) 1821 B.C.# – Abraham died around five years after he sent Keturah's children away (see 6).

Supporting Evidence
1. **Abraham Takes a Concubine** (Keturah) [p.92]
2. **Isaac Takes Rebekah to be His Wife** (at age 40) [p.102]
3. **Birth of Nimrod** – son of Cush & grandson of Ham [p.45]
   After the flood new generations were born approximately every 31 years.
4. **Isaac Becomes Abraham's Heir** – [p.105]
5. **Abraham Sends Keturah's Children Away** – [p.105]
6. **Death of Abraham** (at age 175) [p.106]

Probable age of contemporaries
Shem 571 – Abraham 121 – Sarah 111 – Isaac 21

Abraham Agrees to a Covenant with Abimelech I

Abimelech I Seeks Abraham to Insure Safety of His Dynasty –   [1875 B.C.?]
Gen.21:22-23 – 22 And it came to pass at that time, that Abimelech and Phichol the chief captain of his host spake unto Abraham, saying, God *is* with thee in all that thou doest: 23 Now therefore swear unto me here by God that thou wilt not deal falsely with me, nor with my son, nor with my son's son: *but* according to the kindness that I have done unto thee, thou shalt do unto me, and to the land wherein thou hast sojourned.

Probability Scenario
It appears that Abimelech I may be advanced in years and is seeking a peace agreement with Abraham on behalf of his son (v.23 & see 1) and his grand-son (v.23). Abimelech may have become concerned that Abraham, living so near to Gerar, was beginning to increase his family, and that Isaac might also soon marry and build a family. This event likely occurred soon after Abraham began having children with Keturah around 1875 B.C.? (see 2).

Supporting Evidence
1. **Abimelech II Seeks Isaac to Insure Safety of His Kingdom** – [p.116]

(This event is destined to occur approximately 111 years in the future)
2. **Keturah Begins Having Children** – Abraham's concubine [p.92]
Probable age of contemporaries
Shem 571 – Abraham 121 – Sarah 111 – Isaac 21

Abraham Agrees but Adds One Stipulation – [1875 B.C.?]

Gen.21:24-27 – 24 And Abraham said, I will swear. 25 And Abraham reproved Abimelech because of a well of water, which Abimelech's servants had violently taken away. 26 And Abimelech said, I wot not who hath done this thing: neither didst thou tell me, neither yet heard I *of it*, but to day. 27 And Abraham took sheep and oxen, and gave them unto Abimelech; and both of them made a covenant.

Abraham Sets a Seal on the Agreement – [1875 B.C.?]

Gen.21:28-32 – 28 And Abraham set seven ewe lambs of the flock by themselves. 29 And Abimelech said unto Abraham, What *mean* these seven ewe lambs which thou hast set by themselves? 30 And he said, For *these* seven ewe lambs shalt thou take of my hand, that they may be a witness unto me, that I have digged this well. 31 Wherefore he called that place Beersheba; because there they sware both of them. 32 Thus they made a covenant at Beersheba: ...

Abraham and Abimelech I Part – [1875 B.C.?]

Gen.21:32-34 – 32 ... then Abimelech rose up, and Phichol the chief captain of his host, and they returned into the land of the Philistines.

33 And *Abraham* planted a grove in Beersheba, and called there on the name of the LORD, the everlasting God. 34 And Abraham sojourned in the Philistines' land many days.

Abraham's Descendants through Ishmael

Future Descendants of Ishmael –

Gen.25:12-16 – 12 Now these *are* the generations of Ishmael, Abraham's son, whom Hagar the Egyptian, Sarah's handmaid, bare unto Abraham: 13 And these *are* the names of the sons of Ishmael, by their names, according to their generations: the firstborn of Ishmael, Nebajoth; and Kedar, and Adbeel, and Mibsam, 14 And Mishma, and Dumah, and Massa, 15 Hadar, and Tema, Jetur, Naphish, and Kedemah: 16 These *are* the sons of Ishmael, and these *are* their names, by their towns, and by their castles; twelve princes according to their nations.

1Chron.1:28-31 – [28] The sons of Abraham; Isaac, and Ishmael. [29] These *are* their generations: The firstborn of Ishmael, Nebaioth; then Kedar, and Adbeel, and Mibsam, [30] Mishma, and Dumah, Massa, Hadad, and Tema, [31] Jetur, Naphish, and Kedemah. These are the sons of Ishmael.

Probability Scenario
God promised Abraham that Ishmael would be the father of twelve princes (see 1). It appears that God fulfilled His promise during Abraham's life time. If Ishmael married around age 35, about 1875 B.C.? (see 2), and if Ishmael fathered one child approximately every 4 years or less, he would have fathered all twelve of the children God promised by 1827 B.C.?, before Abraham died in 1821 B.C.# at age 175 (see 3).
Supporting Evidence
1. **God Encourages Hagar and Blesses Ishmael** – [p.88]
2. See Note at **Birth of Nimrod** – son of Cush & grandson of Ham [p.45]
(for average frequency of new generations born after the flood)
3. **Death of Abraham** (at age 175) [p.106]

Birth of Rebekah – daughter of Bethuel/Abraham's nephew   [1874 B.C.?]

    Gen.22:23 – [23] And Bethuel begat Rebekah: …

Probability Scenario
Rebekah is destined to marry Isaac, son of Abraham, approximately eighteen years from this point in time, when Isaac reaches age 40 (see 1).
Supporting Evidence
1. **Isaac Takes Rebekah to be His Wife** (at age 40) [p.102]
Factors involved in the calculation
x = 1856 B.C.# – year Isaac and Rebekah marry
y = 18 ? – Rebekah's probable age in 1856 B.C.?
z = 1874 B.C.? – Birth of Rebekah
Formula
(x) - (y) = z
(1856 B.C.#) + (18 ?) = 1874 B.C.?
Probable age of contemporaries
Shem 572 – Abraham 122 – Sarah 112 – Isaac 22 – Bethuel 30

Birth of Laban – son of Bethuel/Abraham's nephew   [1873 B.C.?]

    Gen.24:29 – [29] And Rebekah had a brother, and his name *was* Laban:

Probability Scenario
It seems that Laban may have been born after his sister Rebekah. There is no mention of Laban's birth, other than he was Rebekah's brother (v.29 & see 1). It seems possible that Laban could have been about one year younger than Rebekah. Laban could have been born around 1873 B.C.?.
Supporting Evidence
1. **Birth of Rebekah** – daughter of Bethuel/Abraham's nephew [p.95]

Factors involved in the calculation
x = 1874 B.C.? – Birth of Rebekah
y = 1 ? – year between birth of Rebekah and birth of Laban
z = 1873 B.C.? – Birth of Laban
Formula
(x) + (y) = z
(1874 B.C.?) - (1 ?) = 1873 B.C.?
Probable age of contemporaries
Shem 577 – Abraham 127 – Sarah 117 – Isaac 27 – Bethuel 35

Death of Sarah

Death of Sarah at Kirjatharba / Hebron (at age 127)　　　　　[1859 B.C.#]

    Gen.23:1 – [1] And Sarah was an hundred and seven and twenty years old: *these were* the years of the life of Sarah.

Years are Calculated from Scripture References
Factors involved in the calculation
x = 1986 B.C.# – Birth of Sarai/Sarah
y = 127 – age at death (v.1)
z = 1859 B.C.# – Death of Sarah
Formula
(x) + (y) = z
(1986 B.C.#) - (127) = 1859 B.C.#
Probable age of contemporaries
Shem 587 – Abraham 137 – Isaac 37

Abraham Journeys to Hebron
- see Map 3(6) p.213 -

Abraham Journeys to Hebron to Mourn for Sarah –　　　　[1859 B.C.?]

    Gen.23:2 – [2] And Sarah died in Kirjatharba; the same *is* Hebron in the land of Canaan: and Abraham came to mourn for Sarah, and to weep for her.

Probability Scenario
After the sacrifice of Isaac, "… *Abraham dwelt at Beersheba*" (Gen.22:19 & see 1). There appears to be no further mention of Abraham being with Sarah until Sarah's death in Hebron (see 2). One might wonder if Sarah might have been so overwhelmed with the anguish surrounding Abraham's intention to sacrifice her only son Isaac that she departed from Abraham and moved back to Hebron (v.2). Abraham's journey likely occurred within a very few days of Sarah's death in 1859 B.C.#.

Supporting Evidence	
1. **Abraham Dwells in Beersheba** – [p.91]	
2. **Death of Sarah at Kirjatharba** / Hebron (at age 127) [p.96]	
Probable age of contemporaries	
Shem 587 – Abraham 137 – Isaac 37	

Abraham Negotiates for the Field and Cave of Ephron –   [1859 B.C.?]

Gen.23:3-20 – 3 And Abraham stood up from before his dead, and spake unto the sons of Heth, saying, 4 I *am* a stranger and a sojourner with you: give me a possession of a burying place with you, that I may bury my dead out of my sight. 5 And the children of Heth answered Abraham, saying unto him, 6 Hear us, my lord: thou *art* a mighty prince among us: in the choice of our sepulchres bury thy dead; none of us shall withhold from thee his sepulchre, but that thou mayest bury thy dead. 7 And Abraham stood up, and bowed himself to the people of the land, *even* to the children of Heth. 8 And he communed with them, saying, If it be your mind that I should bury my dead out of my sight; hear me, and intreat for me to Ephron the son of Zohar, 9 That he may give me the cave of Machpelah, which he hath, which *is* in the end of his field; for as much money as it is worth he shall give it me for a possession of a burying place amongst you. 10 And Ephron dwelt among the children of Heth: and Ephron the Hittite answered Abraham in the audience of the children of Heth, *even* of all that went in at the gate of his city, saying, 11 Nay, my lord, hear me: the field give I thee, and the cave that *is* therein, I give it thee; in the presence of the sons of my people give I it thee: bury thy dead. 12 And Abraham bowed down himself before the people of the land. 13 And he spake unto Ephron in the audience of the people of the land, saying, But if thou *wilt give it*, I pray thee, hear me: I will give thee money for the field; take *it* of me, and I will bury my dead there. 14 And Ephron answered Abraham, saying unto him, 15 My lord, hearken unto me: the land *is worth* four hundred shekels of silver; what *is* that betwixt me and thee? bury therefore thy dead.

16 And Abraham hearkened unto Ephron; and Abraham weighed to Ephron the silver, which he had named in the audience of the sons of Heth, four hundred shekels of silver, current *money* with the merchant. 17 And the field of Ephron, which *was* in Machpelah, which *was* before Mamre, the field, and the cave which *was* therein, and all the trees that *were* in the field, that *were* in all the borders round about, were made sure 18 Unto Abraham for a possession in the presence of the children of Heth, before all that went in at the gate of his city. 19 And after this, Abraham buried Sarah his wife in the cave of the field of Machpelah before Mamre: the same *is* Hebron in the land of Canaan. 20 And the field, and the cave that *is* therein, were made sure unto Abraham for a possession of a burying place by the sons of Heth.

Abraham Returns to Beersheba

- see Map 3(7) p.213 -

Abraham Returns to Beersheba After Burying Sarah –   [1859 B.C.?]

Probability Scenario

After Abraham and Isaac buried Sarah, it is likely that he returned to Beersheba (☺ Gen.23:21 ☺) where he appears to have been living before Sarah's death (see 1). It would seem that Abraham's concubine, Keturah, and his children by her would be there waiting for his return (see 2 & 3). It is probable that this event occurred after approximately forty days of mourning for Sarah likely still in 1859 B.C.?.

Supporting Evidence

1. **Abraham Dwells in Beersheba** – [p.91]
2. **Abraham Takes a Concubine** (Keturah) [p.92]
3. **Keturah Begins Having children** – Abraham's concubine [p.92]

Probable age of contemporaries

Shem 587 – Abraham 137 – Isaac 37

Abraham had No Inheritance in Canaan –

Acts 7:5 – [5] And he gave him none inheritance in it, no, not *so much as* to set his foot on: yet he promised that he would give it to him for a possession, and to his seed after him …

Isaac Dwells at Lahairoi

- see Map 4(1) p.214 -

Probability Scenario

After Abraham and Isaac buried Sarah, it is possible that Isaac may have begun going back and forth between Beersheba and Lahairoi, perhaps spending more and more time in Lahairoi. Isaac likely established a more permanent residence in Lahairoi (Gen.24:62; 25:11), thereby causing Abraham to be concerned Isaac might marry a foreign wife (see 1). This likely occurred around 1856 B.C.?.

Supporting Evidence

1. **Abraham Sends His Servant to Seek a Wife for Isaac** – [p.98]

Probable age of contemporaries

Shem 587 – Abraham 137 – Isaac 37

Abraham Sends His Servant to Seek a Wife for Isaac –   [1856 B.C.?]

Gen.24:1-9 – [1] And Abraham was old, *and* well stricken in age: and the LORD had blessed Abraham in all things. [2] And Abraham said unto his eldest servant of his house, that ruled over all that he had, Put, I pray thee, thy hand under my thigh: 3 And I will make thee swear by the LORD, the God of heaven, and the God of the earth, that thou shalt not take a wife unto my son of the daughters of the Canaanites, among whom I dwell: 4 But thou shalt go unto my country, and to my kindred, and take a wife unto my son Isaac. 5 And the servant said unto him, Peradventure the woman will not be willing to follow me unto this land: must I needs bring thy son again unto the land from whence thou camest? 6 And Abraham said unto him, Beware thou that thou bring not my son thither again. 7 The LORD God of heaven, which took me from my father's house, and from the land of my kindred, and which spake unto me, and that sware unto me, saying, Unto thy seed will I give this land; he shall send his angel before thee, and thou shalt take a wife unto my son from thence. 8 And if the woman will not be willing to follow thee, then thou shalt be clear from this my oath: only bring not my son thither again. 9 And the servant put his hand under the thigh of Abraham his master, and sware to him concerning that matter.

Probability Scenario

Isaac was 37 years of age when Sarah died in 1859 B.C.# (see 1 & 2). Isaac is destined to meet and marry Rebekah, daughter of Bethuel, at age 40 in 1856 B.C.# (see 3 & 4). It appears that Abraham's servant wasted no time in departing and accomplishing his mission, likely taking no longer than several weeks in the year 1856 B.C.?.

Supporting Evidence

1. **Birth of Isaac** – son of Abraham (at age 100) [p.84]
2. **Death of Sarah at Kirjatharba** / Hebron (at age 127) [p.96]
3. **Birth of Rebekah** – daughter of Bethuel/Abraham's nephew [p.95]
4. **Isaac Takes Rebekah to be His Wife** (at age 40) [p.102]

Factors involved in the calculation

x = 1896 B.C.# – Birth of Isaac
y = 40 – Isaac's age at marriage (Gen.25:20)
z = 1856 B.C.? – year of Abraham's servant sent to seek a wife for Isaac

Formula

$$(x) + (y) = z$$
$$(1896 \text{ B.C.\#}) - (40) = 1856 \text{ B.C.?}$$

Probable age of contemporaries

Shem 590 – Abraham 140 – Isaac 40 – Bethuel 48 – Rebekah 18

The Servant Goes to the City of Nahor II (Abraham's brother)   [1856 B.C.?]

Gen.24:10-14 – 10 And the servant took ten camels of the camels of his master, and departed; for all the goods of his master *were* in his hand: and he arose, and went to Mesopotamia, unto the city of Nahor. 11 And he made his camels to kneel down without the city by a well of water at the time of the evening, *even* the time that women go out to draw *water*. 12 And he said, O LORD God of my master Abraham, I pray thee, send me good speed this day, and shew kindness unto my master Abraham. ¹³ Behold, I stand *here* by the well of water; and the daughters of the men of the city come out to draw water: ¹⁴ And let it come to pass, that the damsel to whom I shall say, Let down thy pitcher, I pray thee, that I may drink; and she shall say, Drink, and I will give thy camels drink also: *let the same be* she *that* thou hast appointed for thy servant Isaac; and thereby shall I know that thou hast shewed kindness unto my master.

The Servant Encounters Rebekah –   [1856 B.C.?]

Gen.24:15-23 – ¹⁵ And it came to pass, before he had done speaking, that, behold, Rebekah came out, who was born to Bethuel, son of Milcah, the wife of Nahor, Abraham's brother, with her pitcher upon her shoulder. ¹⁶ And the damsel *was* very fair to look upon, a virgin, neither had any man known her: and she went down to the well, and filled her pitcher, and came up. ¹⁷ And the servant ran to meet her, and said, Let me, I pray thee, drink a little water of thy pitcher. ¹⁸ And she said, Drink, my lord: and she hasted, and let down her pitcher upon her hand, and gave him drink. ¹⁹ And when she had done giving him drink, she said, I will draw *water* for thy camels also, until they have done drinking. ²⁰ And she hasted, and emptied her pitcher into the trough, and ran again unto the well to draw *water*, and drew for all his camels. ²¹ And the man wondering at her held his peace, to wit whether the LORD had made his journey prosperous or not. ²² And it came to pass, as the camels had done drinking, that the man took a golden earring of half a shekel weight, and two bracelets for her hands of ten *shekels* weight of gold; ²³ And said, Whose daughter *art* thou? tell me, I pray thee: is there room *in* thy father's house for us to lodge in?

The Servant Learns that Rebekah is Isaac's Cousin –   [1856 B.C.?]

Gen.24:24-33 – ²⁴ And she said unto him, I *am* the daughter of Bethuel the son of Milcah, which she bare unto Nahor. ²⁵ She said moreover unto him, We have both straw and provender enough, and room to lodge in. ²⁶ And the man bowed down his head, and worshipped the LORD. ²⁷ And he said, Blessed *be* the LORD God of my master Abraham, who hath not left destitute my master of his mercy and his truth: I *being* in the way, the LORD led me to the house of my master's brethren. ²⁸ And the damsel ran, and told *them of* her mother's house these things.

²⁹ And Rebekah had a brother, and his name *was* Laban: and Laban ran out unto the man, unto the well. ³⁰ And it came to pass, when he saw the earring and bracelets upon his sister's hands, and when he heard the words of Rebekah his sister, saying, Thus spake the man unto me; that he came unto the man; and, behold, he stood by the camels at the well. ³¹ And he said, Come in, thou blessed of the LORD; wherefore standest thou without?

for I have prepared the house, and room for the camels. 32 And the man came into the house: and he ungirded his camels, and gave straw and provender for the camels, and water to wash his feet, and the men's feet that *were* with him. 33 And there was set *meat* before him to eat: but he said, I will not eat, until I have told mine errand. And he said, Speak on.

The Servant Explains His Purpose to Laban (Rebekah's brother) [1856 B.C.?]
Gen.24:34-49 – 34 And he said, I *am* Abraham's servant. 35 And the LORD hath blessed my master greatly; and he is become great: and he hath given him flocks, and herds, and silver, and gold, and menservants, and maidservants, and camels, and asses. 36 And Sarah my master's wife bare a son to my master when she was old: and unto him hath he given all that he hath. 37 And my master made me swear, saying, Thou shalt not take a wife to my son of the daughters of the Canaanites, in whose land I dwell: 38 But thou shalt go unto my father's house, and to my kindred, and take a wife unto my son. 39 And I said unto my master, Peradventure the woman will not follow me. 40 And he said unto me, The LORD, before whom I walk, will send his angel with thee, and prosper thy way; and thou shalt take a wife for my son of my kindred, and of my father's house: 41 Then shalt thou be clear from *this* my oath, when thou comest to my kindred; and if they give not thee *one*, thou shalt be clear from my oath. 42 And I came this day unto the well, and said, O LORD God of my master Abraham, if now thou do prosper my way which I go: 43 Behold, I stand by the well of water; and it shall come to pass, that when the virgin cometh forth to draw *water*, and I say to her, Give me, I pray thee, a little water of thy pitcher to drink; 44 And she say to me, Both drink thou, and I will also draw for thy camels: *let* the same *be* the woman whom the LORD hath appointed out for my master's son. 45 And before I had done speaking in mine heart, behold, Rebekah came forth with her pitcher on her shoulder; and she went down unto the well, and drew *water*: and I said unto her, Let me drink, I pray thee. 46 And she made haste, and let down her pitcher from her *shoulder*, and said, Drink, and I will give thy camels drink also: so I drank, and she made the camels drink also. 47 And I asked her, and said, Whose daughter *art* thou? And she said, The daughter of Bethuel, Nahor's son, whom Milcah bare unto him: and I put the earring upon her face, and the bracelets upon her hands. 48 And I bowed down my head, and worshipped the LORD, and blessed the LORD God of my master Abraham, which had led me in the right way to take my master's brother's daughter unto his son. 49 And now if ye will deal kindly and truly with my master, tell me: and if not, tell me; that I may turn to the right hand, or to the left.

Laban, Bethuel and Rebekah Agree to the Servant's Request –   [1856 B.C.?]

Gen.24:50-61 – ⁵⁰ Then Laban and Bethuel answered and said, The thing proceedeth from the LORD: we cannot speak unto thee bad or good. ⁵¹ Behold, Rebekah *is* before thee, take *her*, and go, and let her be thy master's son's wife, as the LORD hath spoken. ⁵² And it came to pass, that, when Abraham's servant heard their words, he worshipped the LORD, *bowing himself* to the earth. ⁵³ And the servant brought forth jewels of silver, and jewels of gold, and raiment, and gave *them* to Rebekah: he gave also to her brother and to her mother precious things.

⁵⁴ And they did eat and drink, he and the men that *were* with him, and tarried all night; and they rose up in the morning, and he said, Send me away unto my master. ⁵⁵ And her brother and her mother said, Let the damsel abide with us *a few* days, at the least ten; after that she shall go. ⁵⁶ And he said unto them, Hinder me not, seeing the LORD hath prospered my way; send me away that I may go to my master. ⁵⁷ And they said, We will call the damsel, and enquire at her mouth. ⁵⁸ And they called Rebekah, and said unto her, Wilt thou go with this man? And she said, I will go. ⁵⁹ And they sent away Rebekah their sister, and her nurse, and Abraham's servant, and his men. ⁶⁰ And they blessed Rebekah, and said unto her, Thou *art* our sister, be thou *the mother* of thousands of millions, and let thy seed possess the gate of those which hate them. ⁶¹ And Rebekah arose, and her damsels, and they rode upon the camels, and followed the man: and the servant took Rebekah, and went his way.

Isaac and Rebekah Meet –   [1856 B.C.?]

Gen.24:62-66 – ⁶² And Isaac came from the way of the well Lahairoi; for he dwelt in the south country. ⁶³ And Isaac went out to meditate in the field at the eventide: and he lifted up his eyes, and saw, and, behold, the camels *were* coming. ⁶⁴ And Rebekah lifted up her eyes, and when she saw Isaac, she lighted off the camel. ⁶⁵ For she *had* said unto the servant, What man *is* this that walketh in the field to meet us? And the servant *had* said, It *is* my master: therefore she took a vail, and covered herself. ⁶⁶ And the servant told Isaac all things that he had done.

Isaac Takes Rebekah to be His Wife (at age 40)   [1856 B.C.#]

Gen.24:67 – ⁶⁷ And Isaac brought her into his mother Sarah's tent, and took Rebekah, and she became his wife; and he loved her: and Isaac was comforted after his mother's *death.*

Gen.25:20 – ²⁰ And Isaac was forty years old when he took Rebekah to wife, the daughter of Bethuel the Syrian of Padanaram, the sister to Laban the Syrian.

Years are Calculated from Scripture References
Factors involved in the calculation
x = 1896 B.C.# – Birth of Isaac
y = 40 – Isaac's age at marriage (v.20) *Issac's Marriage to Rebekah*
z = 1856 B.C.# – ~~Death of Sarah~~
Formula
(x) + (y) = z
(1896 B.C.#) - (40) = 1856 B.C.#
Probable age of contemporaries
Shem 590 – Abraham 140 – Isaac 40 – Rebekah 18

Abraham Dignifies His Concubine Keturah

Abraham Marries Keturah –   [1855 B.C.?]

Gen.25:1 – ¹ Then again Abraham took a wife, and her name *was* Keturah.

Probability Scenario
It appears that Abraham took Keturah as a concubine around 1876 B.C.?, about 3 years after God told Abraham to sacrifice Isaac (see 1 & 2). It seems that Abraham chose to dignify his concubine Keturah by raising her to the status of a wife (v.1).
Supporting Evidence
1. **Abraham Takes a Concubine** (Keturah) [p.92]
2. **God Tells Abraham to Sacrifice His ONLY Son Isaac** – [p.88]
Probable age of contemporaries
Shem 591 – Abraham 141 – Isaac 41 – Rebekah 19 – Keturah ?

Death of Shem (at age 600)   [1846 B.C.#]

Gen.11:11 – ¹¹ And Shem lived after he begat Arphaxad five hundred years, and begat sons and daughters.

Years are Calculated from Scripture References
see "Genesis Genealogical Chart"
Probable age of contemporaries
Abraham 150 – Isaac 50 – Rebekah 28

Birth of Jacob and Esau – sons of Isaac   [1836 B.C.#]

Gen.25:19-26 – ¹⁹ And these *are* the generations of Isaac, Abraham's son: Abraham begat Isaac: ²⁰ And Isaac was forty years old when he took Rebekah to wife, the daughter of Bethuel the Syrian of Padanaram, the sister to Laban the Syrian. ²¹ And Isaac intreated the LORD for his wife, because she *was* barren: and the LORD was intreated of him, and Rebekah his wife conceived. ²² And the children struggled together within her; and she said, If *it be* so, why *am* I thus? And she went to enquire of the LORD. [23] And the LORD said unto her, Two nations *are* in thy womb, and two manner of people shall be separated from thy bowels; and *the one* people shall be stronger than *the other* people; and the elder shall serve the younger. [24] And when her days to be delivered were fulfilled, behold, *there were* twins in her womb. [25] And the first came out red, all over like an hairy garment; and they called his name Esau. [26] And after that came his brother out, and his hand took hold on Esau's heel; and his name was called Jacob: and Isaac *was* threescore years old when she bare them.

1Chron.1:34 – [34] The sons of Isaac; Esau and Israel.

Year is Calculated from Scripture References see "Genesis Genealogical Chart" **Probable age of contemporaries** Abraham 160 – Isaac 60 – Rebekah 38

Chapter 8

Jacob to Joseph

Isaac Becomes Abraham's Heir –   [1826 B.C.?]

Gen.25:5 – 5 And Abraham gave all that he had unto Isaac.

Probability Scenario

It appears that Abraham faithfully passed the inheritance to Isaac (see 1 & Gen.17:19). Although Abraham is destined to live another five years (see 2), one might wonder if Abraham may have considered that his life was nearing the end. Later, both Jacob (Gen.47:29) and Joseph (Gen.50:24) have the same awareness. It seems that this event likely occurred around 1826 B.C.?.

Supporting Evidence

1. **God Promises to Pass the Covenant through Isaac** – [p.76]
2. **Death of Abraham** (at age 175) [p.106]

Factors involved in the calculation

x = 1821 B.C.# – Death of Abraham (at age 175)
y = 5 ? – years before Abraham's death
z = 1826 B.C.? – year Isaac became Abraham's heir

Formula

$$(x) - (y) = z$$
$$(1821 \text{ B.C.\#}) + (5\ ?) = 1826 \text{ B.C.?}$$

Probable age of contemporaries

Abraham 170 – Isaac 70 – Rebekah 48 – Jacob & Esau 10

Abraham Sends Keturah's Children Away –   [1826 B.C.?]

Gen.25:6 – 6 But unto the sons of the concubines, which Abraham had, Abraham gave gifts, and sent them away from Isaac his son, while he yet

105

lived, eastward, unto the east country.

Probability Scenario

It appears that at this point in time there were other concubines (v.6). Hagar and Ishmael may have returned (see 1). It seems that by also giving gifts to the sons of the concubines, Abraham is making sure that Isaac's inheritance and God's intentions would be undisputed. It seems that this event likely occurred on the same day as the previous event, in 1826 B.C.?.

Supporting Evidence

1. **Abraham Sends Hagar and Ishmael Away with Provisions** [p.88]

Probable age of contemporaries

Abraham 170 – Isaac 70 – Rebekah 48 – Jacob & Esau 10

Death of Abraham (at age 175)   [1821 B.C.#]

Gen.25:7-8 – 7 And these *are* the days of the years of Abraham's life which he lived, an hundred threescore and fifteen years. 8 Then Abraham gave up the ghost, and died in a good old age, an old man, and full *of years*; and was gathered to his people.

Years are Calculated from Scripture References
see "Genesis Genealogical Chart"
Probable age of contemporaries
Isaac 75 – Rebekah 53 – Jacob & Esau 15

Abraham's Sons Bury Him (Isaac and Ishmael)   [1821 B.C.?]

Gen.25:9-10 – 9 And his sons Isaac and Ishmael buried him in the cave of Machpelah, in the field of Ephron the son of Zohar the Hittite, which *is* before Mamre; 10 The field which Abraham purchased of the sons of Heth: there was Abraham buried, and Sarah his wife.

1Chron.1:28 – 28 The sons of Abraham; Isaac, and Ishmael.

God Blesses Isaac –   [1821 B.C.?]

Gen.25:11 – 11 And it came to pass after the death of Abraham, that God blessed his son Isaac; and Isaac dwelt by the well Lahairoi.

Birth of Leah – daughter of Laban/Abraham's kinsman   [1819 B.C.?]

Gen.29:16 – 16 And Laban had two daughters: the name of the elder *was* Leah ...

Probability Scenario

Jacob, son of Isaac, is destined to arrive in Padan Aram to take a wife in 1759 B.C.# (see 1 & 2). By that time it seems that Leah will no longer be doing the work of a shepherdess (see 3 & Gen.29:5-6). At that time Leah will be described as having delicate or weak eyes (see 4 & Gen.29:17) - a possible

---

indication of illness or an indication of advanced years. It is probable that Leah may be approximately 60 years of age when Jacob arrives in Padan Aram.

<u>Supporting Evidence</u>
1. **Jacob Sent to Take a Wife from Rebekah's Relatives** – [p.120]
2. **Jacob Meets the People of the East** – [p.122]
3. **Jacob Meets Rachel** – [p.123]
4. **Jacob Offers to Work Seven Years for Rachel** – [p.124]

<u>Factors involved in the calculation</u>
x = 1759 B.C.# – year of Jacob's arrival in Padan Aram
y = 60 ? – Leah's approximate age in 1759 B.C.
z = 1819 B.C.? – year of Leah's birth

<u>Formula</u>
(x) - (y) = z
(1759 B.C.#) + (60 ?) = 1819 B.C.?

<u>Probable age of contemporaries</u>
Isaac 77 – Rebekah 55 – Laban 54 – Jacob & Esau 17

Death of Eber (at age 464)   [1817 B.C.#]

Gen.11:17 – [17] And Eber lived after he begat Peleg four hundred and thirty years, and begat sons and daughters.

<u>Years are Calculated from Scripture References</u>
see "Genesis Genealogical Chart"
<u>Probable age of contemporaries</u>
Isaac 79 – Rebekah 57 – Jacob & Esau 19

Jacob Acquires Esau's Birthright

Esau Becomes an Outdoors Man & Jacob a Homebody   [1811 B.C.?]

Gen.25:27 – [27] And the boys grew: and Esau was a cunning hunter, a man of the field; and Jacob *was* a plain man, dwelling in tents.

<u>Probability Scenario</u>
It is probable that by the age of 25 Esau and Jacob may have gravitated into their preferred life style.

<u>Factors involved in the calculation</u>
x = 1836 B.C.# – Jacob and Esau's year of birth
y = 25 ? – approximate age of Jacob and Esau
z = 1811 B.C.? – year of this event

<u>Formula</u>
(x) + (y) = z
(1836 B.C.#) - (25 ?) = 1811 B.C.?

<u>Probable age of contemporaries</u>
Isaac 85 – Rebekah 63 – Jacob & Esau 25

Isaac Loved Esau & Rebekah Loved Jacob   [1811 B.C.?]
    Gen.25:28 – ²⁸ And Isaac loved Esau, because he did eat of *his* venison: but Rebekah loved Jacob.

Birth of Rachel – daughter of Laban/Abraham's kinsman   [1799 B.C.?]
    Gen.29:16 – ¹⁶ And Laban had two daughters: ... and the name of the younger *was* Rachel.

Probability Scenario
Jacob is destined to arrive in Padan Aram to take a wife in 1759 B.C.# (see 1 & 2). It seems that Leah, Rachel's older sister, will no longer be doing the rigorous work of a shepherdess (see 3 & Gen.29:5-6). At that time Leah will be described as having delicate or weak eyes (see 4 & Gen.29:17) - a possible indication of illness or an indication of advanced years. Rachel may be as much as 20 years younger than Leah (see 5), and in 1759 B.C. likely still able to function in the work of a shepherdess at around 40 years of age.
<u>Supporting Evidence</u>
1. **Jacob Sent to Take a Wife from Rebekah's Relatives** – [p.120]
2. **Jacob Meets the People of the East** – [p.122]
3. **Jacob Meets Rachel** – [p.123]
4. **Jacob Offers to Work Seven Years for Rachel** – [p.124]
5. **Birth of Leah** – daughter of Laban/Abraham's kinsman [p.106]
<u>Factors involved in the calculation</u>
x = 1759 B.C.# – year of Jacob's arrival in Padan Aram
y = 40 ? – Rachel's approximate age in 1759 B.C.
z = 1799 B.C.? – year of Rachel's birth
<u>Formula</u>
(x) - (y) = z
(1759 B.C.#) + (40 ?) = 1799 B.C.?
<u>Probable age of contemporaries</u>
Isaac 97– Rebekah 75– Laban 74– Jacob & Esau 37

Esau Sells His Birthright –   [1796 B.C.?]
    Gen.25:29-34 – ²⁹ And Jacob sod pottage: and Esau came from the field, and he *was* faint: ³⁰ And Esau said to Jacob, Feed me, I pray thee, with that same red *pottage*; for I *am* faint: therefore was his name called Edom. ³¹ And Jacob said, Sell me this day thy birthright. ³² And Esau said, Behold, I *am* at the point to die: and what profit shall this birthright do to me? ³³ And Jacob said, Swear to me this day; and he sware unto him: and he sold his birthright unto Jacob. ³⁴ Then Jacob gave Esau bread and pottage of lentiles; and he did eat and drink, and rose up, and went his way: thus Esau despised *his* birthright.

Probability Scenario
It seems that acceptance from one parent and complacency or rejection from

the other parent may have eventually fostered a spirit of hostility and competitiveness between Jacob and Esau (see 1). Jacob may have sought to take advantage of Esau's moment of vulnerability to embarrass him and gain favor in Isaac's eyes. This event likely occurred the same year Esau married foreign wives in 1796 B.C.? (see 2).

Supporting Evidence
1. **Isaac Loved Esau & Rebekah Loved Jacob** [p.108]
2. **Esau Marries Foreign Wives** – Isaac and Rebekah grieved [p.109]

Note
It seems that this event may prove to be the pivotal point for several future events.

Factors involved in the calculation
x = 1836 B.C.# – year of Jacob and Esau's birth
y = 40 ? – age at time of this event
z = 1796 B.C.? – year of this event

Formula
(x) + (y) = z
(1836 B.C.#) - (40 ?) = 1796 B.C.?

Probable age of contemporaries
Isaac 100 – Rebekah 78 – Jacob & Esau 40

Esau Marries Foreign Wives – Isaac and Rebekah grieved   [1796 B.C.#]

Gen.26:34-35 – 34 And Esau was forty years old when he took to wife Judith the daughter of Beeri the Hittite, and Bashemath the daughter of Elon the Hittite: 35 Which were a grief of mind unto Isaac and to Rebekah.

Gen.36:2 – 2 Esau took his wives of the daughters of Canaan; Adah the daughter of Elon the Hittite, and Aholibamah the daughter of Anah the daughter of Zibeon the Hivite;

This year is calculated from Scripture References
Note
It appears that earlier in this same year, Jacob may have taken advantage of Esau during a moment of vulnerability (see **Esau Sells His Birthright** – [p.108]). It is possible that Esau was deeply embarrassed and is attempting to regain favor with Isaac, and win the favor of Rebekah, by marrying in preparation to present them with grandchildren before his brother Jacob does.

Factors involved in the calculation
x = 1836 B.C.# – year of Jacob and Esau's birth
y = 40 – age at time of this event (v.34)
z = 1796 B.C.# – year of this event

Formula
(x) + (y) = z
(1836 B.C.#) - (40) = 1796 B.C.#

Probable age of contemporaries
Isaac 100 – Rebekah 78 – Jacob & Esau 40

BEGIN PARALLEL ACCOUNTS OF ELIPHAZ AND JOB

Events Associated with Eliphaz (son of Esau)	Events Associated with Job (friend of Eliphaz)
Birth of Eliphaz (the Teamanite?) [1795 B.C.?]	**Birth of Job –** [1795 B.C.?]

Events Associated with Eliphaz (son of Esau)

Birth of Eliphaz (the Teamanite?)
[1795 B.C.?]

Gen.36:1 – [1] Now these *are* the generations of Esau, who *is* Edom.

Gen.36:4-5 – [4] And Adah bare to Esau Eliphaz; and Bashemath bare Reuel; [5] And Aholibamah bare Jeush, and Jaalam, and Korah: these *are* the sons of Esau, which were born unto him in the land of Canaan.

Gen.36:10 – [10] These *are* the names of Esau's sons; Eliphaz the son of Adah the wife of Esau, Reuel the son of Bashemath the wife of Esau.

1Chron.1:35 – [35] The sons of Esau; Eliphaz, Reuel, and Jeush, and Jaalam, and Korah.

> **Probability Scenario**
> It seems that Esau might have begun fathering children very soon after getting married (see 1). It is likely that Eliphaz could have been born 1 year later around 1795 B.C.?.
> **Supporting Evidence**
> 1. **Esau Marries Foreign Wives –** [p.109]
> **Probable age of contemporaries**
> Isaac 101 – Rebekah 79 – Esau 41

Events Associated with Job (friend of Eliphaz)

Birth of Job – [1795 B.C.?]

> **Probability Scenario**
> It seems that Job is destined to be confronted by Eliphaz and some of his other friends in the distant future (see 1). Considering that Eliphaz is named before Job's other friends (Job 2:11), and that he spoke first (Job 4-5), is a possible indication that Eliphaz was the eldest of the three friends, and possibly the closest in age to Job. It seems probable that Job might have been born very near to the time that Eliphaz was born around 1795 B.C.?.
> **Supporting Evidence**
> 1. **Job's Loyalty to God Disputed by His Friends –** [p.111]
> **Probable age of contemporaries**
> Isaac 101 – Rebekah 79 – Esau 41

Job's Early Adult / Married Life –
[1765–1745 B.C.?]

Job 1:1-5

(This is a future event and will appear again)

> **Probability Scenario**
> It is probable that Job may have married about age 30 (around 1765 B.C.?), and may have fathered a child approximately every two years after that. Job could likely have fathered all of his 10 children by age 50.
> **Probable age of contemporaries in 1765 B.C.**
> Isaac 131 – Rebekah 109 – Esau 71
> Eliphaz 30

Birth of Teman – son of Eliphaz
[1764 B.C.?]
(This is a future event and will appear again)

Gen.36:11 – 11 And the sons of Eliphaz were Teman, Omar, Zepho, and Gatam, and Kenaz.

1Chron.1:36 – 36 The sons of Eliphaz; Teman, and Omar, Zephi, and Gatam, Kenaz, and Timna, and Amalek.

Probability Scenario
It is probable that Eliphaz may have married around age 30 (around 1765 B.C.?), and fathered Teman about one year later around 1764 B.C.?.
Note
It appears that Teman was destined to become a Duke "... *according to their habitations in the land of their possession*" (Gen.36:43). If Eliphaz lived in his son's city, or a city that he built and named after his son, he may be Eliphaz the Temanite who visited Job (Job 2:11).
Probable age of contemporaries
Isaac 132 – Rebekah 110 – Esau 72
Eliphaz 31

Job's Loyalty to God Disputed by satan – [1725 B.C.?]
Job 1:6-2:10
(This is a future event and will appear again)

Probability Scenario
It seems that Job might have enjoyed his peaceful and bountiful life until about 70 years of age when satan questioned his loyalty to God around 1725 B.C.?.
Note
It seems that Job's youngest child could be about 20 years of age.
Probable age of contemporaries:
Isaac 171 – Esau 111 – Eliphaz 70
Joseph 20

Job's Loyalty to God Disputed by His Friends – [1725 B.C.?]
Job 2:11-37:24 (future event – see p.155)

Job Confronted by God – [1725 B.C.?]
Job 38:1-42:6 (future event – see p.155)

Job's Friends Confronted by God –
[1725 B.C.?]
Job 42:7-9 (future event – see p.155)

Job Blessed by God – [1725 B.C.?]
Job 42:10-15 (future event – see p.155)

Death of Job – [1585 B.C.?]
Job 42:16-17 (future event – see p.183)

* END PARALLEL ACCOUNTS OF ELIPHAZ AND JOB *

Isaac Journeys from Lahairoi to Gerar
- see Map 4(2) p.214 -

Isaac Encounters Famine –   [1794 B.C.?]

Gen.26:1 – ¹ And there was a famine in the land, beside the first famine that was in the days of Abraham. And Isaac went unto Abimelech king of the Philistines unto Gerar.

Probability Scenario
After the death of Abraham, *"Isaac dwelt by the well Lahairoi"* (Gen.25:11). The land God promised as an inheritance stretched from Dan to Beersheba. Lahairoi was about 50 miles south-west of Beersheba in the area of the Negev. Now with Isaac and Rebekah failing to disallow their son Esau to marry foreign wives (see 1), God may have sent this famine as a means of forcing Isaac back into the promised land. It might take approximately two years for the effects of the famine to force departure - likely around 1794 B.C.?.
Supporting Evidence
1. **Esau Marries Foreign Wives** – Isaac and Rebekah grieved [p.109]
Factors involved in the calculation
x = 1796 B.C.# – year of Esau's marriage
y = 2 ? – years for famine to cause concern
z = 1794 B.C.? – year of this event
Formula
(x) + (y) = z
(1796 B.C.#) - (2 ?) = 1794 B.C.?
Probable age of contemporaries
Isaac 102 – Rebekah 80 – Jacob & Esau 42

God Warns Isaac Not to go to Egypt (covenant renewed)   [1794 B.C.?]

Gen.26:2-5 – ² And the LORD appeared unto him, and said, Go not down into Egypt; dwell in the land which I shall tell thee of: ³ Sojourn in this land, and I will be with thee, and will bless thee; for unto thee, and unto thy seed, I will give all these countries, and I will perform the oath which I sware unto Abraham thy father; ⁴ And I will make thy seed to multiply as the stars of heaven, and will give unto thy seed all these countries; and in thy seed shall all the nations of the earth be blessed; ⁵ Because that Abraham obeyed my voice, and kept my charge, my commandments, my statutes, and my laws.

Isaac Obscures His Full Relationship with His Wife –   [1794 B.C.?]

Gen.26:6-7 – ⁶ And Isaac dwelt in Gerar: ⁷ And the men of the place asked *him* of his wife; and he said, She *is* my sister: for he feared to say, *She is* my wife; lest, *said he*, the men of the place should kill me for Rebekah; because she *was* fair to look upon.

Abimelech II Observes Isaac with Rebekah (Isaac rebuked) [1788 B.C.?]

Gen.26:8-11 – 8 And it came to pass, when he had been there a long time, that Abimelech king of the Philistines looked out at a window, and saw, and, behold, Isaac *was* sporting with Rebekah his wife. 9 And Abimelech called Isaac, and said, Behold, of a surety she *is* thy wife: and how saidst thou, She *is* my sister? And Isaac said unto him, Because I said, Lest I die for her. 10 And Abimelech said, What *is* this thou hast done unto us? one of the people might lightly have lien with thy wife, and thou shouldest have brought guiltiness upon us. 11 And Abimelech charged all *his* people, saying, He that toucheth this man or his wife shall surely be put to death.

Probability Scenario
Isaac had been in Gerar a long time (v.8). It seems probable that Isaac may have been in Gerar as long as six years (see 1). This event may have occurred around 1788 B.C.?.
Supporting Evidence
1. **Isaac Encounters Famine** – [p.112]
Note
It seems that Isaac is following very closely in his father's footsteps (v.10 & see **Abraham is Rebuked by Abimelech I** – [p.82]).
Factors involved in the calculation
x = 1794 B.C.? – year Isaac entered Gerar
y = 6 ? – years sojourn in Gerar
z = 1788 B.C.? – year of this event
Formula
(x) + (y) = z
(1794 B.C.?) - (6 ?) = 1788 B.C.?
Probable age of contemporaries
Isaac 108 – Rebekah 86 – Jacob & Esau 48

Isaac Envied – asked to depart [1782 B.C.?]

Gen.26:12-16 – 12 Then Isaac sowed in that land, and received in the same year an hundredfold: and the LORD blessed him. 13 And the man waxed great, and went forward, and grew until he became very great: 14 For he had possession of flocks, and possession of herds, and great store of servants: and the Philistines envied him. 15 For all the wells which his father's servants had digged in the days of Abraham his father, the Philistines had stopped them, and filled them with earth. 16 And Abimelech said unto Isaac, Go from us; for thou art much mightier than we.

Probability Scenario

It seems probable that under Abimelech's order of protection (see 1 & Gen.26:11), Isaac may have felt confident to remain in Gerar approximately six additional years (v.13) before being asked to leave (v.16). One might wonder if Isaac forgot God's promise of protection and blessing (see 2 & Gen.26:3-4). This event may have occurred around 1782 B.C.?.

Supporting Evidence

1. **Abimelech II Observes Isaac with Rebekah** (Isaac rebuked) [p.113]
2. **God Warns Isaac Not to go to Egypt** (covenant renewed) [p.112]

Note

It seems that Isaac is following very closely in his father's footsteps (Gen.26:10 & see **Abraham is Rebuked by Abimelech I** – [p.82]).

Factors involved in the calculation

x = 1788 B.C.? – year Abimelech II observes Isaac with Rebekah
y = 6 ? – years additional sojourn in Gerar
z = 1782 B.C.? – year of this event

Formula

(x) + (y) = z
(1788 B.C.?) - (6 ?) = 1782 B.C.?

Probable age of contemporaries

Isaac 114 – Rebekah 92 – Jacob & Esau 54

Isaac Journeys to the Valley of Gerar
- see Map 4(3) p.214 -

Isaac Re-opens the Wells of Abraham (receives strife)   [1782 B.C.?]
Gen.26:17-21 – 17 And Isaac departed thence, and pitched his tent in the valley of Gerar, and dwelt there. 18 And Isaac digged again the wells of water, which they had digged in the days of Abraham his father; for the Philistines had stopped them after the death of Abraham: and he called their names after the names by which his father had called them. 19 And Isaac's servants digged in the valley, and found there a well of springing water. 20 And the herdmen of Gerar did strive with Isaac's herdmen, saying, The water *is* ours: and he called the name of the well Esek; because they strove with him. 21 And they digged another well, and strove for that also: and he called the name of it Sitnah.

Isaac Moves Again – digs another well (finds God's blessing)   [1780 B.C.?]
Gen.26:22 – 22 And he removed from thence, and digged another well; and for that they strove not: and he called the name of it Rehoboth; and he said, For now the LORD hath made room for us, and we shall be fruitful in the land.

Isaac Journeys to Beersheba
- see Map 4(4) p.214 -

God Appears (blesses Isaac)   [1773 B.C.?]

Gen.26:23-25 – 23 And he went up from thence to Beersheba. 24 And the LORD appeared unto him the same night, and said, I *am* the God of Abraham thy father: fear not, for I *am* with thee, and will bless thee, and multiply thy seed for my servant Abraham's sake. 25 And he builded an altar there, and called upon the name of the LORD, and pitched his tent there: and there Isaac's servants digged a well.

Formula
(x) + (y) = z
(1780 B.C.?) - (7 ?) = 1773 B.C.?
Probable age of contemporaries
Isaac 123 – Rebekah 101 – Jacob & Esau 63

Death of Ishmael (at age 137)   [1773 B.C.#]

Gen.25:17-18 – ¹⁷ And these *are* the years of the life of Ishmael, an hundred and thirty and seven years: and he gave up the ghost and died; and was gathered unto his people. ¹⁸ And they dwelt from Havilah unto Shur, that *is* before Egypt, as thou goest toward Assyria: *and* he died in the presence of all his brethren.

Years are Calculated from Scripture References
Factors involved in the calculation
x = 1910 B.C.# – year Ishmael was born
y = 137 – age at death (v.17)
z = 1773 B.C.# – year of death
Formula
(x) + (y) = z
(1910 B.C.#) - (137) = 1773 B.C.#
Probable age of contemporaries
Isaac 123 – Rebekah 101 – Jacob & Esau 63

Birth of Teman – son of Eliphaz   [1764 B.C.?]

Previously documented
at
* * * * * * BEGIN PARALLEL ACCOUNTS OF ELIPHAZ AND JOB * * * * * *
Birth of Eliphaz (the Teamanite?) [p.110]
Birth of Teman – son of Eliphaz [p.111]
Probable age of contemporaries
Isaac 132 – Rebekah 110 – Esau 72 – Eliphaz 31

Isaac Agrees to a Covenant with Abimelech II

Abimelech II Seeks Isaac to Insure Safety of His Kingdom –   [1764 B.C.?]

Gen.26:26-30 – ²⁶ Then Abimelech went to him from Gerar, and Ahuzzath one of his friends, and Phichol the chief captain of his army. ²⁷ And Isaac said unto them, Wherefore come ye to me, seeing ye hate me, and have sent me away from you? ²⁸ And they said, We saw certainly that the LORD was with thee: and we said, Let there be now an oath betwixt us, *even* betwixt us and thee, and let us make a covenant with thee; 29 That thou wilt do us no hurt, as we have not touched thee, and as we have done unto thee nothing but good, and have sent thee away in peace: thou *art* now the blessed of the LORD. 30 And he made them a feast, and they did eat and drink.

Probability Scenario

It appears that God's continued blessing of Isaac's prosperity has become very apparent to Abimelech II (see 1, 2, 3 & v.28). It seems probable that Isaac may have remained in Beersheba approximately nine years before Abimelech came to make a covenant of peace with Isaac. This event may have occurred around 1764 B.C.?.

Supporting Evidence

1. **Isaac Envied** – asked to depart [p.113]
2. **Isaac Re-opens the Wells of Abraham** (receives strife) [p.114]
3. **Isaac Moves Again** – digs another well (finds God's blessing) [p.114]

Factors involved in the calculation

x = 1773 B.C.? – year Isaac journeyed to Beersheba
y = 9 ? – years sojourn at Beersheba
z = 1764 B.C.? – year of this event

Formula

(x) + (y) = z
(1773 B.C.?) - (9 ?) = 1764 B.C.?

Probable age of contemporaries

Isaac 132 – Rebekah 110 – Jacob & Esau 72

Isaac Agrees and Abimelech II Departs –   [1764 B.C.?]

Gen.26:31 – 31 And they rose up betimes in the morning, and sware one to another: and Isaac sent them away, and they departed from him in peace.

Isaac Digs Another Well (there is peace)   [1764 B.C.?]

Gen.26:32-33 – 32 And it came to pass the same day, that Isaac's servants came, and told him concerning the well which they had digged, and said unto him, We have found water. 33 And he called it Shebah: therefore the name of the city *is* Beersheba unto this day.

Jacob Acquires Esau's Blessing

Isaac Plans to Pass the Inheritance to Esau –   [1759 B.C.?]

Gen.27:1-4 – 1 And it came to pass, that when Isaac was old, and his eyes were dim, so that he could not see, he called Esau his eldest son, and said unto him, My son: and he said unto him, Behold, *here am* I. 2 And he said,

Behold now, I am old, I know not the day of my death: ³ Now therefore take, I pray thee, thy weapons, thy quiver and thy bow, and go out to the field, and take me *some* venison; ⁴ And make me savoury meat, such as I love, and bring *it* to me, that I may eat; that my soul may bless thee before I die.

Probability Scenario

It appears that Isaac may have either considered that his life was nearing its end (v.1), or he had a real craving for the savory food that he loved (v.4). He still has approximately 43 years yet to live (see 1). It seems probable that this event and the events that follow occurred in rapid succession, resulting in Jacob's hasty journey from Beersheba to Padan Aram (see 2 & 3). This event likely occurred in 1759 B.C.?.

Supporting Evidence

1. **Death of Isaac** (at age 180) [p.158]
2. **Jacob Sent to Take a Wife from Rebekah's Relatives** – [p.120]
3. **Jacob Offers to Work Seven Years for Rachel** – [p.124]

Probable age of contemporaries
Isaac 137 – Rebekah 115 – Jacob & Esau 77

Rebekah Plans to Alter Isaac's Intentions –   [1759 B.C.?]

Gen.27:5-10 – ⁵ And Rebekah heard when Isaac spake to Esau his son. And Esau went to the field to hunt *for* venison, *and* to bring *it*.

⁶ And Rebekah spake unto Jacob her son, saying, Behold, I heard thy father speak unto Esau thy brother, saying, ⁷ Bring me venison, and make me savoury meat, that I may eat, and bless thee before the LORD before my death. ⁸ Now therefore, my son, obey my voice according to that which I command thee. ⁹ Go now to the flock, and fetch me from thence two good kids of the goats; and I will make them savoury meat for thy father, such as he loveth: ¹⁰ And thou shalt bring *it* to thy father, that he may eat, and that he may bless thee before his death.

Jacob is Concerned but Rebekah is Determined –   [1759 B.C.?]

Gen.27:11-14 – ¹¹ And Jacob said to Rebekah his mother, Behold, Esau my brother *is* a hairy man, and I *am* a smooth man: ¹² My father peradventure will feel me, and I shall seem to him as a deceiver; and I shall bring a curse upon me, and not a blessing. ¹³ And his mother said unto him, Upon me *be* thy curse, my son: only obey my voice, and go fetch me *them*.
¹⁴ And he went, and fetched, and brought *them* to his mother: and his mother made savoury meat, such as his father loved.

Deception and Lies Prevail –   [1759 B.C.?]

Gen.27:15-29 – ¹⁵ And Rebekah took goodly raiment of her eldest son Esau, which *were* with her in the house, and put them upon Jacob her younger son: ¹⁶ And she put the skins of the kids of the goats upon his hands, and upon the smooth of his neck: ¹⁷ And she gave the savoury meat and the bread, which she had prepared, into the hand of her son Jacob.

¹⁸ And he came unto his father, and said, My father: and he said, Here *am* I; who *art* thou, my son? ¹⁹ And Jacob said unto his father, I *am* Esau thy firstborn; I have done according as thou badest me: arise, I pray thee, sit and eat of my venison, that thy soul may bless me. ²⁰ And Isaac said unto his son, How *is it* that thou hast found *it* so quickly, my son? And he said, Because the LORD thy God brought *it* to me. ²¹ And Isaac said unto Jacob, Come near, I pray thee, that I may feel thee, my son, whether thou *be* my very son Esau or not. ²² And Jacob went near unto Isaac his father; and he felt him, and said, The voice *is* Jacob's voice, but the hands *are* the hands of Esau. ²³ And he discerned him not, because his hands were hairy, as his brother Esau's hands: so he blessed him. ²⁴ And he said, *Art* thou my very son Esau? And he said, I *am*. ²⁵ And he said, Bring *it* near to me, and I will eat of my son's venison, that my soul may bless thee. And he brought *it* near to him, and he did eat: and he brought him wine, and he drank. ²⁶ And his father Isaac said unto him, Come near now, and kiss me, my son. ²⁷ And he came near, and kissed him: and he smelled the smell of his raiment, and blessed him, and said, See, the smell of my son *is* as the smell of a field which the LORD hath blessed: ²⁸ Therefore God give thee of the dew of heaven, and the fatness of the earth, and plenty of corn and wine: ²⁹ Let people serve thee, and nations bow down to thee: be lord over thy brethren, and let thy mother's sons bow down to thee: cursed *be* every one that curseth thee, and blessed *be* he that blesseth thee.

The Deception is Revealed –   [1759 B.C.?]
Gen.27:30-40 – ³⁰ And it came to pass, as soon as Isaac had made an end of blessing Jacob, and Jacob was yet scarce gone out from the presence of Isaac his father, that Esau his brother came in from his hunting. ³¹ And he also had made savoury meat, and brought it unto his father, and said unto his father, Let my father arise, and eat of his son's venison, that thy soul may bless me. ³² And Isaac his father said unto him, Who *art* thou? And he said, I *am* thy son, thy firstborn Esau. ³³ And Isaac trembled very exceedingly, and said, Who? where *is* he that hath taken venison, and brought *it* me, and I have eaten of all before thou camest, and have blessed him? yea, *and* he shall be blessed. ³⁴ And when Esau heard the words of his father, he cried with a great and exceeding bitter cry, and said unto his father, Bless me, *even* me also, O my father. ³⁵ And he said, Thy brother came with subtilty, and hath taken away thy blessing. ³⁶ And he said, Is not he rightly named Jacob? for he hath supplanted me these two times: he took away my birthright; and, behold, now he hath taken away my

blessing. And he said, Hast thou not reserved a blessing for me? [37] And Isaac answered and said unto Esau, Behold, I have made him thy lord, and all his brethren have I given to him for servants; and with corn and wine have I sustained him: and what shall I do now unto thee, my son? [38] And Esau said unto his father, Hast thou but one blessing, my father? bless me, *even* me also, O my father. And Esau lifted up his voice, and wept. [39] And Isaac his father answered and said unto him, Behold, thy dwelling shall be the fatness of the earth, and of the dew of heaven from above; [40] And by thy sword shalt thou live, and shalt serve thy brother; and it shall come to pass when thou shalt have the dominion, that thou shalt break his yoke from off thy neck.

Esau Plans to Kill Jacob –   [1759 B.C.?]
Gen.27:41 – [41] And Esau hated Jacob because of the blessing wherewith his father blessed him: and Esau said in his heart, The days of mourning for my father are at hand; then will I slay my brother Jacob.

Rebekah Seeks to Protect Jacob's Life –   [1759 B.C.?]
Gen.27:42-46 – [42] And these words of Esau her elder son were told to Rebekah: and she sent and called Jacob her younger son, and said unto him, Behold, thy brother Esau, as touching thee, doth comfort himself, *purposing* to kill thee. [43] Now therefore, my son, obey my voice; and arise, flee thou to Laban my brother to Haran; [44] And tarry with him a few days, until thy brother's fury turn away; [45] Until thy brother's anger turn away from thee, and he forget *that* which thou hast done to him: then I will send, and fetch thee from thence: why should I be deprived also of you both in one day? [46] And Rebekah said to Isaac, I am weary of my life because of the daughters of Heth: if Jacob take a wife of the daughters of Heth, such as these *which are* of the daughters of the land, what good shall my life do me?

Jacob Flees from Esau

Jacob Sent to Take a Wife from Rebekah's Relatives –   [1759 B.C.?]
Gen.28:1-5 – [1] And Isaac called Jacob, and blessed him, and charged him, and said unto him, Thou shalt not take a wife of the daughters of Canaan. [2] Arise, go to Padanaram, to the house of Bethuel thy mother's father; and take thee a wife from thence of the daughters of Laban thy mother's brother. [3] And God Almighty bless thee, and make thee fruitful, and multiply thee, that thou mayest be a multitude of people; [4] And give thee the blessing of Abraham, to thee, and to thy seed with thee; that thou

mayest inherit the land wherein thou art a stranger, which God gave unto Abraham. ⁵ And Isaac sent away Jacob: and he went to Padanaram unto Laban, son of Bethuel the Syrian, the brother of Rebekah, Jacob's and Esau's mother.

Esau's Murder Plot is Thwarted by Isaac and Rebekah –   [1759 B.C.?]
Gen.28:6-7 – ⁶ When Esau saw that Isaac had blessed Jacob, and sent him away to Padanaram, to take him a wife from thence; and that as he blessed him he gave him a charge, saying, Thou shalt not take a wife of the daughters of Canaan; ⁷ And that Jacob obeyed his father and his mother, and was gone to Padanaram;

Esau Marries the Daughter of Ishmael –   [1759 B.C.?]
Gen.28:8-9 – ⁸ And Esau seeing that the daughters of Canaan pleased not Isaac his father; ⁹ Then went Esau unto Ishmael, and took unto the wives which he had Mahalath the daughter of Ishmael Abraham's son, the sister of Nebajoth, to be his wife.

Gen.36:3 – ³ And Bashemath Ishmael's daughter, sister of Nebajoth.

Probability Scenario

It seems that thirty-seven years earlier Jacob took advantage of Esau during a moment of vulnerability (see 1). It appears that Esau was deeply embarrassed and attempted to regain favor with Isaac, and win the favor of Rebekah, by marrying foreign wives in hopes of presenting them with grandchildren before his brother Jacob did (see 2). Now, however, Esau's previous embarrassment and present humiliation appears to have turned to anger even against Isaac and Rebekah (v.8). It seems probable that this event occurred within the same year previously noted - 1759 B.C.?.

Supporting Evidence

1. **Esau Sells His Birthright** – [p.108]
2. **Esau Marries Foreign Wives** – Isaac and Rebekah grieved [p.109]

Probable age of contemporaries

Isaac 137 – Rebekah 115 – Jacob & Esau 77

Jacob Journeys to Luz (Bethel)
- see Map 5(1) & (2) p.215 -

Jacob Receives God's Covenant (in a dream)   [1759 B.C.?]
Gen.28:10-17 – ¹⁰ And Jacob went out from Beersheba, and went toward Haran. ¹¹ And he lighted upon a certain place, and tarried there all night, because the sun was set; and he took of the stones of that place, and put *them for* his pillows, and lay down in that place to sleep. ¹² And he

dreamed, and behold a ladder set up on the earth, and the top of it reached to heaven: and behold the angels of God ascending and descending on it. 13 And, behold, the LORD stood above it, and said, I *am* the LORD God of Abraham thy father, and the God of Isaac: the land whereon thou liest, to thee will I give it, and to thy seed; 14 And thy seed shall be as the dust of the earth, and thou shalt spread abroad to the west, and to the east, and to the north, and to the south: and in thee and in thy seed shall all the families of the earth be blessed. 15 And, behold, I *am* with thee, and will keep thee in all *places* whither thou goest, and will bring thee again into this land; for I will not leave thee, until I have done *that* which I have spoken to thee of.

16 And Jacob awaked out of his sleep, and he said, Surely the LORD is in this place; and I knew *it* not. 17 And he was afraid, and said, How dreadful *is* this place! this *is* none other but the house of God, and this *is* the gate of heaven.

Jacob Makes a Vow at Luz (Bethel) [1759 B.C.?]

Gen.28:18-22 – 18 And Jacob rose up early in the morning, and took the stone that he had put *for* his pillows, and set it up *for* a pillar, and poured oil upon the top of it. 19 And he called the name of that place Bethel: but the name of that city *was called* Luz at the first. 20 And Jacob vowed a vow, saying, If God will be with me, and will keep me in this way that I go, and will give me bread to eat, and raiment to put on, 21 So that I come again to my father's house in peace; then shall the LORD be my God: 22 And this stone, which I have set *for* a pillar, shall be God's house: and of all that thou shalt give me I will surely give the tenth unto thee.

Jacob Journeys to Haran
- see Map 5(3) p.215 also Map 6(1) p.216 -

Jacob Meets the People of the East – [1759 B.C.?]

Gen.29:1-4 – 1 Then Jacob went on his journey, and came into the land of the people of the east. 2 And he looked, and behold a well in the field, and, lo, there *were* three flocks of sheep lying by it; for out of that well they watered the flocks: and a great stone *was* upon the well's mouth. 3 And thither were all the flocks gathered: and they rolled the stone from the well's mouth, and watered the sheep, and put the stone again upon the well's mouth in his place. 4 And Jacob said unto them, My brethren, whence *be* ye? And they said, Of Haran *are* we.

Jacob Meets Rachel – [1759 B.C.?]

Gen.29:5-11 – 5 And he said unto them, Know ye Laban the son of Nahor? And they said, We know *him*. 6 And he said unto them, *Is* he well? And they said, *He is* well: and, behold, Rachel his daughter cometh with the sheep. 7 And he said, Lo, *it is* yet high day, neither *is it* time that the cattle should be gathered together: water ye the sheep, and go *and* feed *them*. 8 And they said, We cannot, until all the flocks be gathered together, and *till* they roll the stone from the well's mouth; then we water the sheep.

9 And while he yet spake with them, Rachel came with her father's sheep: for she kept them. 10 And it came to pass, when Jacob saw Rachel the daughter of Laban his mother's brother, and the sheep of Laban his mother's brother, that Jacob went near, and rolled the stone from the well's mouth, and watered the flock of Laban his mother's brother. 11 And Jacob kissed Rachel, and lifted up his voice, and wept.

Probability Scenario

It seems that Rachel's older sister, Leah, is no longer doing the work of a shepherdess, and is described as having delicate or weak eyes (see 1 & Gen.29:17) – a possible indication of illness or being advanced in years. It appears that Rachel may be as much as 20 years younger than Leah, and still quite able to function in the rigorous work of a shepherdess (vv.5-6). It seems likely that Rachel might be approximately 40 years of age. It seems probable that this event occurred within the same year previously noted - 1759 B.C.?.

Supporting Evidence

1. **Jacob Offers to Work Seven Years for Rachel** – [p.124]

Factors involved in the calculation

x = 1799 B.C.? – birth of Rachel
y = 40 ? – age at time of this event
z = 1759 B.C.? – year of this event

Formula

$(x) + (y) = z$
$(1799 \text{ B.C.?}) - (40\ ?) = 1759 \text{ B.C.?}$

Probable age of contemporaries

Isaac 137 – Rebekah 115 – Laban 114 – Jacob & Esau 77 – Leah 60 – Rachel 40

Jacob Welcomed by Laban – [1759 B.C.?]

Gen.29:12-14 – 12 And Jacob told Rachel that he *was* her father's brother, and that he *was* Rebekah's son: and she ran and told her father. 13 And it came to pass, when Laban heard the tidings of Jacob his sister's son, that he ran to meet him, and embraced him, and kissed him, and brought him to his house. And he told Laban all these things. 14 And Laban said to him, Surely thou *art* my bone and my flesh. And he abode with him the space of a month.

Laban and Jacob Establish a Working Relationship

Jacob Offers to Work Seven Years for Rachel –   [1759 B.C.#]

Gen.29:15-20 – 15 And Laban said unto Jacob, Because thou *art* my brother, shouldest thou therefore serve me for nought? tell me, what *shall* thy wages *be*? 16 And Laban had two daughters: the name of the elder *was* Leah, and the name of the younger *was* Rachel. 17 Leah *was* tender eyed; but Rachel was beautiful and well favoured. 18 And Jacob loved Rachel; and said, I will serve thee seven years for Rachel thy younger daughter. 19 And Laban said, *It is* better that I give her to thee, than that I should give her to another man: abide with me. 20 And Jacob served seven years for Rachel; and they seemed unto him *but* a few days, for the love he had to her.

This year calculated from scripture references

1. First, steps must be taken to determine the year of Joseph's birth.
2. Then, steps may be taken to determine the year of this event.

Factors involved in step #1 to determine the year of Joseph's birth.

x = 1836 B.C.# – Birth of Jacob (see "Genesis Genealogical Chart")
$y1$ = 147 – Jacob's age at death (Gen.47:28)
$y2$ = 30 – Joseph's age before Pharaoh (Gen.41:46)
$y3$ = 7 – years of good crops (Gen.41:48)
$y4$ = 2 – years of famine passed when Jacob entered Egypt (Gen.45:6)
$y5$ = 17 – year Jacob lived in Egypt (Gen.47:28)
z = 1745 B.C.# – Birth of Joseph (see "Genesis Genealogical Chart")

Formula

$$(x) + (y1 - (y2 + y3 + y4 + y5)) = z$$
$$(1836\ B.C.\#) - ((147) - (30 + 7 + 2 + 17)) = \text{Child's year of birth}$$
$$(1836\ B.C.\#) - (147 - 56) = \text{Child's year of birth}$$
$$(1836\ B.C.\#) - (91) = 1745\ B.C.\#$$

Factors involved in step #2 to determine the year of this event.

x = 1745 B.C.# – Birth of Joseph (see "Genesis Genealogical Chart")
$y1$ = 7 – years Jacob agreed to serve Laban for Rachel (Gen.29:18)
$y2$ = 7 – additional years Jacob agreed to serve Laban for Rachel (Gen.29: 26-30) to the birth of Joseph (Gen.30:25)
z = 1759 B.C.# – year of this event

Formula

$$(x) - (y1 + y2) = z$$
$$(1745\ B.C.\#) + (14) = 1759\ B.C.\#$$

Probable age of contemporaries

Isaac 137 – Rebekah 115 – Laban 114 – Jacob & Esau 77 – Leah 60 – Rachel 40

Jacob Fulfills His Obligation – asks for Rachel   [1752 B.C.#]

Gen.29:21-22 – 21 And Jacob said unto Laban, Give *me* my wife, for my days are fulfilled, that I may go in unto her. 22 And Laban gathered together all the men of the place, and made a feast.

Factors involved in calculating the year
x = 1759 B.C.# – Jacob offers to work seven years for Rachel
y = 7 – years of agreed servitude
z = 1752 B.C.# – Jacob fulfills his obligation – asks for Rachel

Formula
$$(x) + (y) = z$$
$$(1759 \text{ B.C.\#}) - (7) = 1752 \text{ B.C.\#}$$

Probable age of contemporaries
Isaac 144 – Rebekah 122 – Laban 121 – Jacob & Esau 84 – Leah 67 – Rachel 47

Laban Gives Jacob a Surprise (and Leah a servant)   [1752 B.C.?]

Gen.29:23-26 – 23 And it came to pass in the evening, that he took Leah his daughter, and brought her to him; and he went in unto her. 24 And Laban gave unto his daughter Leah Zilpah his maid *for* an handmaid. 25 And it came to pass, that in the morning, behold, it *was* Leah: and he said to Laban, What *is* this thou hast done unto me? did not I serve with thee for Rachel? wherefore then hast thou beguiled me? 26 And Laban said, It must not be so done in our country, to give the younger before the firstborn.

Probability Scenario
It seems that Laban may be supplanting (tripping up) Jacob, the supplanter, and at the same time esteeming his daughter Leah. It is probable that Laban might have given Leah a maid young enough to be strong and able to serve for many years, but old enough to show proper respect to her mistress. Zilpah might possibly have been around 34, approximately half Leah's age. It seems probable that this event occurred within days of the previous event and in the same year previously noted - 1752 B.C.?.

Probable age of contemporaries
Isaac 144 – Rebekah 122 – Laban 121 – Jacob & Esau 84 – Leah 67 – Rachel 47

Jacob Agrees to Work Seven More Years for Rachel –   [1752 B.C.?]

Gen.29:27-30 – 27 Fulfil her week, and we will give thee this also for the service which thou shalt serve with me yet seven other years. 28 And Jacob did so, and fulfilled her week: and he gave him Rachel his daughter to wife also. 29 And Laban gave to Rachel his daughter Bilhah his handmaid to be her maid. 30 And he went in also unto Rachel, and he loved also Rachel more than Leah, and served with him yet seven other years.

Probability Scenario
It seems that Laban may still be supplanting (tripping up) Jacob, the supplanter, and at the same time esteeming his daughter Rachel. It is probable that Laban might have given Rachel a maid young enough to be strong and

---

able to serve for many years, but old enough to show proper respect to her mistress. Bilhah might possibly have been around 24, approximately half Rachel's age. It is apparent that this event occurred within seven days of the previous event and in the same year previously noted - 1752 B.C.?.

<u>**Probable age of contemporaries**</u>
Isaac 144 – Rebekah 122 – Laban 121 – Jacob & Esau 84 – Leah 67 – Rachel 47

Jacob Begins Having Children

<u>**Probability Scenario**</u>
Within a span of seven years, between 1752 B.C.# and 1745 B.C.#, Jacob is destined to father 12 children (11 sons and 1 daughter). Within those seven years, Leah will seemingly do the impossible. Leah is destined to bear seven children in seven years (6 sons and 1 daughter), and also be unable to bear for a time in that same period.

<u>**Note**</u>
It seems that the women of Biblical times focused the validation of their identity on their ability to bear children. Sarai (Gen.16:1-3), Leah (Gen.29:31-34), Rachel (Gen.30:1-3), Hannah (1Sam.1:1-20), Elizabeth (Lk.1:24-25).

<u>**Probable age of contemporaries**</u>
Isaac 144 – Rebekah 122 – Laban 121 – Jacob & Esau 84 – Leah 67 – Rachel 47

* * * BEGIN PARALLEL ACCOUNTS OF LEAH AND RACHEL * * *

Children of Jacob and Leah	**Children of Jacob and Rachel**
(and Leah's handmaid - Zilpah)	(and Rachel's handmaid - Bilhah)
Birth of Ruben – [03/1751 B.C.?]	
(son of Jacob/Leah)	
Gen.29:31-32 – 31 And when the LORD saw that Leah *was* hated, he opened her womb: but Rachel *was* barren. 32 And Leah conceived, and bare a son, and she called his name Reuben: for she said, Surely the LORD hath looked upon my affliction; now therefore my husband will love me.	
<u>Probability Scenario</u> It seems likely that Jacob took Leah in marriage around June of 1752 B.C.? (see 1). It is probable that Leah conceived during "... *her week*"	

126

(Gen.29:27-28 & see 2) or very soon after and bore Ruben around March of 1751 B.C.?.

Supporting Evidence
1. **Laban Gives Jacob a Surprise (and Leah a servant) [p.125].**
2. **Jacob Agrees to Work Seven More Years for Rachel – [p.125].**

Probable age of contemporaries
Isaac 145 – Rebekah 123 – Jacob 85
Laban 122 – Leah 68 – Rachel 48

Birth of Simeon – [02/1750 B.C.?]
(son of Jacob/Leah)

Gen.29:33 – 33 And she conceived again, and bare a son; and said, Because the LORD hath heard that I *was* hated, he hath therefore given me this *son* also: and she called his name Simeon.

Probability Scenario
It seems probable that approximately 4-6 weeks after the birth of Ruben (see 1), Leah likely became pregnant and bore Simeon around February of 1750 B.C.?.

Supporting Evidence
1. **Birth of Ruben** – by Leah [p.126]

Probable age of contemporaries
Isaac 146 – Rebekah 124 – Jacob 86
Laban 123 – Leah 69 – Rachel 49

Birth of Levi – [02/1749 B.C.?]
(son of Jacob/Leah)

Gen.29:34 – 34 And she conceived again, and bare a son; and said, Now this time will my husband be joined unto me, because I have born him three sons: therefore was his name called Levi.

(continued – next page)

Rachel Offers Bilhah to Jacob - [09/1750 B.C.?]

Gen.30:1-3 – 1 And when Rachel saw that she bare Jacob no children, Rachel envied her sister; and said unto Jacob, Give me children, or else I die. 2 And Jacob's anger was kindled against Rachel: and he said, *Am* I in God's stead, who hath withheld from thee the fruit of the womb? 3 And she said, Behold my maid Bilhah, go in unto her; and she shall bear upon my knees, that I may also have children by her.

Probability Scenario
It seems probable that after Leah's second son was born (see 1) and Leah had began to show signs of being pregnant with her third child (see 2), Rachel's envy may have become unbearable causing her to offer her maid to Jacob to bear children for her around September of 1750 B.C.?.

Supporting Evidence
1. **Birth of Simeon** – by Leah [p.127]
2. **Birth of Levi** – by Leah [p.127]

Probable age of contemporaries:
Isaac 146 – Rebekah 124 – Jacob 86
Laban 123 – Leah 69 – Rachel 49

Probability Scenario

It seems probable that around 8 – 10 weeks after the birth of Simeon (see 1), Leah likely became pregnant and bore Levi around February of 1749 B.C.?.

Supporting Evidence

1. **Birth of Simeon** – by Leah [p.127]

Probable age of contemporaries

Isaac 147 – Rebekah 125 – Jacob 87
Laban 124 – Leah 70 – Rachel 50

Birth of Judah – [01/1748 B.C.?]
(son of Jacob/Leah)

Gen.29:35 – 35 And she conceived again, and bare a son: and she said, Now will I praise the LORD: therefore she called his name Judah; and left bearing.

Probability Scenario

It seems probable that around 4 – 6 weeks after the birth of Levi (see 1), Leah likely became pregnant and bore Judah around January of 1748 B.C.?.

Supporting Evidence

1. **Birth of Levi** – by Leah [p.127]

Probable age of contemporaries

Isaac 148 – Rebekah 126 – Jacob 88
Laban 125 – Leah 71 – Rachel 51

Leah Offers Zilpah to Jacob -
[07/1748 B.C.?]

Gen.30:9 – 9 When Leah saw that she had left bearing, she took Zilpah her maid, and gave her Jacob to wife.

Probability Scenario

It seems probable that about six months may have passed after the birth of Judah (see 1), around

Birth of Dan – [07/1749 B.C.?]
(son of Jacob/Bilhah)

Gen.30:4-6 – 4 And she gave him Bilhah her handmaid to wife: and Jacob went in unto her. 5 And Bilhah conceived, and bare Jacob a son. 6 And Rachel said, God hath judged me, and hath also heard my voice, and hath given me a son: therefore called she his name Dan.

Probability Scenario

It seems probable that Bilhah conceived shortly after being offered to Jacob (see 1) and bore Dan around July of 1749 B.C.?.

Supporting Evidence

1. **Rachel Offers Bilhah to Jacob** [p.127]

Probable age of contemporaries

Isaac 147 – Rebekah 125 – Jacob 87
Laban 124 – Leah 70 – Rachel 50

Birth of Naphtali – [06/1748 B.C.?]
(son of Jacob/Bilhah)

Gen.30:7-8 – 7 And Bilhah Rachel's maid conceived again, and bare Jacob a second son. 8 And Rachel said, With great wrestlings have I wrestled with my sister, and I have prevailed: and she called his name Naphtali.

Probability Scenario

It seems probable that around 4 – 6 weeks after the birth of Dan (see 1), Bilhah likely became pregnant and bore Naphtali around June of 1748 B.C.?.

Supporting Evidence

1. **Birth of Dan** – by Bilhah [p.128]

Probable age of contemporaries

Isaac 148 – Rebekah 126 – Jacob 88
Laban 125 – Leah 71 – Rachel 51

January of 1748 B.C.?, when Leah "... *saw that she had left bearing*" (Gen.30:9). Not to be out done by her sister Rachel (see 2), Leah likely gave Zilpah her maid to Jacob as wife around July of 1748 B.C.?. **Supporting Evidence** 1. **Birth of Judah** – by Leah [p.128] 2. **Rachel Offers Bilhah** [p.127] **Probable age of contemporaries** Isaac 148 – Rebekah 126 – Jacob 88 Laban 125 – Leah 71 – Rachel 51	

* * * PAUSE PARALLEL ACCOUNTS OF LEAH AND RACHEL * * *

Leah and Rachel Barter Over Mandrakes –   [07/1748 B.C.?]

Gen.30:14-16 – [14] And Reuben went in the days of wheat harvest, and found mandrakes in the field, and brought them unto his mother Leah. Then Rachel said to Leah, Give me, I pray thee, of thy son's mandrakes. [15] And she said unto her, *Is it* a small matter that thou hast taken my husband? and wouldest thou take away my son's mandrakes also? And Rachel said, Therefore he shall lie with thee to night for thy son's mandrakes. [16] And Jacob came out of the field in the evening, and Leah went out to meet him, and said, Thou must come in unto me; for surely I have hired thee with my son's mandrakes. And he lay with her that night.

Probability Scenario
It seems probable that Ruben may have been out in the field with Leah, or possibly Leah's servant, Zilpah. Ruben likely saw some flowering mandrake plants that he just had to give to his mommy. Ruben was likely no older than three years and four months.
Probable age of contemporaries
Jacob 88 – Leah 71 – Rachel 51 – Ruben 3 years 4 months

* * RESUME PARALLEL ACCOUNTS OF LEAH AND RACHEL * *

Children of Jacob and Leah (and Leah's handmaid - Zilpah)	Children of Jacob and Rachel (and Rachel's handmaid - Bilhah)
Birth of Gad – [04/1747 B.C.?] (son of Jacob/Zilpah) Gen.30:10-11 – [10] And Zilpah, Leah's maid bare Jacob a son. [11] And	

Leah said, A troop cometh: and she called his name Gad.

> **Probability Scenario**
> It seems probable that Zilpah conceived shortly after being offered to Jacob (see 1) and bore Gad around April of 1747 B.C.?.
> **Supporting Evidence**
> 1. **Leah Offers Zilpah to Jacob**
> [p.128]
> **Probable age of contemporaries**
> Isaac 149 – Rebekah 127 – Jacob 89
> Laban 126 – Leah 72 – Rachel 52

Birth of Issachar – [05/1747 B.C.?]
(son of Jacob/Leah)

Gen.30:17-18 – 17 And God hearkened unto Leah, and she conceived, and bare Jacob the fifth son. 18 And Leah said, God hath given me my hire, because I have given my maiden to my husband: and she called his name Issachar.

> **Probability Scenario**
> It seems probable that shortly after Leah offered her maid, Zilpah, to Jacob (see 1), that Leah again conceived and bore Issachar around May of 1747 B.C.?.
> **Supporting Evidence**
> 1. **Leah Offers Zilpah to Jacob**
> [p.128]
> **Probable age of contemporaries**
> Isaac 149 – Rebekah 127 – Jacob 89
> Laban 126 – Leah 72 – Rachel 52

Birth of Asher – [03/1746 B.C.?]
(son of Jacob/Zilpah)

Gen.30:12-13 – 12 And Zilpah, Leah's maid bare Jacob a second son. 13 And Leah said, Happy am I, for the daughters will call me blessed: and she called his name Asher.

> **Probability Scenario**
> It seems probable that around 4 – 6 weeks after the birth of Gad (see 1), Zilpah likely became pregnant and bore Asher around March of 1746 B.C.?.
> **Supporting Evidence**
> 1. **Birth of Gad** – by Zilpah [p.129]
> **Probable age of contemporaries**
> Isaac 150 – Rebekah 128 – Jacob 90
> Laban 127 – Leah 73 – Rachel 53

Birth of Zebulun –   [05/1746 B.C.?]
        (son of Jacob/Leah)

Gen.30:19-20 – 19 And Leah conceived again, and bare Jacob the sixth son. 20 And Leah said, God hath endued me *with* a good dowry; now will my husband dwell with me, because I have born him six sons: and she called his name Zebulun.

> **Probability Scenario**
> It seems probable that around 8 – 10 weeks after the birth of Issachar (see 1), Leah likely became pregnant and bore Zebulun around May of 1746 B.C.?.
> **Supporting Evidence**
> 1. **Birth of Issachar** – by Leah
>   [p.130]
> **Probable age of contemporaries**
> Isaac 150 – Rebekah 128 – Jacob 90
> Laban 127 – Leah 73 – Rachel 53

Birth of Dinah –   [04/1745 B.C.?]
        (daughter of Jacob/Leah)

Gen.30:21 – 21 And afterwards she bare a daughter, and called her name Dinah.

> **Probability Scenario**
> It seems probable that around 4 – 6

Birth of Joseph –   [05?/1745 B.C.#]
        (son of Jacob/Rachel)

Gen.30:22-24 – 22 And God remembered Rachel, and God hearkened to her, and opened her womb. 23 And she conceived, and bare a son; and said, God hath taken away my

weeks after the birth of Zebulun (see 1), Leah likely became pregnant and bore Dinah around April of 1745 B.C.?.

<u>Supporting Evidence</u>
1. **Birth of Zebulun** – by Leah
[p.131]
<u>Probable age of contemporaries</u>
Isaac 151 – Rebekah 129 – Jacob 91
Laban 128 – Leah 74 – Rachel 54

reproach: 24 And she called his name Joseph; and said, The LORD shall add to me another son.

<u>Year is Calculated from Scripture References</u>
see "Genesis Genealogical Chart"
and / or
see "**Factors involved in step #1 to determine the year of Joseph's birth**"
at
Jacob Offers to Work Seven Years for Rachel – [p.124]
<u>Probable age of contemporaries:</u>
Isaac 151 – Rebekah 129 – Jacob 91
Laban 128 – Leah 74 – Rachel 54

* * * * END PARALLEL ACCOUNTS OF LEAH AND RACHEL * * * *

Chapter 9

Joseph

Jacob Plans to Depart from Laban –   [1745 B.C.?]

    Gen.30:25-28 – ²⁵ And it came to pass, when Rachel had born Joseph, that Jacob said unto Laban, Send me away, that I may go unto mine own place, and to my country. ²⁶ Give *me* my wives and my children, for whom I have served thee, and let me go: for thou knowest my service which I have done thee. ²⁷ And Laban said unto him, I pray thee, if I have found favour in thine eyes, *tarry: for* I have learned by experience that the LORD hath blessed me for thy sake. ²⁸ And he said, Appoint me thy wages, and I will give *it*.

Jacob Negotiates to Work Additional Years for Livestock –   [1745 B.C.?]

    Gen.30:29-43 – ²⁹ And he said unto him, Thou knowest how I have served thee, and how thy cattle was with me. ³⁰ For *it was* little which thou hadst before I *came*, and it is *now* increased unto a multitude; and the LORD hath blessed thee since my coming: and now when shall I provide for mine own house also? ³¹ And he said, What shall I give thee? And Jacob said, Thou shalt not give me any thing: if thou wilt do this thing for me, I will again feed *and* keep thy flock: ³² I will pass through all thy flock to day, removing from thence all the speckled and spotted cattle, and all the brown cattle among the sheep, and the spotted and speckled among the goats: and *of such* shall be my hire. ³³ So shall my righteousness answer for me in time to come, when it shall come for my hire before thy face: every one that *is* not speckled and spotted among the goats, and brown among the sheep, that shall be counted stolen with me. 34 And Laban said, Behold, I would it might be according to thy word. 35 And he removed that day the he goats that were ringstraked and spotted, and all the she goats that were speckled and spotted, *and* every one that had *some* white in it, and all the brown among the sheep, and gave *them* into the hand of his sons. 36 And he set three days' journey betwixt himself and Jacob: and Jacob fed the rest of Laban's flocks.

37 And Jacob took him rods of green poplar, and of the hazel and chesnut tree; and pilled white strakes in them, and made the white appear which *was* in the rods. 38 And he set the rods which he had pilled before the flocks in the gutters in the watering troughs when the flocks came to drink, that they should conceive when they came to drink. 39 And the flocks conceived before the rods, and brought forth cattle ringstraked, speckled, and spotted. 40 And Jacob did separate the lambs, and set the faces of the flocks toward the ringstraked, and all the brown in the flock of Laban; and he put his own flocks by themselves, and put them not unto Laban's cattle. 41 And it came to pass, whensoever the stronger cattle did conceive, that Jacob laid the rods before the eyes of the cattle in the gutters, that they might conceive among the rods. 42 But when the cattle were feeble, he put *them* not in: so the feebler were Laban's, and the stronger Jacob's. 43 And the man increased exceedingly, and had much cattle, and maidservants, and menservants, and camels, and asses.

Death of Rebekah (mother of Jacob and Esau)   [1739 B.C.?]

Probability Scenario
Deborah, Rebekah's nurse, is destined to be journeying back to Canaan with Jacob at the time of her death, around 1729 B.C.? (see 1). It is unlikely that Deborah would leave Rebekah as long as she was alive.
Supporting Evidence
1. **Death of Deborah** (nurse to Jacob's mother, Rebekah) [p.146]
Probable age of contemporaries
Isaac 157 – Laban 134 – Jacob & Esau 97 – Leah 80 – Rachel 60 – Joseph 6

Deborah Brings News from Isaac (nurse of Rebekah)   [1739 B.C.?]

Probability Scenario
It is reckoned that Rebekah, Jacob's mother, may have died (see 1); and that Deborah, her nurse, was sent to inform Jacob of his mother's death and to return to her former homeland in Padan Aram. It is also probable that Isaac, Jacob's father, sent Deborah to warn Jacob against returning to Canaan (see 2).
Supporting Evidence
1. **Death of Rebekah** (mother of Jacob and Esau) [p.134]

> 2. **Esau Plans to Kill Jacob** – [p.120]
> **Probable age of contemporaries**
> Isaac 157 – Laban 134 – Jacob & Esau 97 – Leah 80 – Rachel 60 – Joseph 6

Laban and His Sons Turn Against Jacob –   [1739 B.C.?]

Gen.31:1-2 – 1 And he heard the words of Laban's sons, saying, Jacob hath taken away all that *was* our father's; and of *that* which *was* our father's hath he gotten all this glory. 2 And Jacob beheld the countenance of Laban, and, behold, it *was* not toward him as before.

> **Probability Scenario**
> It appears that this change in attitude toward Jacob, on the part of Laban and his sons, might have come about through a perceived change in their personal and financial relationship. Considering that Deborah, Rebekah's nurse, may have brought news of Rebekah's death (see 1 & 2), Laban and his sons might no longer see Jacob as family but as a hired hand or even a servant. In this case, Jacob's wives, children and possessions could possibly belong to Laban (Ex.21:4).
> **Supporting Evidence**
> 1. **Death of Rebekah** (mother of Jacob and Esau) [p.134]
> 2. **Deborah Brings News from Isaac** (nurse of Rebekah) [p.134]
> **Factors involved in calculating the year**
> x = 1759 B.C.# – Jacob offers to work seven years for Rachel
> y = 20 – years of agreed servitude (Gen.31:41)
> z = 1739 B.C.? – year of this event
> **Formula**
> $(x) + (y) = z$
> (1759 B.C.#) - (20) = 1739 B.C.?
> **Probable age of contemporaries**
> Isaac 157 – Jacob & Esau 97 – Laban 134 – Leah 80 – Rachel 60 – Joseph 6

God Tells Jacob to Return to Canaan –   [1739 B.C.?]

Gen.31:3-16 – 3 And the LORD said unto Jacob, Return unto the land of thy fathers, and to thy kindred; and I will be with thee. 4 And Jacob sent and called Rachel and Leah to the field unto his flock, 5 And said unto them, I see your father's countenance, that it *is* not toward me as before; but the God of my father hath been with me. 6 And ye know that with all my power I have served your father. 7 And your father hath deceived me, and changed my wages ten times; but God suffered him not to hurt me. 8 If he said thus, The speckled shall be thy wages; then all the cattle bare speckled: and if he said thus, The ringstraked shall be thy hire; then bare all the cattle ringstraked. 9 Thus God hath taken away the cattle of your father, and given *them* to me. 10 And it came to pass at the time that the cattle conceived, that I lifted up mine eyes, and saw in a dream, and, behold, the rams which leaped upon the cattle *were* ringstraked, speckled, and grisled.

¹¹ And the angel of God spake unto me in a dream, *saying*, Jacob: And I said, Here *am* I. ¹² And he said, Lift up now thine eyes, and see, all the rams which leap upon the cattle *are* ringstraked, speckled, and grisled: for I have seen all that Laban doeth unto thee. ¹³ I *am* the God of Bethel, where thou anointedst the pillar, *and* where thou vowedst a vow unto me: now arise, get thee out from this land, and return unto the land of thy kindred. ¹⁴ And Rachel and Leah answered and said unto him, *Is there* yet any portion or inheritance for us in our father's house? ¹⁵ Are we not counted of him strangers? for he hath sold us, and hath quite devoured also our money. ¹⁶ For all the riches which God hath taken from our father, that *is* ours, and our children's: now then, whatsoever God hath said unto thee, do.

Jacob Departs for Canaan

Jacob Slips Away from Laban –   [1739 B.C.#]
   Gen.31:17-21 – ¹⁷ Then Jacob rose up, and set his sons and his wives upon camels; ¹⁸ And he carried away all his cattle, and all his goods which he had gotten, the cattle of his getting, which he had gotten in Padanaram, for to go to Isaac his father in the land of Canaan. ¹⁹ And Laban went to shear his sheep: and Rachel had stolen the images that *were* her father's. ²⁰ And Jacob stole away unawares to Laban the Syrian, in that he told him not that he fled. ²¹ So he fled with all that he had; and he rose up, and passed over the river, and set his face *toward* the mount Gilead.

Factors involved in calculating the year
x = 1759 B.C.# – Jacob offers to work seven years for Rachel
y = 20 – years of agreed servitude (Gen.31:38, 41)
z = 1739 B.C.? – year of this event
Formula
(x) + (y) = z
(1759 B.C.#) - (20) = 1739 B.C.#
Probable age of contemporaries
Isaac 157 – Jacob & Esau 97 – Laban 134 – Leah 80 – Rachel 60 – Joseph 6

Jacob Reaches Gilead
- see Map 6(2) p.216 -

Jacob Pursued and Confronted by Laban in Gilead –   [1739 B.C.?]
   Gen.31:22-42 – ²² And it was told Laban on the third day that Jacob was fled. ²³ And he took his brethren with him, and pursued after him seven days' journey; and they overtook him in the mount Gilead. ²⁴ And God

came to Laban the Syrian in a dream by night, and said unto him, Take heed that thou speak not to Jacob either good or bad.

25 Then Laban overtook Jacob. Now Jacob had pitched his tent in the mount: and Laban with his brethren pitched in the mount of Gilead. 26 And Laban said to Jacob, What hast thou done, that thou hast stolen away unawares to me, and carried away my daughters, as captives *taken* with the sword? 27 Wherefore didst thou flee away secretly, and steal away from me; and didst not tell me, that I might have sent thee away with mirth, and with songs, with tabret, and with harp? 28 And hast not suffered me to kiss my sons and my daughters? thou hast now done foolishly in *so* doing. 29 It is in the power of my hand to do you hurt: but the God of your father spake unto me yesternight, saying, Take thou heed that thou speak not to Jacob either good or bad. 30 And now, *though* thou wouldest needs be gone, because thou sore longedst after thy father's house, *yet* wherefore hast thou stolen my gods? 31 And Jacob answered and said to Laban, Because I was afraid: for I said, Peradventure thou wouldest take by force thy daughters from me. 32 With whomsoever thou findest thy gods, let him not live: before our brethren discern thou what *is* thine with me, and take *it* to thee. For Jacob knew not that Rachel had stolen them. 33 And Laban went into Jacob's tent, and into Leah's tent, and into the two maidservants' tents; but he found *them* not. Then went he out of Leah's tent, and entered into Rachel's tent. 34 Now Rachel had taken the images, and put them in the camel's furniture, and sat upon them. And Laban searched all the tent, but found *them* not. 35 And she said to her father, Let it not displease my lord that I cannot rise up before thee; for the custom of women *is* upon me. And he searched, but found not the images.

36 And Jacob was wroth, and chode with Laban: and Jacob answered and said to Laban, What *is* my trespass? what *is* my sin, that thou hast so hotly pursued after me? 37 Whereas thou hast searched all my stuff, what hast thou found of all thy household stuff? set *it* here before my brethren and thy brethren, that they may judge betwixt us both. 38 This twenty years *have* I *been* with thee; thy ewes and thy she goats have not cast their young, and the rams of thy flock have I not eaten. 39 That which was torn *of beasts* I brought not unto thee; I bare the loss of it; of my hand didst thou require it, *whether* stolen by day, or stolen by night. 40 *Thus* I was; in the day the drought consumed me, and the frost by night; and my sleep departed from mine eyes. 41 Thus have I been twenty years in thy house; I served thee fourteen years for thy two daughters, and six years for thy cattle: and thou hast changed my wages ten times. 42 Except the God of my father, the God of Abraham, and the fear of Isaac, had been with me, surely thou hadst sent me away now empty. God hath seen mine affliction and the labour of my hands, and rebuked *thee* yesternight.

Jacob and Laban Make a Covenant of Peace –   [1739 B.C.?]

Gen.31:43-55 – ⁴³ And Laban answered and said unto Jacob, *These* daughters *are* my daughters, and *these* children *are* my children, and *these* cattle *are* my cattle, and all that thou seest *is* mine: and what can I do this day unto these my daughters, or unto their children which they have born? ⁴⁴ Now therefore come thou, let us make a covenant, I and thou; and let it be for a witness between me and thee. ⁴⁵ And Jacob took a stone, and set it up *for* a pillar. ⁴⁶ And Jacob said unto his brethren, Gather stones; and they took stones, and made an heap: and they did eat there upon the heap. ⁴⁷ And Laban called it Jegarsahadutha: but Jacob called it Galeed. ⁴⁸ And Laban said, This heap *is* a witness between me and thee this day. Therefore was the name of it called Galeed; ⁴⁹ And Mizpah; for he said, The LORD watch between me and thee, when we are absent one from another. ⁵⁰ If thou shalt afflict my daughters, or if thou shalt take *other* wives beside my daughters, no man *is* with us; see, God *is* witness betwixt me and thee. ⁵¹ And Laban said to Jacob, Behold this heap, and behold *this* pillar, which I have cast betwixt me and thee; ⁵² This heap *be* witness, and *this* pillar *be* witness, that I will not pass over this heap to thee, and that thou shalt not pass over this heap and this pillar unto me, for harm. ⁵³ The God of Abraham, and the God of Nahor, the God of their father, judge betwixt us. And Jacob sware by the fear of his father Isaac. ⁵⁴ Then Jacob offered sacrifice upon the mount, and called his brethren to eat bread: and they did eat bread, and tarried all night in the mount. ⁵⁵ And early in the morning Laban rose up, and kissed his sons and his daughters, and blessed them: and Laban departed, and returned unto his place.

Jacob Reaches Mahanaim
- see Map 6(3) p.216 -

Jacob Encounters Angels at Mahanaim –   [1739 B.C.?]

Gen.32:1-2 – ¹ And Jacob went on his way, and the angels of God met him. ² And when Jacob saw them, he said, This *is* God's host: and he called the name of that place Mahanaim.

Jacob Sends Messengers to Esau –   [1739 B.C.?]

Gen.32:3-12 – ³ And Jacob sent messengers before him to Esau his brother unto the land of Seir, the country of Edom. ⁴ And he commanded them, saying, Thus shall ye speak unto my lord Esau; Thy servant Jacob saith thus, I have sojourned with Laban, and stayed there until now: ⁵ And I have oxen, and asses, flocks, and menservants, and womenservants: and I have sent to tell my lord, that I may find grace in thy sight. ⁶ And the messengers returned to Jacob, saying, We came to thy brother Esau, and also he cometh to meet thee, and four hundred men with him. 7 Then Jacob was greatly afraid and distressed: and he divided the people that *was* with him, and the flocks, and herds, and the camels, into two bands; 8 And said, If Esau come to the one company, and smite it, then the other company which is left shall escape.

9 And Jacob said, O God of my father Abraham, and God of my father Isaac, the LORD which saidst unto me, Return unto thy country, and to thy kindred, and I will deal well with thee: 10 I am not worthy of the least of all the mercies, and of all the truth, which thou hast shewed unto thy servant; for with my staff I passed over this Jordan; and now I am become two bands. 11 Deliver me, I pray thee, from the hand of my brother, from the hand of Esau: for I fear him, lest he will come and smite me, *and* the mother with the children. 12 And thou saidst, I will surely do thee good, and make thy seed as the sand of the sea, which cannot be numbered for multitude.

Jacob Prepares a Present for Esau – [1739 B.C.?]

Gen.32:13-23 – 13 And he lodged there that same night; and took of that which came to his hand a present for Esau his brother; 14 Two hundred she goats, and twenty he goats, two hundred ewes, and twenty rams, 15 Thirty milch camels with their colts, forty kine, and ten bulls, twenty she asses, and ten foals. 16 And he delivered *them* into the hand of his servants, every drove by themselves; and said unto his servants, Pass over before me, and put a space betwixt drove and drove. 17 And he commanded the foremost, saying, When Esau my brother meeteth thee, and asketh thee, saying, Whose *art* thou? and whither goest thou? and whose *are* these before thee? 18 Then thou shalt say, *They be* thy servant Jacob's; it *is* a present sent unto my lord Esau: and, behold, also he *is* behind us. 19 And so commanded he the second, and the third, and all that followed the droves, saying, On this manner shall ye speak unto Esau, when ye find him. 20 And say ye moreover, Behold, thy servant Jacob *is* behind us. For he said, I will appease him with the present that goeth before me, and afterward I will see his face; peradventure he will accept of me. 21 So went the present over before him: and himself lodged that night in the company. 22 And he rose up that night, and took his two wives, and his two womenservants, and his eleven sons, and passed over the ford Jabbok. 23 And he took them, and sent them over the brook, and sent over that he had.

Jacob Wrestles with God (asks for a blessing) [1739 B.C.?]

Gen.32:24-26 – 24 And Jacob was left alone; and there wrestled a man with him until the breaking of the day. 25 And when he saw that he prevailed not against him, he touched the hollow of his thigh; and the hollow of Jacob's thigh was out of joint, as he wrestled with him. ²⁶ And he said, Let me go, for the day breaketh. And he said, I will not let thee go, except thou bless me.

Jacob at Peniel
- see Map 6(4) p.216 -

Jacob is Renamed Israel –   [1739 B.C.?]

Gen.32:27-32 – ²⁷ And he said unto him, What *is* thy name? And he said, Jacob. ²⁸ And he said, Thy name shall be called no more Jacob, but Israel: for as a prince hast thou power with God and with men, and hast prevailed. ²⁹ And Jacob asked *him*, and said, Tell *me*, I pray thee, thy name. And he said, Wherefore *is* it *that* thou dost ask after my name? And he blessed him there. ³⁰ And Jacob called the name of the place Peniel: for I have seen God face to face, and my life is preserved. ³¹ And as he passed over Penuel the sun rose upon him, and he halted upon his thigh.
³² Therefore the children of Israel eat not *of* the sinew which shrank, which *is* upon the hollow of the thigh, unto this day: because he touched the hollow of Jacob's thigh in the sinew that shrank.

Jacob Prepares and Meets Esau –   [1739 B.C.?]

Gen.33:1-15 – ¹ And Jacob lifted up his eyes, and looked, and, behold, Esau came, and with him four hundred men. And he divided the children unto Leah, and unto Rachel, and unto the two handmaids. ² And he put the handmaids and their children foremost, and Leah and her children after, and Rachel and Joseph hindermost. ³ And he passed over before them, and bowed himself to the ground seven times, until he came near to his brother. ⁴ And Esau ran to meet him, and embraced him, and fell on his neck, and kissed him: and they wept.

⁵ And he lifted up his eyes, and saw the women and the children; and said, Who *are* those with thee? And he said, The children which God hath graciously given thy servant. ⁶ Then the handmaidens came near, they and their children, and they bowed themselves. ⁷ And Leah also with her children came near, and bowed themselves: and after came Joseph near and Rachel, and they bowed themselves. ⁸ And he said, What *meanest* thou by all this drove which I met? And he said, *These are* to find grace in the sight of my lord. ⁹ And Esau said, I have enough, my brother; keep that thou hast unto thyself. ¹⁰ And Jacob said, Nay, I pray thee, if now I have found grace in thy sight, then receive my present at my hand: for therefore I have seen thy face, as though I had seen the face of God, and thou wast pleased with me. ¹¹ Take, I pray thee, my blessing that is brought to thee;

because God hath dealt graciously with me, and because I have enough. And he urged him, and he took *it*. 12 And he said, Let us take our journey, and let us go, and I will go before thee. 13 And he said unto him, My lord knoweth that the children *are* tender, and the flocks and herds with young *are* with me: and if men should overdrive them one day, all the flock will die. 14 Let my lord, I pray thee, pass over before his servant: and I will lead on softly, according as the cattle that goeth before me and the children be able to endure, until I come unto my lord unto Seir. 15 And Esau said, Let me now leave with thee *some* of the folk that *are* with me. And he said, What needeth it? let me find grace in the sight of my lord.

Jacob Journeys to Succoth
- see Map 6(5) p.216 -

Jacob Builds a House –   [1739 B.C.?]
Gen.33:17 – 17 And Jacob journeyed to Succoth, and built him an house, and made booths for his cattle: therefore the name of the place is called Succoth.

Probability Scenario
It seems that Jacob's journey from Padan Aram, including all of the trials along the way, likely occurred over a short period of time – likely within the same year previously noted - 1739 B.C.?. It appears that Jacob intended to remain in Succoth for an extended period of time (v.17).
Probable age of contemporaries
Isaac 157 – Jacob 97 – Leah 80 – Rachel 60 – Dinah 6 – Joseph 6

Esau Journeys to Seir –   [1739 B.C.?]
Gen.33:16 – 16 So Esau returned that day on his way unto Seir.

Gen.36:6-8 – 6 And Esau took his wives, and his sons, and his daughters, and all the persons of his house, and his cattle, and all his beasts, and all his substance, which he had got in the land of Canaan; and went into the country from the face of his brother Jacob. 7 For their riches were more than that they might dwell together; and the land wherein they were strangers could not bear them because of their cattle. 8 Thus dwelt Esau in mount Seir: Esau *is* Edom.

Esau's Descendants –
Gen.36:9-19 – 9 And these *are* the generations of Esau the father of the Edomites in mount Seir: 10 These *are* the names of Esau's sons; Eliphaz the son of Adah the wife of Esau, Reuel the son of Bashemath the wife of Esau.

¹¹ And the sons of Eliphaz were Teman, Omar, Zepho, and Gatam, and Kenaz. ¹² And Timna was concubine to Eliphaz Esau's son; and she bare to Eliphaz Amalek: these *were* the sons of Adah Esau's wife. ¹³ And these *are* the sons of Reuel; Nahath, and Zerah, Shammah, and Mizzah: these were the sons of Bashemath Esau's wife. ¹⁴ And these were the sons of Aholibamah, the daughter of Anah the daughter of Zibeon, Esau's wife: and she bare to Esau Jeush, and Jaalam, and Korah. ¹⁵ These *were* dukes of the sons of Esau: the sons of Eliphaz the firstborn *son* of Esau; duke Teman, duke Omar, duke Zepho, duke Kenaz, ¹⁶ Duke Korah, duke Gatam, *and* duke Amalek: these *are* the dukes *that came* of Eliphaz in the land of Edom; these *were* the sons of Adah. ¹⁷ And these *are* the sons of Reuel Esau's son; duke Nahath, duke Zerah, duke Shammah, duke Mizzah: these *are* the dukes *that came* of Reuel in the land of Edom; these *are* the sons of Bashemath Esau's wife. ¹⁸ And these *are* the sons of Aholibamah Esau's wife; duke Jeush, duke Jaalam, duke Korah: these *were* the dukes *that came* of Aholibamah the daughter of Anah, Esau's wife. ¹⁹ These *are* the sons of Esau, who *is* Edom, and these *are* their dukes.

Seir's Descendants (Seir inhabited the land of Seir)

Gen.36:20-30 – ²⁰ These *are* the sons of Seir the Horite, who inhabited the land; Lotan, and Shobal, and Zibeon, and Anah, ²¹ And Dishon, and Ezer, and Dishan: these *are* the dukes of the Horites, the children of Seir in the land of Edom. ²² And the children of Lotan were Hori and Hemam; and Lotan's sister *was* Timna. ²³ And the children of Shobal *were* these; Alvan, and Manahath, and Ebal, Shepho, and Onam. ²⁴ And these *are* the children of Zibeon; both Ajah, and Anah: this *was that* Anah that found the mules in the wilderness, as he fed the asses of Zibeon his father. ²⁵ And the children of Anah *were* these; Dishon, and Aholibamah the daughter of Anah. ²⁶ And these *are* the children of Dishon; Hemdan, and Eshban, and Ithran, and Cheran. ²⁷ The children of Ezer *are* these; Bilhan, and Zaavan, and Akan. ²⁸ The children of Dishan *are* these; Uz, and Aran. ²⁹ These *are* the dukes *that came* of the Horites; duke Lotan, duke Shobal, duke Zibeon, duke Anah, ³⁰ Duke Dishon, duke Ezer, duke Dishan: these *are* the dukes *that came* of Hori, among their dukes in the land of Seir.

Edomite Kings (kings descended from Esau)

Gen.36:31-43 – ³¹ And these *are* the kings that reigned in the land of Edom, before there reigned any king over the children of Israel. ³² And Bela the son of Beor reigned in Edom: and the name of his city *was* Dinhabah.

³³ And Bela died, and Jobab the son of Zerah of Bozrah reigned in his stead. ³⁴ And Jobab died, and Husham of the land of Temani reigned in his stead. ³⁵ And Husham died, and Hadad the son of Bedad, who smote

Midian in the field of Moab, reigned in his stead: and the name of his city *was* Avith. ³⁶ And Hadad died, and Samlah of Masrekah reigned in his stead. ³⁷ And Samlah died, and Saul of Rehoboth *by* the river reigned in his stead. ³⁸ And Saul died, and Baalhanan the son of Achbor reigned in his stead. ³⁹ And Baalhanan the son of Achbor died, and Hadar reigned in his stead: and the name of his city *was* Pau; and his wife's name *was* Mehetabel, the daughter of Matred, the daughter of Mezahab. ⁴⁰ And these *are* the names of the dukes *that came* of Esau, according to their families, after their places, by their names; duke Timnah, duke Alvah, duke Jetheth, ⁴¹ Duke Aholibamah, duke Elah, duke Pinon, ⁴² Duke Kenaz, duke Teman, duke Mibzar, ⁴³ Duke Magdiel, duke Iram: these *be* the dukes of Edom, according to their habitations in the land of their possession: he *is* Esau the father of the Edomites.

Jacob Journeys to Shalem
- see Map 6(6) p.216 -

Jacob Pitches His Tent in Shalem (a city of Shechem)   [1730 B.C.?]
   Gen.33:18-20 – ¹⁸ And Jacob came to Shalem, a city of Shechem, which *is* in the land of Canaan, when he came from Padanaram; and pitched his tent before the city. ¹⁹ And he bought a parcel of a field, where he had spread his tent, at the hand of the children of Hamor, Shechem's father, for an hundred pieces of money. ²⁰ And he erected there an altar, and called it Elelohe-Israel.

Probability Scenario

It is probable that Jacob may have remained in Succoth before journeying to Shechem as long as nine years (see 1). Jacob's daughter, Dinah, is destined to be defiled by the "... *prince of the country*" (Gen.34:2 & see 2) before Joseph is sold by his brothers into slavery (see 3). It is reckoned that Dinah would be around age 15 at this point in time around 1730 B.C.?.

Supporting Evidence

1. **Jacob Builds a House** – [p.141]
2. **Dinah Defiled** – [p.144]
3. **Joseph Sold into Slavery** – [p.152]

Factors involved in calculating the year

x = 1739 B.C.? – Jacob journeys to Succoth then to Shalem
y = 9 ? – years probable sojourn in Shalem
z = 1730 B.C.? – year of this event

Formula

(x) + (y) = z
(1739 B.C.?) - (9) = 1730 B.C.?

Probable age of contemporaries

Isaac 166 – Jacob 106 – Leah 89 – Rachel 69 – Dinah 15 – Joseph 15

Dinah Defiled –   [1729 B.C.?]

Gen.34:1-12 – ¹ And Dinah the daughter of Leah, which she bare unto Jacob, went out to see the daughters of the land. ² And when Shechem the son of Hamor the Hivite, prince of the country, saw her, he took her, and lay with her, and defiled her. ³ And his soul clave unto Dinah the daughter of Jacob, and he loved the damsel, and spake kindly unto the damsel. ⁴ And Shechem spake unto his father Hamor, saying, Get me this damsel to wife. ⁵ And Jacob heard that he had defiled Dinah his daughter: now his sons were with his cattle in the field: and Jacob held his peace until they were come.

⁶ And Hamor the father of Shechem went out unto Jacob to commune with him. ⁷ And the sons of Jacob came out of the field when they heard *it*: and the men were grieved, and they were very wroth, because he had wrought folly in Israel in lying with Jacob's daughter; which thing ought not to be done. ⁸ And Hamor communed with them, saying, The soul of my son Shechem longeth for your daughter: I pray you give her him to wife. ⁹ And make ye marriages with us, *and* give your daughters unto us, and take our daughters unto you. ¹⁰ And ye shall dwell with us: and the land shall be before you; dwell and trade ye therein, and get you possessions therein. ¹¹ And Shechem said unto her father and unto her brethren, Let me find grace in your eyes, and what ye shall say unto me I will give. ¹² Ask me never so much dowry and gift, and I will give according as ye shall say unto me: but give me the damsel to wife.

Probability Scenario

It is probable that Jacob may have been in Shechem about a year when Dinah decided to meet the other young girls of the land (v.1). This event likely occurred after Dinah reached age 16 around 1729 B.C.?.

Factors involved in calculating the year

x = 1730 B.C.? – Jacob journeys to Shalem (a city of Shechem)
y = 1 ? – year probable sojourn in Shalem
z = 1729 B.C.? – year of this event

Formula

$(x) + (y) = z$

(1730 B.C.?) - (1) = 1729 B.C.?

Probable age of contemporaries

Isaac 167 – Jacob 107 – Leah 90 – Rachel 70 – Dinah 16 – Joseph 16

Deception and Lies Prevail – Jacob's earlier traits inherited   [1729 B.C.?]

Gen.34:13-24 – ¹³ And the sons of Jacob answered Shechem and Hamor his father deceitfully, and said, because he had defiled Dinah their sister: ¹⁴ And they said unto them, We cannot do this thing, to give our sister to one that is uncircumcised; for that *were* a reproach unto us: ¹⁵ But in this will we consent unto you: If ye will be as we *be*, that every male of you be circumcised; ¹⁶ Then will we give our daughters unto you, and we will take your daughters to us, and we will dwell with you, and we will become one people. ¹⁷ But if ye will not hearken unto us, to be circumcised; then will we take our daughter, and we will be gone.

¹⁸ And their words pleased Hamor, and Shechem Hamor's son. ¹⁹ And the young man deferred not to do the thing, because he had delight in Jacob's daughter: and he *was* more honourable than all the house of his father. ²⁰ And Hamor and Shechem his son came unto the gate of their city, and communed with the men of their city, saying, ²¹ These men *are* peaceable with us; therefore let them dwell in the land, and trade therein; for the land, behold, *it is* large enough for them; let us take their daughters to us for wives, and let us give them our daughters. ²² Only herein will the men consent unto us for to dwell with us, to be one people, if every male among us be circumcised, as they *are* circumcised. ²³ *Shall* not their cattle and their substance and every beast of theirs *be* ours? only let us consent unto them, and they will dwell with us. ²⁴ And unto Hamor and unto Shechem his son hearkened all that went out of the gate of his city; and every male was circumcised, all that went out of the gate of his city.

Anger Escalates into Murder –   [1729 B.C.?]

Gen.34:25-31 – ²⁵ And it came to pass on the third day, when they were sore, that two of the sons of Jacob, Simeon and Levi, Dinah's brethren, took each man his sword, and came upon the city boldly, and slew all the males. ²⁶ And they slew Hamor and Shechem his son with the edge of the sword, and took Dinah out of Shechem's house, and went out. ²⁷ The sons of Jacob came upon the slain, and spoiled the city, because they had defiled their sister. ²⁸ They took their sheep, and their oxen, and their asses, and that which *was* in the city, and that which *was* in the field, ²⁹ And all their wealth, and all their little ones, and their wives took they captive, and spoiled even all that *was* in the house. ³⁰ And Jacob said to Simeon and Levi, Ye have troubled me to make me to stink among the inhabitants of the land, among the Canaanites and the Perizzites: and I *being* few in number, they shall gather themselves together against me, and slay me; and I shall be destroyed, I and my house. ³¹ And they said, Should he deal with our sister as with an harlot?

God Tells Jacob to Leave Shechem –   [1729 B.C.?]

Gen.35:1 – ¹ And God said unto Jacob, Arise, go up to Bethel, and dwell there: and make there an altar unto God, that appeared unto thee when thou fleddest from the face of Esau thy brother.

Jacob Makes Preparation to Appear Before God –   [1729 B.C.?]
   Gen.35:2-4 – ² Then Jacob said unto his household, and to all that *were* with him, Put away the strange gods that *are* among you, and be clean, and change your garments: ³ And let us arise, and go up to Bethel; and I will make there an altar unto God, who answered me in the day of my distress, and was with me in the way which I went. ⁴ And they gave unto Jacob all the strange gods which *were* in their hand, and *all their* earrings which *were* in their ears; and Jacob hid them under the oak which *was* by Shechem.

Jacob Journeys to Bethel
- see Map 6(7) p.216 -

The Inhabitants of Shechem Fear God –   [1729 B.C.?]
   Gen.35:5-7 – ⁵ And they journeyed: and the terror of God was upon the cities that *were* round about them, and they did not pursue after the sons of Jacob.
   ⁶ So Jacob came to Luz, which *is* in the land of Canaan, that *is*, Bethel, he and all the people that *were* with him. ⁷ And he built there an altar, and called the place Elbethel: because there God appeared unto him, when he fled from the face of his brother.

Probability Scenario

It is reckoned that the actions of Jacob's sons, Simeon and Levi (see 1 & Gen.34:30), not only caused Jacob and his household to be obnoxious (loathsome) to the inhabitants of the land; but it would seem that God may have found them to be loathsome also. It seems that Jacob and his household were becoming more enamored with the gods of the world (v.2), than with the God Jacob met at Bethel (see 2) when he fled from Esau ("*the* LORD *God of Abraham … and the God of Isaac*" - Gen.28:13). It seems that the trials Jacob and his household were going through occurred in rapid succession, and were possibly orchestrated for the purpose of forcing Jacob to leave Shalem – likely within the same year previously noted, 1729 B.C.?.

Supporting Evidence
1. **Anger Escalates into Murder** – [p.145]
2. **Jacob Receives God's Covenant** (in a dream) [p.121]

Probable age of contemporaries
Isaac 167 – Jacob 107 – Leah 90 – Rachel 70 – Joseph 16

Death of Deborah (nurse to Jacob's mother, Rebekah)   [1729 B.C.?]
   Gen.35:8 – ⁸ But Deborah Rebekah's nurse died, and she was buried beneath Bethel under an oak: and the name of it was called Allonbachuth.

Probability Scenario

Deborah may have become Rebekah's nurse (v.8) at Rebekah's birth (see 1), and likely grew to love Rebekah so much that she accompanied Rebekah (see 2) when she went to become Isaac's wife (see 3). It is apparent that Deborah remained and journeyed with Jacob (see 4), Rebekah's favorite son, after Rebekah's death (see 5).

Supporting Evidence

1. **Birth of Rebekah** – daughter of Bethuel/Abraham's nephew [p.95]
2. **Laban, Bethuel and Rebekah Agree to the Servant's Request** – [p.102]
3. **Isaac Takes Rebekah to be His Wife** (at age 40) [p.102]
4. **Deborah Brings News from Isaac** (nurse of Rebekah) [p.134]
5. **Death of Rebekah** (mother of Jacob and Esau) [p.134]

Probable age of contemporaries

Isaac 167 – Jacob 107 – Leah 90 – Rachel 70 – Joseph 16

Jacob Blessed and Renamed Israel (supplanter/God prevails)   [1729 B.C.?]

Gen.35:9-10 – 9 And God appeared unto Jacob again, when he came out of Padanaram, and blessed him. 10 And God said unto him, Thy name is Jacob: thy name shall not be called any more Jacob, but Israel shall be thy name: and he called his name Israel.

God Renews the Covenant with Jacob –   [1729 B.C.?]

Gen.35:11-15 – 11 And God said unto him, I am God Almighty: be fruitful and multiply; a nation and a company of nations shall be of thee, and kings shall come out of thy loins; 12 And the land which I gave Abraham and Isaac, to thee I will give it, and to thy seed after thee will I give the land. 13 And God went up from him in the place where he talked with him. 14 And Jacob set up a pillar in the place where he talked with him, even a pillar of stone: and he poured a drink offering thereon, and he poured oil thereon. 15 And Jacob called the name of the place where God spake with him, Bethel.

Jacob Journeys to Ephrath / Bethlehem
- see Map 6(8) p.216 -

Jacob Leaves Bethel –   [1729 B.C.?]

Gen.35:16 – 16 And they journeyed from Bethel; and there was but a little way to come to Ephrath: …

Birth of Benjamin (son of Jacob and Rachel)   [1729 B.C.?]

Gen.35:16-18 – 16 … and Rachel travailed, and she had hard labour. 17 And it came to pass, when she was in hard labour, that the midwife said unto her, Fear not; thou shalt have this son also. 18 And it came to pass, as her soul was in departing, (for she died) that she called his name Benoni: but his father called him Benjamin.

Probability Scenario

It is probable that Rachel was pregnant around 1729 B.C., during the time of Dinah's defilement (see 1). It would seem likely that the ensuing deception, lies (see 2) and murder of the Shechemites (see 3), the fear of possible reprisal from the inhabitants of the land, and her delicate condition could have put tremendous stress on Rachel. It seems that the events following Diana's defilement occurred in rapid succession – likely within days of one another within the year 1729 B.C.?.

Supporting Evidence

1. **Dinah Defiled** – [p.144]
2. **Deception and Lies Prevail** – Jacob's earlier traits inherited [pp.118 & 144]
3. **Anger Escalates into Murder** – [p.145]

Probable age of contemporaries

Isaac 167 – Jacob 107 – Leah 90
Ruben 22 – Simeon 21 – Levi 20 – Dan 20 – Judah 19 – Naphtali 19 – Gad 18
Issachar 18 – Asher 17 – Zebulun 17 – Dinah 16 – Joseph 16

Death of Rachel –   [1729 B.C.?]

Gen.35:19-20 – [19] And Rachel died, and was buried in the way to Ephrath, which *is* Bethlehem. [20] And Jacob set a pillar upon her grave: that *is* the pillar of Rachel's grave unto this day.

Probability Scenario

Rachel's year of birth was likely around 1799 B.C.?. Rachel's probable life span is estimated at 70 years.

Supporting Evidence

1. **Birth of Rachel** – daughter of Laban/Abraham's kinsman [p.108]

Factors involved in calculating the year

x = 1799 B.C.? – Rachel's year of birth
y = 70 ? – years of life span
z = 1729 B.C.? – year of death

Formula

$(x) + (y) = z$
$(1799 \text{ B.C.?}) - (70) = 1729 \text{ B.C.?}$

Jacob's Sons Now Number Twelve –   [1729 B.C.?]

Gen.35:22-26 – [22] ... Now the sons of Jacob were twelve: [23] The sons of Leah; Reuben, Jacob's firstborn, and Simeon, and Levi, and Judah, and Issachar, and Zebulun: [24] The sons of Rachel; Joseph, and Benjamin: [25] And the sons of Bilhah, Rachel's handmaid; Dan, and Naphtali: [26] And the sons of Zilpah, Leah's handmaid; Gad, and Asher: these *are* the sons of Jacob, which were born to him in Padanaram.

1Chron.2:1-2 – [1] These *are* the sons of Israel; Reuben, Simeon, Levi, and Judah, Issachar, and Zebulun, [2] Dan, Joseph, and Benjamin, Naphtali, Gad, and Asher.

Israel (Jacob) Arrives in Bethlehem –   [1729 B.C.?]
Gen.35:21 – [21] And Israel journeyed, and spread his tent beyond the tower of Edar.

Reuben Defiles His Father's Bed –   [1729 B.C.?]
Gen.35:22 – [22] And it came to pass, when Israel dwelt in that land, that Reuben went and lay with Bilhah his father's concubine: and Israel heard *it...*

Probability Scenario

It is probable that the coat of many colors may have already been made - showing Israel's favoritism toward Joseph (see 1 & Gen.37:3-4). It is possible that Ruben did not actually intend to defile his father's bed; but that he was expressing his contempt for Joseph by defiling the maid of Joseph's deceased mother. There are incidents where it is quite apparent that Ruben chose not to direct vengeance toward Joseph, because of his respect for his father (Gen.37:17-22, 29-30). Ruben likely felt that, as the firstborn son, he should have the place of honor - certainly not the eleventh son. However, no matter what his intent was, the end result is that Ruben ultimately defiled his father's bed. This event likely occurred in the same year that Rachel died 1729 B.C.? (see 2).

Supporting Evidence
1. **Joseph Favored by Jacob –** hated by his brothers [p.150]
2. **Death of Rachel [p.148]**

Probable age of contemporaries:
Isaac 167 – Jacob 107 – Leah 90
Ruben 22 – Simeon 21 – Levi 20 – Dan 20 – Judah 19 – Naphtali 19 – Gad 18
Issachar 18 – Asher 17 – Zebulun 17 – Dinah 16 – Joseph 16
Benjamin (weeks)

Jacob Journeys to Hebron
- see Map 6(9) p.216 -

Jacob Returns to Isaac –   [1728 B.C.?]
Gen.35:27 – [27] And Jacob came unto Isaac his father unto Mamre, unto the city of Arbah, which *is* Hebron, where Abraham and Isaac sojourned.

Joseph at Hebron
- see Map 7(1) p.217 also Map 6(9) p.216 -

Joseph and His Brothers Dwell at Hebron –   [1728 B.C.?]

   Gen.37:1 – ¹ And Jacob dwelt in the land wherein his father was a stranger, in the land of Canaan.

Probability Scenario
It is important to note that Joseph, Jacob's favorite (see 1), along with his other brothers, is also dwelling in Hebron with his father Jacob (see 2).
Supporting Evidence
1. **Joseph Favored by Jacob** – hated by his brothers [p.150]
2. **Jacob Returns to Isaac** – [p.149]
Probable age of contemporaries
Isaac 168 – Jacob 108 – Leah 91
Ruben 23 – Simeon 22 – Levi 21 – Dan 21 – Judah 20 – Naphtali 20 – Gad 19
Issachar 19 – Asher 18 – Zebulun 18 – Dinah 17 – Joseph 17 – Benjamin 1

Joseph Favored by Jacob – hated by his brothers   [1728 B.C.#]

   Gen.37:2-11 – ² These *are* the generations of Jacob. Joseph, *being* seventeen years old, was feeding the flock with his brethren; and the lad *was* with the sons of Bilhah, and with the sons of Zilpah, his father's wives: and Joseph brought unto his father their evil report. ³ Now Israel loved Joseph more than all his children, because he *was* the son of his old age: and he made him a coat of *many* colours. ⁴ And when his brethren saw that their father loved him more than all his brethren, they hated him, and could not speak peaceably unto him.

   ⁵ And Joseph dreamed a dream, and he told *it* his brethren: and they hated him yet the more. ⁶ And he said unto them, Hear, I pray you, this dream which I have dreamed: ⁷ For, behold, we *were* binding sheaves in the field, and, lo, my sheaf arose, and also stood upright; and, behold, your sheaves stood round about, and made obeisance to my sheaf. ⁸ And his brethren said to him, Shalt thou indeed reign over us? or shalt thou indeed have dominion over us? And they hated him yet the more for his dreams, and for his words. ⁹ And he dreamed yet another dream, and told it his brethren, and said, Behold, I have dreamed a dream more; and, behold, the sun and the moon and the eleven stars made obeisance to me. ¹⁰ And he told *it* to his father, and to his brethren: and his father rebuked him, and said unto him, What *is* this dream that thou hast dreamed? Shall I and thy mother and thy brethren indeed come to bow down ourselves to thee to the earth? ¹¹ And his brethren envied him; but his father observed the saying.

Joseph Sent to Shechem –   [1728 B.C.?]
Gen.37:12-14 – 12 And his brethren went to feed their father's flock in Shechem. 13 And Israel said unto Joseph, Do not thy brethren feed *the flock* in Shechem? come, and I will send thee unto them. And he said to him, Here *am I*. 14 And he said to him, Go, I pray thee, see whether it be well with thy brethren, and well with the flocks; and bring me word again. So he sent him out of the vale of Hebron ...

Joseph Journeys to Shechem
- see Map 7(2) p.217 -

Joseph Sent to Dothan –   [1728 B.C.?]
Gen.37:14-17 – 14 ... and he came to Shechem. 15 And a certain man found him, and, behold, *he was* wandering in the field: and the man asked him, saying, What seekest thou? 16 And he said, I seek my brethren: tell me, I pray thee, where they feed *their flocks*. 17 And the man said, They are departed hence; for I heard them say, Let us go to Dothan. ...

Joseph Journeys to Dothan
- see Map 7(3) p.217 -

Joseph's Brothers Plot to Kill Him – Reuben defends Joseph   [1728 B.C.?]
Gen.37:17-24 – 17 ... And Joseph went after his brethren, and found them in Dothan. 18 And when they saw him afar off, even before he came near unto them, they conspired against him to slay him. 19 And they said one to

another, Behold, this dreamer cometh. ²⁰ Come now therefore, and let us
slay him, and cast him into some pit, and we will say, Some evil beast hath
devoured him: and we shall see what will become of his dreams. ²¹ And
Reuben heard *it*, and he delivered him out of their hands; and said, Let us
not kill him. ²² And Reuben said unto them, Shed no blood, *but* cast him
into this pit that *is* in the wilderness, and lay no hand upon him; that he
might rid him out of their hands, to deliver him to his father again.

²³ And it came to pass, when Joseph was come unto his brethren, that
they stript Joseph out of his coat, *his* coat of *many* colours that *was* on him; ²⁴
And they took him, and cast him into a pit: and the pit *was* empty, *there was*
no water in it.

Judah Incites His Brothers to Sell Joseph – while Reuben is away [1728 B.C.?]
Gen.37:25-27 – ²⁵ And they sat down to eat bread: and they lifted up
their eyes and looked, and, behold, a company of Ishmeelites came from
Gilead with their camels bearing spicery and balm and myrrh, going to
carry *it* down to Egypt. ²⁶ And Judah said unto his brethren, What profit *is
it* if we slay our brother, and conceal his blood? ²⁷ Come, and let us sell him
to the Ishmeelites, and let not our hand be upon him; for he *is* our brother
and our flesh. And his brethren were content.

Probability Scenario

It is probable that Judah, the fourth in line for the inheritance, might be
considering the possibility of getting rid of Joseph, the primary obstacle to his
becoming the next family patriarch if normal protocol is followed. It appears
that Ruben has disqualified himself from the inheritance of the firstborn by
defiling his father's bed (see 1 & Gen.49:4). It seems that Simeon and Levi, the
second and third born, have disqualified themselves as well, after murdering
the Shechemites in retaliation for Dinah's defilement (see 2 & Gen.49:5-7). This
event likely occurred within the first year Jacob's family settled in Hebron -
1728 B.C.? (see 3).

Supporting Evidence

1. **Reuben Defiles His Father's Bed** – [p.149]
2. **Anger Escalates into Murder** – [p.145]
3. **Joseph and His Brothers Dwell at Hebron** – [p.150]

Probable age of contemporaries

Isaac 168 – Jacob 108 – Leah 91

Ruben 23 – Simeon 22 – Levi 21 – Dan 21 – Judah 20 – Naphtali 20 – Gad 19

Issachar 19 – Asher 18 – Zebulun 18 – Dinah 17 – Joseph 17 – Benjamin 1

Joseph Journeys to Egypt
- see Map 7(4) p.217 -

Joseph Sold into Slavery –   [1728 B.C.#]
Gen.37:28 – ²⁸ Then there passed by Midianites merchantmen; and they

drew and lifted up Joseph out of the pit, and sold Joseph to the Ishmeelites for twenty *pieces* of silver: and they brought Joseph into Egypt.

Deception and Lies Prevail – Jacob reaps what he has sown   [1728 B.C.?]
    Gen.37:29-35 – ²⁹ And Reuben returned unto the pit; and, behold, Joseph *was* not in the pit; and he rent his clothes. ³⁰ And he returned unto his brethren, and said, The child *is* not; and I, whither shall I go? ³¹ And they took Joseph's coat, and killed a kid of the goats, and dipped the coat in the blood; ³² And they sent the coat of *many* colours, and they brought *it* to their father; and said, This have we found: know now whether it *be* thy son's coat or no. ³³ And he knew it, and said, *It is* my son's coat; an evil beast hath devoured him; Joseph is without doubt rent in pieces. ³⁴ And Jacob rent his clothes, and put sackcloth upon his loins, and mourned for his son many days. ³⁵ And all his sons and all his daughters rose up to comfort him; but he refused to be comforted; and he said, For I will go down into the grave unto my son mourning. Thus his father wept for him.

Note
It seems that Jacob's sons are following very closely in theirs father's deceptive ways (see **Deception and Lies Prevail** – [pp.118 & 144])

* BEGIN PARALLEL ACCOUNTS OF JOSEPH AND JUDAH / JOB *

Events Associated with Joseph	Events Associated with Judah / Job
Joseph in Egypt – [1728 B.C.?]	**Judah Departs from His Brothers -** [1728 B.C.?]
Gen.37:36 – ³⁶ And the Midianites sold him into Egypt unto Potiphar, an officer of Pharaoh's, *and* captain of the guard.	Gen.38:1 – ¹ And it came to pass at that time, that Judah went down from his brethren, and turned in to a certain Adullamite, whose name *was* Hirah.
Gen.39:1 – ¹ And Joseph was brought down to Egypt; and Potiphar, an officer of Pharaoh, captain of the guard, an Egyptian, bought him of the hands of the Ishmeelites, which had brought him down thither.	**Probability Scenario** It was Judah who proposed the idea that his brothers sell Joseph to the Ishmaelites (see 1 & Gen.37:26-27). It is probable that Judah may have been deeply remorseful after seeing his father's anguish over the loss of Joseph (Gen.37:34-35).
Probability Scenario This event likely occurred within	**Supporting Evidence**

153

several weeks of Joseph's brothers selling him into slavery (see 1) and likely in the same year - 1728 B.C.?.

Supporting Evidence

1. **Joseph Sold into Slavery** – [p.152]

<u>Probable age of contemporaries</u>
Isaac 168 – Jacob 108 – Leah 91
Ruben 23 – Simeon 22 – Levi 21
Dan 21 – Judah 20 – Naphtali 20
Gad 19 – Issachar 19 – Asher 18
Zebulun 18 – Dinah 17 – Joseph 17
Benjamin 1

The LORD Blesses Joseph –
[1725 B.C.?]

Gen.39:2-6 – ² And the LORD was with Joseph, and he was a prosperous man; and he was in the house of his master the Egyptian. ³ And his master saw that the LORD *was* with him, and that the LORD made all that he did to prosper in his hand. ⁴ And Joseph found grace in his sight, and he served him: and he made him overseer over his house, and all *that* he had he put into his hand. ⁵ And it came to pass from the time *that* he had made him overseer in his house, and over all that he had, that the LORD blessed the Egyptian's house for Joseph's sake; and the blessing of the LORD was upon all that he had in the house, and in the field. ⁶ And he left all that he had in Joseph's hand; and he knew not ought he had, save

1. **Judah Incites His Brothers to Sell Joseph** – [p.152]

<u>Probable age of contemporaries</u>
Isaac 168 – Jacob 108 – Leah 91
Ruben 23 – Simeon 22 – Levi 21
Dan 21 – Judah 20 – Naphtali 20
Gad 19 – Issachar 19 – Asher 18
Zebulun 18 – Dinah 17 – Joseph 17
Benjamin 1

Birth of Er – [1727 B.C.?]
(son of Judah)

Gen.38:2-3 – ² And Judah saw there a daughter of a certain Canaanite, whose name *was* Shuah; and he took her, and went in unto her. ³ And she conceived, and bare a son; and he called his name Er.

Birth of Onan – [1726 B.C.?]
(son of Judah)

Gen.38:4 – ⁴ And she conceived again, and bare a son; and she called his name Onan.

Birth of Shelah – [1725 B.C.?]
(son of Judah)

Gen.38:5 – ⁵ And she yet again conceived, and bare a son; and called his name Shelah: and he was at Chezib, when she bare him.

Job's Loyalty to God Disputed by satan – [1725B.C.?]

Job 1:6-2:10

<u>Probability Scenario</u>
It seems that satan's challenge of Job's loyalty to God may have occurred when Job was about 70 years of age (see 1 & 2), around 1725 B.C.?.

Supporting Evidence
1. **Birth of Job** - [p.110]

the bread which he did eat...
(Note: v.6 continues at –
Joseph Accused of Improper Conduct –
[p.155])

Probability Scenario
It is probable that Joseph was assigned menial tasks at first and then gradually tasks of greater importance (v.2). It seems that Joseph excelled in his assignments above and beyond his masters expectations and beyond normal human capability, to the degree that divine intervention was apparent (v.3). Joseph is destined to be enticed by the wife of his master (see 1). At this point in time, it would seem that approximately three years may have passed, giving Joseph enough time to learn the Egyptian language and to be made overseer of Potiphar's house - around 1725 B.C.?.
Supporting Evidence
1. **Joseph Accused of Improper Conduct** – [p.155]
Probable age of contemporaries
Isaac 171 – Jacob 111 – Leah 94
Ruben 26 – Simeon 25 – Levi 24
Dan 24 – Judah 23 – Naphtali 23
Gad 22 – Issachar 22 – Asher 21
Zebulun 21 – Dinah 20 – Joseph 20
Benjamin 4

2. **Job Blessed by God** - [p.155]
Probable age of contemporaries
Isaac 171 – Esau 111 – Eliphaz 70
Teman 39 – Joseph 20

Job's Loyalty to God Disputed by His Friends –   [1725B.C.?]
Job 2:11-37:24

Job Confronted by God – [1725B.C.?]
Job 38:1-42:6

Job's Friends Confronted by God –
[1725B.C.?]
Job 42:7-9

Job Blessed by God –   [1725B.C.?]
Job 42:10-15

Probability Scenario
It is possible that God's blessing upon Job not only included "... *twice as much as he had before*" (Job 42:10), but also twice as many years of life than he had before. "*After this lived Job an hundred and forty years, and saw his sons, and his sons' sons, even four generations*" (Job 42:16).
Supporting Evidence
1. **Birth of Job** – [p.110]
2. **Death of Job** (at age 210) [p.183]

* PAUSE PARALLEL ACCOUNTS OF JOSEPH AND JUDAH / JOB *

God Prepares Joseph to Save Israel

Joseph Accused of Improper Conduct –   [1719 B.C.?]
(Note: v.6 continued from – **The LORD Blesses Joseph** [p.154])
Gen.39:6-19 – ⁶ ... And Joseph was *a goodly person*, and well favoured.
⁷ And it came to pass after these things, that his master's wife cast her

155

eyes upon Joseph; and she said, Lie with me. 8 But he refused, and said unto his master's wife, Behold, my master wotteth not what *is* with me in the house, and he hath committed all that he hath to my hand; 9 *There is* none greater in this house than I; neither hath he kept back any thing from me but thee, because thou *art* his wife: how then can I do this great wickedness, and sin against God? 10 And it came to pass, as she spake to Joseph day by day, that he hearkened not unto her, to lie by her, *or* to be with her. 11 And it came to pass about this time, that *Joseph* went into the house to do his business; and *there was* none of the men of the house there within. 12 And she caught him by his garment, saying, Lie with me: and he left his garment in her hand, and fled, and got him out.

13 And it came to pass, when she saw that he had left his garment in her hand, and was fled forth, 14 That she called unto the men of her house, and spake unto them, saying, See, he hath brought in an Hebrew unto us to mock us; he came in unto me to lie with me, and I cried with a loud voice: 15 And it came to pass, when he heard that I lifted up my voice and cried, that he left his garment with me, and fled, and got him out. 16 And she laid up his garment by her, until his lord came home. 17 And she spake unto him according to these words, saying, The Hebrew servant, which thou hast brought unto us, came in unto me to mock me: 18 And it came to pass, as I lifted up my voice and cried, that he left his garment with me, and fled out.

19 And it came to pass, when his master heard the words of his wife, which she spake unto him, saying, After this manner did thy servant to me; that his wrath was kindled.

Probability Scenario

It seems likely that it would take Joseph a few years to reach a level of confidence and physical maturity that would appeal to Potiphar's wife (vv.6-7). It is probable that Joseph could have faithfully served as many as six years as overseer in Potiphar's house. The year could likely be around 1719 B.C.?.

Probable age of contemporaries

Isaac 177 – Jacob 117 –Joseph 26

Joseph Thrown in Prison – the LORD continues to bless   [1719 B.C.?]

Gen.39:20-23 – 20 And Joseph's master took him, and put him into the prison, a place where the king's prisoners *were* bound: and he was there in the prison. 21 But the LORD was with Joseph, and shewed him mercy, and gave him favour in the sight of the keeper of the prison. 22 And the keeper of the prison committed to Joseph's hand all the prisoners that *were* in the prison; and whatsoever they did there, he was the doer *of it.* 23 The keeper of the prison looked not to any thing *that was* under his hand; because the LORD was with him, and *that* which he did, the LORD made *it* to prosper.

Joseph Interprets Dreams of Pharaoh's Servants –   [1717 B.C.#]

Gen.40:1-23 – ¹ And it came to pass after these things, *that* the butler of the king of Egypt and *his* baker had offended their lord the king of Egypt. ² And Pharaoh was wroth against two *of* his officers, against the chief of the butlers, and against the chief of the bakers. ³ And he put them in ward in the house of the captain of the guard, into the prison, the place where Joseph *was* bound. ⁴ And the captain of the guard charged Joseph with them, and he served them: and they continued a season in ward.

⁵ And they dreamed a dream both of them, each man his dream in one night, each man according to the interpretation of his dream, the butler and the baker of the king of Egypt, which *were* bound in the prison. ⁶ And Joseph came in unto them in the morning, and looked upon them, and, behold, they *were* sad. ⁷ And he asked Pharaoh's officers that *were* with him in the ward of his lord's house, saying, Wherefore look ye *so* sadly to day? ⁸ And they said unto him, We have dreamed a dream, and *there is* no interpreter of it. And Joseph said unto them, *Do* not interpretations *belong* to God? tell me *them*, I pray you. ⁹ And the chief butler told his dream to Joseph, and said to him, In my dream, behold, a vine *was* before me; ¹⁰ And in the vine *were* three branches: and it *was* as though it budded, *and* her blossoms shot forth; and the clusters thereof brought forth ripe grapes: ¹¹ And Pharaoh's cup *was* in my hand: and I took the grapes, and pressed them into Pharaoh's cup, and I gave the cup into Pharaoh's hand. ¹² And Joseph said unto him, This *is* the interpretation of it: The three branches *are* three days: ¹³ Yet within three days shall Pharaoh lift up thine head, and restore thee unto thy place: and thou shalt deliver Pharaoh's cup into his hand, after the former manner when thou wast his butler. ¹⁴ But think on me when it shall be well with thee, and shew kindness, I pray thee, unto me, and make mention of me unto Pharaoh, and bring me out of this house: ¹⁵ For indeed I was stolen away out of the land of the Hebrews: and here also have I done nothing that they should put me into the dungeon. ¹⁶ When the chief baker saw that the interpretation was good, he said unto Joseph, I also *was* in my dream, and, behold, *I had* three white baskets on my head: ¹⁷ And in the uppermost basket *there was* of all manner of bake-meats for Pharaoh; and the birds did eat them out of the basket upon my had. ¹⁸ And Joseph answered and said, This *is* the interpretation thereof: The three baskets *are* three days: ¹⁹ Yet within three days shall Pharaoh lift up thy head from off thee, and shall hang thee on a tree; and the birds shall eat thy flesh from off thee.

²⁰ And it came to pass the third day, *which was* Pharaoh's birthday, that he made a feast unto all his servants: and he lifted up the head of the chief

butler and of the chief baker among his servants. 21 And he restored the chief butler unto his butlership again; and he gave the cup into Pharaoh's hand: 22 But he hanged the chief baker: as Joseph had interpreted to them. 23 Yet did not the chief butler remember Joseph, but forgat him.

Probability Scenario

It seems likely that it would take Joseph a few months after being thrown in prison to gain "… *favour in the sight of the keeper of the prison*" (Gen.39:21 & see 1). These events occurred "… *two full years*" (Gen.41:1) before Joseph interpreted Pharaoh's dreams (see 2) and was elevated to governor over all Egypt (see 3). The year of these events was 1717 B.C.#.

Supporting Evidence

1. **Joseph Thrown in Prison** – the LORD continues to bless [p.156]
2. **Joseph Interprets Dreams of Pharaoh** – [p.158]
3. **Joseph Elevated to Governor in Egypt** (at age 30) [p.160]

Probable age of contemporaries

Isaac 179 – Jacob 119 –Joseph 28

Death of Isaac (at age 180)   [1716 B.C.#]

Gen.35:28-29 – 28 And the days of Isaac were an hundred and fourscore years. 29 And Isaac gave up the ghost, and died, and was gathered unto his people, *being* old and full of days: and his sons Esau and Jacob buried him.

Years are Calculated from Scripture References

see "Genesis Genealogical Chart"

Probable age of contemporaries

Jacob 120 –Joseph 29

Joseph Interprets Dreams of Pharaoh –   [1715 B.C.#]

Gen.41:1-36 – 1 And it came to pass at the end of two full years, that Pharaoh dreamed: and, behold, he stood by the river. 2 And, behold, there came up out of the river seven well favoured kine and fatfleshed; and they fed in a meadow. 3 And, behold, seven other kine came up after them out of the river, ill favoured and leanfleshed; and stood by the *other* kine upon the brink of the river. 4 And the ill favoured and leanfleshed kine did eat up the seven well favoured and fat kine. So Pharaoh awoke. 5 And he slept and dreamed the second time: and, behold, seven ears of corn came up upon one stalk, rank and good. 6 And, behold, seven thin ears and blasted with the east wind sprung up after them. 7 And the seven thin ears devoured the seven rank and full ears. And Pharaoh awoke, and, behold, *it was* a dream. 8 And it came to pass in the morning that his spirit was troubled; and he sent and called for all the magicians of Egypt, and all the wise men thereof: and Pharaoh told them his dream; but *there was* none that could interpret them unto Pharaoh.

⁹ Then spake the chief butler unto Pharaoh, saying, I do remember my faults this day: ¹⁰ Pharaoh was wroth with his servants, and put me in ward in the captain of the guard's house, *both* me and the chief baker: ¹¹ And we dreamed a dream in one night, I and he; we dreamed each man according to the interpretation of his dream. ¹² And *there was* there with us a young man, an Hebrew, servant to the captain of the guard; and we told him, and he interpreted to us our dreams; to each man according to his dream he did interpret. ¹³ And it came to pass, as he interpreted to us, so it was; me he restored unto mine office, and him he hanged. ¹⁴ Then Pharaoh sent and called Joseph, and they brought him hastily out of the dungeon: and he shaved *himself*, and changed his raiment, and came in unto Pharaoh. ¹⁵ And Pharaoh said unto Joseph, I have dreamed a dream, and *there is* none that can interpret it: and I have heard say of thee, *that* thou canst understand a dream to interpret it. ¹⁶ And Joseph answered Pharaoh, saying, *It is* not in me: God shall give Pharaoh an answer of peace.

¹⁷ And Pharaoh said unto Joseph, In my dream, behold, I stood upon the bank of the river: ¹⁸ And, behold, there came up out of the river seven kine, fatfleshed and well favoured; and they fed in a meadow: ¹⁹ And, behold, seven other kine came up after them, poor and very ill favoured and leanfleshed, such as I never saw in all the land of Egypt for badness: ²⁰ And the lean and the ill favoured kine did eat up the first seven fat kine: ²¹ And when they had eaten them up, it could not be known that they had eaten them; but they *were* still ill favoured, as at the beginning. So I awoke. ²² And I saw in my dream, and, behold, seven ears came up in one stalk, full and good: ²³ And, behold, seven ears, withered, thin, *and* blasted with the east wind, sprung up after them: ²⁴ And the thin ears devoured the seven good ears: and I told *this* unto the magicians; but *there was* none that could declare *it* to me. ²⁵ And Joseph said unto Pharaoh, The dream of Pharaoh *is* one: God hath shewed Pharaoh what he *is* about to do. ²⁶ The seven good kine *are* seven years; and the seven good ears *are* seven years: the dream *is* one. ²⁷ And the seven thin and ill favoured kine that came up after them *are* seven years; and the seven empty ears blasted with the east wind shall be seven years of famine. ²⁸ This *is* the thing which I have spoken unto Pharaoh: What God *is* about to do he sheweth unto Pharaoh. ²⁹ Behold, there come seven years of great plenty throughout all the land of Egypt: ³⁰ And there shall arise after them seven years of famine; and all the plenty shall be forgotten in the land of Egypt; and the famine shall consume the land; ³¹ And the plenty shall not be known in the land by reason of that famine following; for it *shall be* very grievous. ³² And for that the dream was doubled unto Pharaoh twice; *it is* because the thing *is* established by God, and God will shortly bring it to pass.

³³ Now therefore let Pharaoh look out a man discreet and wise, and set

him over the land of Egypt. ³⁴ Let Pharaoh do *this*, and let him appoint officers over the land, and take up the fifth part of the land of Egypt in the seven plenteous years. ³⁵ And let them gather all the food of those good years that come, and lay up corn under the hand of Pharaoh, and let them keep food in the cities. ³⁶ And that food shall be for store to the land against the seven years of famine, which shall be in the land of Egypt; that the land perish not through the famine.

Probability Scenario

These events occurred "... *two full years*" (v.1) after Joseph interpreted the dreams of Pharaoh's servants (see 1), and culminated in the elevation of Joseph to governor over all Egypt (see 2). The year of these events was 1715 B.C.#.

Supporting Evidence
1. **Joseph Interprets Dreams of Pharaoh's Servants** – [p.157]
2. **Joseph Elevated to Governor in Egypt** (at age 30) [p.160]

Probable age of contemporaries
Jacob 121 –Joseph 30

Joseph Elevated to Governor in Egypt (at age 30)   [1715 B.C.#]

Gen.41:37-46 – ³⁷ And the thing was good in the eyes of Pharaoh, and in the eyes of all his servants. ³⁸ And Pharaoh said unto his servants, Can we find *such a one* as this *is*, a man in whom the Spirit of God *is*? ³⁹ And Pharaoh said unto Joseph, Forasmuch as God hath shewed thee all this, *there is* none so discreet and wise as thou *art*: ⁴⁰ Thou shalt be over my house, and according unto thy word shall all my people be ruled: only in the throne will I be greater than thou. ⁴¹ And Pharaoh said unto Joseph, See, I have set thee over all the land of Egypt. ⁴² And Pharaoh took off his ring from his hand, and put it upon Joseph's hand, and arrayed him in vestures of fine linen, and put a gold chain about his neck; ⁴³ And he made him to ride in the second chariot which he had; and they cried before him, Bow the knee: and he made him *ruler* over all the land of Egypt. ⁴⁴ And Pharaoh said unto Joseph, I *am* Pharaoh, and without thee shall no man lift up his hand or foot in all the land of Egypt. ⁴⁵ And Pharaoh called Joseph's name Zaphnathpaaneah; and he gave him to wife Asenath the daughter of Potipherah priest of On. And Joseph went out over *all* the land of Egypt.

⁴⁶ And Joseph *was* thirty years old when he stood before Pharaoh king of Egypt. And Joseph went out from the presence of Pharaoh, and went throughout all the land of Egypt.

Factors involved in calculating the year

x = 1745 B.C.# – Birth of Joseph (see "Genesis Genealogical Chart")
y = 30 – years (v.46)
z = 1715 B.C.# – year of this event

Formula

(x) + (y) = z

(1745 B.C.#) - (30) = 1715 B.C.#

Probable age of contemporaries

Jacob 121 –Joseph 30

Joseph Fulfills Asenath's Week –   [1715 B.C.#]

Probability Scenario

Pharaoh's gift to Joseph of Asenath as a wife (see 1 & Gen.41:45) likely postponed Joseph's travels "… *throughout all the land of Egypt*" (Gen.41:46 & see 1) about one week (see 2 & Gen.29:27).

Supporting Evidence

1. **Joseph Elevated to Governor in Egypt** (at age 30) [p.160]
2. **Jacob Agrees to Work Seven More Years for Rachel** - [p.125]

Probable age of contemporaries

Jacob 121 –Joseph 30

Bountiful Harvests Begin –   [1715 B.C.#]

Gen.41:47-49 – [47] And in the seven plenteous years the earth brought forth by handfuls. [48] And he gathered up all the food of the seven years, which were in the land of Egypt, and laid up the food in the cities: the food of the field, which *was* round about every city, laid he up in the same. [49] And Joseph gathered corn as the sand of the sea, very much, until he left numbering; for *it was* without number.

Probability Scenario

It is likely that when Joseph told Pharaoh "… *the thing is established by God, and God will shortly bring it to pass*" (Gen.41:32 & see 1), the signs were already becoming evident in 1715 B.C.#.

Supporting Evidence

1. **Joseph Interprets Dreams of Pharaoh** [p.158]

Probable age of contemporaries

Jacob 121 –Joseph 30

Birth of Manasseh (son of Joseph)   [1714 B.C.?]

Gen.41:50-51 – [50] And unto Joseph were born two sons before the years of famine came, which Asenath the daughter of Potipherah priest of On bare unto him. [51] And Joseph called the name of the firstborn Manasseh: For God, *said he*, hath made me forget all my toil, and all my father's house.

Probability Scenario

It is probable that Asenath conceived during her week (see 1), or very soon after in 1715 B.C.?, baring Manasseh during the following year in 1714 B.C.?.

Supporting Evidence

1. **Joseph Fulfills Asenath's Week –** [p.161]

Birth of Ephraim (son of Joseph)   [1712 B.C.?]

Gen.41:52 – 52 And the name of the second called he Ephraim: For God hath caused me to be fruitful in the land of my affliction.

Probability Scenario

It seems likely that Joseph may have been very focused on his travels "... *throughout all the land of Egypt*" (Gen.41:46 & see 1) and overseeing the building or renovating of the storehouses where "... *he laid up in every city the food of the fields which surrounded them*" (Gen.41:48 & see 2). It seems probable that Ephraim may have been born approximately two years after Manasseh (see 3), around 1712 B.C.?.

Supporting Evidence

1. **Joseph Elevated to Governor in Egypt** (at age 30) [p.160]
2. **Bountiful Harvests Begin** – [p.161]
3. **Birth of Manasseh** (son of Joseph) [p.161]

Probable age of contemporaries
Jacob 124 –Joseph 33

---

* * RESUME PARALLEL ACCOUNTS OF JOSEPH AND JUDAH * *

Events Associated with Joseph	Events Associated with Judah
Bountiful Harvests End –[1708 B.C.#] Gen.41:53 – 53 And the seven years of plenteousness, that was in the land of Egypt, were ended. **Factors involved in calculating the year** x = 1715 B.C.# – Bountiful harvests begin y = 7 – years of plenty ends (v.53) z = 1708 B.C.# – year of this event **Formula** (x) + (y) = z (1715 B.C.#) - (7) = 1708 B.C.# **Probable age of contemporaries** Jacob 128 –Joseph 37	**Judah's Eldest Marries Tamar -** [1708 B.C.?] Gen.38:6 – 6 And Judah took a wife for Er his firstborn, whose name *was* Tamar. **Probability Scenario** It is possible that Er may have been only 19 years of age when Judah took Tamar to be his sons wife (see 1) **Supporting Evidence** 1. **Birth of Er** (son of Judah) [p.154] **Factors involved in calculating the year** x = 1727 B.C.? – Birth of Er y = 19 ? – Er's probable age z = 1708 B.C.? – year of this event

Formula
(x) + (y) = z
(1727 B.C.?) - (19) = 1708 B.C.?
Probable age of contemporaries
Jacob 128 – Judah 40 – Joseph 37
Onan 18 – Shelah 17

Seven Years of Famine Begin –
                    [1708 B.C.#]

Gen.41:54-57 – ⁵⁴ And the seven years of dearth began to come, according as Joseph had said: and the dearth was in all lands; but in all the land of Egypt there was bread. ⁵⁵ And when all the land of Egypt was famished, the people cried to Pharaoh for bread: and Pharaoh said unto all the Egyptians, Go unto Joseph; what he saith to you, do. ⁵⁶ And the famine was over all the face of the earth: And Joseph opened all the storehouses, and sold unto the Egyptians; and the famine waxed sore in the land of Egypt. ⁵⁷ And all countries came into Egypt to Joseph for to buy *corn*; because that the famine was *so* sore in all lands.

Judah's Two Sons Die – [1708 B.C.?]

Gen.38:7-10 – ⁷ And Er, Judah's firstborn, was wicked in the sight of the LORD; and the LORD slew him. ⁸ And Judah said unto Onan, Go in unto thy brother's wife, and marry her, and raise up seed to thy brother. ⁹ And Onan knew that the seed should not be his; and it came to pass, when he went in unto his brother's wife, that he spilled *it* on the ground, lest that he should give seed to his brother. ¹⁰ And the thing which he did displeased the LORD: wherefore he slew him also.

1Chron.2:3 – ³ The sons of Judah; Er, and Onan, and Shelah: *which* three were born unto him of the daughter of Shua the Canaanitess. And Er, the firstborn of Judah, was evil in the sight of the LORD; and he slew him.

Probability Scenario
It is seems that the loss of Judah's two eldest sons may have occurred in the same year, 1708 B.C.?. Er would have been 19 years of age (see 1), and Onan only 18 (see 2) in 1708 B.C.?.
Supporting Evidence
1. **Birth of Er** (son of Judah) [p.154]
2. **Birth of Onan** (son of Judah) [p.154]
Probable age of contemporaries
Jacob 128 – Judah 40 – Joseph 37
Shelah 17

Judah Tricked by Tamar-[1707 B.C.?]

Gen.38:11-23 – [11] Then said Judah to Tamar his daughter in law, Remain a widow at thy father's house, till Shelah my son be grown: for he said, Lest peradventure he die also, as his brethren *did*. And Tamar went and dwelt in her father's house.

[12] And in process of time the daughter of Shuah Judah's wife died; and Judah was comforted, and went up unto his sheepshearers to Timnath, he and his friend Hirah the Adullamite. [13] And it was told Tamar, saying, Behold thy father in law goeth up to Timnath to shear his sheep. [14] And she put her widow's garments off from her, and covered her with a vail, and wrapped herself, and sat in an open place, which *is* by the way to Timnath; for she saw that Shelah was grown, and she was not given unto him to wife. [15] When Judah saw her, he thought her *to be* an harlot; because she had covered her face. [16] And he turned unto her by the way, and said, Go to, I pray thee, let me come in unto thee; (for he knew not that she *was* his daughter in law.) And she said, What wilt thou give me, that thou mayest come in unto me? [17] And he said, I will send *thee* a kid from the flock. And she said, Wilt thou give *me* a pledge, till thou send *it*? [18] And he said, What pledge shall I give thee? And she said, Thy signet, and thy bracelets, and thy staff that *is* in thine hand. And he gave *it* her, and came in unto her, and she conceived by him. [19] And she arose, and went away, and laid

by her vail from her, and put on the garments of her widowhood. ²⁰ And Judah sent the kid by the hand of his friend the Adullamite, to receive *his* pledge from the woman's hand: but he found her not. ²¹ Then he asked the men of that place, saying, Where *is* the harlot, that *was* openly by the way side? And they said, There was no harlot in this *place*. ²² And he returned to Judah, and said, I cannot find her; and also the men of the place said, *that* there was no harlot in this *place*. ²³ And Judah said, Let her take *it* to her, lest we be shamed: behold, I sent this kid, and thou hast not found her.

Probability Scenario

It is seems that Tamar may have reasoned that if Judah considered Onan to be old enough to "*… raise up seed*" (Gen.38:8 & see 1) for his brother at 18 years of age, then Shelah also should have been old enough at age 18 (see 2) in 1707 B.C.?.

Supporting Evidence
1. **Judah's Two Sons Die** – [p.163]
2. **Birth of Shelah** (son of Judah) [p.154]

Probable age of contemporaries
Jacob 129 – Judah 41 – Joseph 38 Shelah 18

Judah Returns to Jacob – in Hebron
[1707 B.C.?]

Gen.38:24-26 – ²⁴ And it came to pass about three months after, that it was told Judah, saying, Tamar thy daughter in law hath played the harlot; and also, behold, she *is* with child by whoredom. And Judah said, Bring her forth, and let her be burnt. ²⁵ When she *was* brought forth, she

Joseph's Brothers go to Egypt –
[1706 B.C.?]

Gen.42:1-5 – ¹ Now when Jacob saw that there was corn in Egypt, Jacob said unto his sons, Why do ye look one upon another? ² And he said, Behold, I have heard that there is corn in Egypt: get you down thither, and buy for us from thence; that we may live, and not die. ³ And Joseph's ten brethren went down to buy corn in Egypt. ⁴ But Benjamin, Joseph's brother, Jacob sent not with his brethren; for he said, Lest peradventure mischief befall him. ⁵ And the sons of Israel came to buy *corn* among those that came: for the famine was in the land of Canaan.

> **Probability Scenario**
> It is probable that all the events from the time Jacob sent his sons to Egypt for grain (v.2), until the time Jacob entered into Egypt at age 130 (see 1), took place during the second year of the famine (see 2 & Gen.45:6) in 1706 B.C.?.
> **Supporting Evidence**
> 1. **Jacob Meets Pharaoh** (at age 130) [p.176]
> 2. **Joseph Reveals His Identity –** [p.172]
> **Factors involved in calculating the year**
> x = 1836 B.C.# – Birth of Jacob
> y = 130 – years of age when Jacob meets Pharaoh (Gen.47:9)
> z = 1706 B.C.? – year of this event
> **Formula**
> (x) + (y) = z
> (1836 B.C.#) - (130) = 1706 B.C.?
> **Probable age of contemporaries**
> Jacob 130 –Joseph 39

sent to her father in law, saying, By the man, whose these *are, am* I with child: and she said, Discern, I pray thee, whose *are* these, the signet, and bracelets, and staff. ²⁶ And Judah acknowledged *them*, and said, She hath been more righteous than I; because that I gave her not to Shelah my son. And he knew her again no more.

> **Probability Scenario**
> It is probable that because "… *the dearth was in all lands*" (Gen.41:54 & see 1), Judah returned to his family in Hebron (see 2 & Gen.42:3) and took Tamar along with him (see 3 & Gen.46:8,12).
> **Supporting Evidence**
> 1. **Seven Years of Famine Begin –** [p.163]
> 2. **Joseph's Brothers go to Egypt –** [p.166]
> 3. **Joseph's Family Enters Egypt –** [p.174]
> **Probable age of contemporaries**
> Jacob 129 – Judah 41 – Joseph 38
> Shelah 18

Birth of Pharez & Zarah -[1706 B.C.?]
sons of Judah/Tamar

Gen.38:27-30 – ²⁷ And it came to pass in the time of her travail, that, behold, twins *were* in her womb. ²⁸ And it came to pass, when she travailed, that *the one* put out *his* hand: and the midwife took and bound upon his hand a scarlet thread, saying, This came out first. ²⁹ And it came to pass, as he drew back his hand, that, behold, his brother came out: and she said, How hast thou broken forth? *this* breach *be* upon thee: therefore his name was called

	Pharez. 30 And afterward came out his brother, that had the scarlet thread upon his hand: and his name was called Zarah. 1Chron.2:4 – 4 And Tamar his daughter in law bare him Pharez and Zerah. All the sons of Judah *were* five.
	Probability Scenario It is likely that Pharez and Zerah were born in Hebron several months before Jacob's family enters into Egypt (see 1 & Gen.46:8,12). **Supporting Evidence** 1. **Joseph's Family Enters Egypt** – [p.174] **Probable age of contemporaries** Jacob 130 – Judah 42 – Joseph 39 Shelah 19

* * * END PARALLEL ACCOUNTS OF JOSEPH AND JUDAH * * *

Joseph Speaks Harshly to His Brothers – accuses them of spying [1706 B.C.?]

Gen.42:6-17 – 6 And Joseph *was* the governor over the land, *and* he *it was* that sold to all the people of the land: and Joseph's brethren came, and bowed down themselves before him *with* their faces to the earth.

7 And Joseph saw his brethren, and he knew them, but made himself strange unto them, and spake roughly unto them; and he said unto them, Whence come ye? And they said, From the land of Canaan to buy food. 8 And Joseph knew his brethren, but they knew not him. 9 And Joseph remembered the dreams which he dreamed of them, and said unto them, Ye *are* spies; to see the nakedness of the land ye are come. 10 And they said unto him, Nay, my lord, but to buy food are thy servants come. 11 We *are* all one man's sons; we *are* true *men*, thy servants are no spies. 12 And he said unto them, Nay, but to see the nakedness of the land ye are come. 13 And they said, Thy servants *are* twelve brethren, the sons of one man in the land of Canaan; and, behold, the youngest *is* this day with our father, and one *is* not. 14 And Joseph said unto them, That *is it* that I spake unto you, saying, Ye *are* spies: 15 Hereby ye shall be proved: By the life of Pharaoh ye shall not go forth hence, except your youngest brother come hither. 16 Send one of you, and let him fetch your brother, and ye shall be kept in prison, that your words may be proved, whether *there be any* truth in you: or else by the

life of Pharaoh surely ye *are* spies. [17] And he put them all together into ward three days.

Probability Scenario

Jacob is destined to live in Egypt 17 years before his death in 1689 B.C.# (see 1 & Gne.47:28). This event likely occurred within several months of Jacob's entry into the land of Egypt, likely in 1706 B.C.? (see 2).

Supporting Evidence

1. **Death of Jacob** (at age 147) [p.181] also see "Genesis Genealogical Chart"
2. **Joseph's Family Enters Egypt** – [p.174]

Probable age of contemporaries

Jacob 130 – Judah 42 – Joseph 39
Shelah 19

Joseph Demands His Brothers Prove Their Integrity –   [1706 B.C.?]

Gen.42:18-23 – [18] And Joseph said unto them the third day, This do, and live; *for* I fear God: [19] If ye *be* true *men*, let one of your brethren be bound in the house of your prison: go ye, carry corn for the famine of your houses: [20] But bring your youngest brother unto me; so shall your words be verified, and ye shall not die. And they did so.

[21] And they said one to another, We *are* verily guilty concerning our brother, in that we saw the anguish of his soul, when he besought us, and we would not hear; therefore is this distress come upon us. [22] And Reuben answered them, saying, Spake I not unto you, saying, Do not sin against the child; and ye would not hear? therefore, behold, also his blood is required. [23] And they knew not that Joseph understood *them*; for he spake unto them by an interpreter.

Joseph Puts Simeon in Custody –   [1706 B.C.?]

Gen.42:24 – [24] And he turned himself about from them, and wept; and returned to them again, and communed with them, and took from them Simeon, and bound him before their eyes.

Joseph's Brothers Return to Jacob in Canaan –   [1706 B.C.?]

Gen.42:25-38 – [25] Then Joseph commanded to fill their sacks with corn, and to restore every man's money into his sack, and to give them provision for the way: and thus did he unto them. [26] And they laded their asses with the corn, and departed thence. [27] And as one of them opened his sack to give his ass provender in the inn, he espied his money; for, behold, it *was* in his sack's mouth. [28] And he said unto his brethren, My money is restored; and, lo, *it is* even in my sack: and their heart failed *them*, and they were afraid, saying one to another, What *is* this *that* God hath done unto us?

[29] And they came unto Jacob their father unto the land of Canaan, and told him all that befell unto them; saying, [30] The man, *who is* the lord of the

land, spake roughly to us, and took us for spies of the country. ³¹ And we said unto him, We *are* true *men*; we are no spies: ³² We *be* twelve brethren, sons of our father; one *is* not, and the youngest *is* this day with our father in the land of Canaan. ³³ And the man, the lord of the country, said unto us, Hereby shall I know that ye *are* true *men*; leave one of your brethren *here* with me, and take *food for* the famine of your households, and be gone: ³⁴ And bring your youngest brother unto me: then shall I know that ye *are* no spies, but *that* ye *are* true *men: so* will I deliver you your brother, and ye shall traffick in the land. ³⁵ And it came to pass as they emptied their sacks, that, behold, every man's bundle of money *was* in his sack: and when *both* they and their father saw the bundles of money, they were afraid. ³⁶ And Jacob their father said unto them, Me have ye bereaved *of my children*: Joseph *is* not, and Simeon *is* not, and ye will take Benjamin *away*: all these things are against me. ³⁷ And Reuben spake unto his father, saying, Slay my two sons, if I bring him not to thee: deliver him into my hand, and I will bring him to thee again. ³⁸ And he said, My son shall not go down with you; for his brother is dead, and he is left alone: if mischief befall him by the way in the which ye go, then shall ye bring down my gray hairs with sorrow to the grave.

Joseph's Brothers Return and Prove Their Integrity –   [1706 B.C.?]
    Gen.43:1-34 – ¹ And the famine *was* sore in the land. ² And it came to pass, when they had eaten up the corn which they had brought out of Egypt, their father said unto them, Go again, buy us a little food. ³ And Judah spake unto him, saying, The man did solemnly protest unto us, saying, Ye shall not see my face, except your brother *be* with you. ⁴ If thou wilt send our brother with us, we will go down and buy thee food: ⁵ But if thou wilt not send *him*, we will not go down: for the man said unto us, Ye shall not see my face, except your brother *be* with you. ⁶ And Israel said, Wherefore dealt ye *so* ill with me, *as* to tell the man whether ye had yet a brother? ⁷ And they said, The man asked us straitly of our state, and of our kindred, saying, *Is* your father yet alive? have ye *another* brother? and we told him according to the tenor of these words: could we certainly know that he would say, Bring your brother down? ⁸ And Judah said unto Israel his father, Send the lad with me, and we will arise and go; that we may live, and not die, both we, and thou, *and* also our little ones. ⁹ I will be surety for him; of my hand shalt thou require him: if I bring him not unto thee, and set him before thee, then let me bear the blame for ever: ¹⁰ For except we had lingered, surely now we had returned this second time.
    ¹¹ And their father Israel said unto them, If *it must be* so now, do this; take of the best fruits in the land in your vessels, and carry down the man a present, a little balm, and a little honey, spices, and myrrh, nuts, and

almonds: 12 And take double money in your hand; and the money that was brought again in the mouth of your sacks, carry *it* again in your hand; peradventure it *was* an oversight: 13 Take also your brother, and arise, go again unto the man: 14 And God Almighty give you mercy before the man, that he may send away your other brother, and Benjamin. If I be bereaved *of my children*, I am bereaved.

15 And the men took that present, and they took double money in their hand, and Benjamin; and rose up, and went down to Egypt, and stood before Joseph. 16 And when Joseph saw Benjamin with them, he said to the ruler of his house, Bring *these* men home, and slay, and make ready; for *these* men shall dine with me at noon. 17 And the man did as Joseph bade; and the man brought the men into Joseph's house. 18 And the men were afraid, because they were brought into Joseph's house; and they said, Because of the money that was returned in our sacks at the first time are we brought in; that he may seek occasion against us, and fall upon us, and take us for bondmen, and our asses. 19 And they came near to the steward of Joseph's house, and they communed with him at the door of the house, 20 And said, O sir, we came indeed down at the first time to buy food: 21 And it came to pass, when we came to the inn, that we opened our sacks, and, behold, *every* man's money *was* in the mouth of his sack, our money in full weight: and we have brought it again in our hand. 22 And other money have we brought down in our hands to buy food: we cannot tell who put our money in our sacks. 23 And he said, Peace *be* to you, fear not: your God, and the God of your father, hath given you treasure in your sacks: I had your money. And he brought Simeon out unto them. 24 And the man brought the men into Joseph's house, and gave *them* water, and they washed their feet; and he gave their asses provender. 25 And they made ready the present against Joseph came at noon: for they heard that they should eat bread there.

26 And when Joseph came home, they brought him the present which *was* in their hand into the house, and bowed themselves to him to the earth. 27 And he asked them of *their* welfare, and said, *Is* your father well, the old man of whom ye spake? *Is* he yet alive? 28 And they answered, Thy servant our father *is* in good health, he *is* yet alive. And they bowed down their heads, and made obeisance. 29 And he lifted up his eyes, and saw his brother Benjamin, his mother's son, and said, *Is* this your younger brother, of whom ye spake unto me? And he said, God be gracious unto thee, my son. 30 And Joseph made haste; for his bowels did yearn upon his brother: and he sought *where* to weep; and he entered into *his* chamber, and wept there. 31 And he washed his face, and went out, and refrained himself, and said, Set on bread. 32 And they set on for him by himself, and for them by themselves, and for the Egyptians, which did eat with him, by themselves:

because the Egyptians might not eat bread with the Hebrews; for that *is* an abomination unto the Egyptians. ³³ And they sat before him, the firstborn according to his birthright, and the youngest according to his youth: and the men marvelled one at another. ³⁴ And he took *and sent* messes unto them from before him: but Benjamin's mess was five times so much as any of theirs. And they drank, and were merry with him.

Joseph Tests His Brothers –   [1706 B.C.?]
    Gen.44:1-13 – ¹ And he commanded the steward of his house, saying, Fill the men's sacks *with* food, as much as they can carry, and put every man's money in his sack's mouth. ² And put my cup, the silver cup, in the sack's mouth of the youngest, and his corn money. And he did according to the word that Joseph had spoken. ³ As soon as the morning was light, the men were sent away, they and their asses. ⁴ *And* when they were gone out of the city, *and* not *yet* far off, Joseph said unto his steward, Up, follow after the men; and when thou dost overtake them, say unto them, Wherefore have ye rewarded evil for good? ⁵ *Is* not this *it* in which my lord drinketh, and whereby indeed he divineth? ye have done evil in so doing. ⁶ And he overtook them, and he spake unto them these same words. ⁷ And they said unto him, Wherefore saith my lord these words? God forbid that thy servants should do according to this thing: ⁸ Behold, the money, which we found in our sacks' mouths, we brought again unto thee out of the land of Canaan: how then should we steal out of thy lord's house silver or gold? ⁹ With whomsoever of thy servants it be found, both let him die, and we also will be my lord's bondmen. ¹⁰ And he said, Now also *let* it *be* according unto your words: he with whom it is found shall be my servant; and ye shall be blameless. ¹¹ Then they speedily took down every man his sack to the ground, and opened every man his sack. ¹² And he searched, *and* began at the eldest, and left at the youngest: and the cup was found in Benjamin's sack. ¹³ Then they rent their clothes, and laded every man his ass, and returned to the city.

Judah Volunteers to Protect Benjamin –   [1706 B.C.?]
    Gen.44:14-34 – ¹⁴ And Judah and his brethren came to Joseph's house; for he *was* yet there: and they fell before him on the ground. ¹⁵ And Joseph said unto them, What deed *is* this that ye have done? wot ye not that such a man as I can certainly divine? ¹⁶ And Judah said, What shall we say unto my lord? what shall we speak? or how shall we clear ourselves? God hath found out the iniquity of thy servants: behold, we *are* my lord's servants, both we, and *he* also with whom the cup is found. ¹⁷ And he said, God forbid that I should do so: *but* the man in whose hand the cup is found, he shall be my servant; and as for you, get you up in peace unto your father.

¹⁸ Then Judah came near unto him, and said, Oh my lord, let thy servant, I pray thee, speak a word in my lord's ears, and let not thine anger burn against thy servant: for thou *art* even as Pharaoh. ¹⁹ My lord asked his servants, saying, Have ye a father, or a brother? ²⁰ And we said unto my lord, We have a father, an old man, and a child of his old age, a little one; and his brother is dead, and he alone is left of his mother, and his father loveth him. ²¹ And thou saidst unto thy servants, Bring him down unto me, that I may set mine eyes upon him. ²² And we said unto my lord, The lad cannot leave his father: for *if* he should leave his father, *his father* would die. ²³ And thou saidst unto thy servants, Except your youngest brother come down with you, ye shall see my face no more. ²⁴ And it came to pass when we came up unto thy servant my father, we told him the words of my lord. ²⁵ And our father said, Go again, *and* buy us a little food. ²⁶ And we said, We cannot go down: if our youngest brother be with us, then will we go down: for we may not see the man's face, except our youngest brother *be* with us. ²⁷ And thy servant my father said unto us, Ye know that my wife bare me two *sons*: ²⁸ And the one went out from me, and I said, Surely he is torn in pieces; and I saw him not since: ²⁹ And if ye take this also from me, and mischief befall him, ye shall bring down my gray hairs with sorrow to the grave. ³⁰ Now therefore when I come to thy servant my father, and the lad *be* not with us; seeing that his life is bound up in the lad's life; ³¹ It shall come to pass, when he seeth that the lad *is* not *with us,* that he will die: and thy servants shall bring down the gray hairs of thy servant our father with sorrow to the grave. ³² For thy servant became surety for the lad unto my father, saying, If I bring him not unto thee, then I shall bear the blame to my father for ever. ³³ Now therefore, I pray thee, let thy servant abide instead of the lad a bondman to my lord; and let the lad go up with his brethren. ³⁴ For how shall I go up to my father, and the lad *be* not with me? lest peradventure I see the evil that shall come on my father.

Joseph Reveals His Identity –   [1706 B.C.?]

Gen.45:1-8 – ¹ Then Joseph could not refrain himself before all them that stood by him; and he cried, Cause every man to go out from me. And there stood no man with him, while Joseph made himself known unto his brethren. ² And he wept aloud: and the Egyptians and the house of Pharaoh heard. ³ And Joseph said unto his brethren, I *am* Joseph; doth my father yet live? And his brethren could not answer him; for they were troubled at his presence. ⁴ And Joseph said unto his brethren, Come near to me, I pray you. And they came near. And he said, I *am* Joseph your brother, whom ye sold into Egypt. ⁵ Now therefore be not grieved, nor angry with yourselves, that ye sold me hither: for God did send me before you to preserve life. ⁶ For these two years *hath* the famine *been* in the land: and yet *there are* five years, in the which *there shall* neither *be* earing nor harvest. 7 And God sent me before you to preserve you a posterity in the earth, and to save your lives by a great deliverance. 8 So now *it was* not you *that* sent me hither, but God: and he hath made me a father to Pharaoh, and lord of all his house, and a ruler throughout all the land of Egypt.

Joseph Sends for Jacob – [1706 B.C.?]

Gen.45:9-20 – 9 Haste ye, and go up to my father, and say unto him, Thus saith thy son Joseph, God hath made me lord of all Egypt: come down unto me, tarry not: 10 And thou shalt dwell in the land of Goshen, and thou shalt be near unto me, thou, and thy children, and thy children's children, and thy flocks, and thy herds, and all that thou hast: 11 And there will I nourish thee; for yet *there are* five years of famine; lest thou, and thy household, and all that thou hast, come to poverty. 12 And, behold, your eyes see, and the eyes of my brother Benjamin, that *it is* my mouth that speaketh unto you. 13 And ye shall tell my father of all my glory in Egypt, and of all that ye have seen; and ye shall haste and bring down my father hither. 14 And he fell upon his brother Benjamin's neck, and wept; and Benjamin wept upon his neck. 15 Moreover he kissed all his brethren, and wept upon them: and after that his brethren talked with him.

16 And the fame thereof was heard in Pharaoh's house, saying, Joseph's brethren are come: and it pleased Pharaoh well, and his servants. 17 And Pharaoh said unto Joseph, Say unto thy brethren, This do ye; lade your beasts, and go, get you unto the land of Canaan; 18 And take your father and your households, and come unto me: and I will give you the good of the land of Egypt, and ye shall eat the fat of the land. 19 Now thou art commanded, this do ye; take you wagons out of the land of Egypt for your little ones, and for your wives, and bring your father, and come. 20 Also regard not your stuff; for the good of all the land of Egypt *is* yours.

Probability Scenario
Jacob is destined to live in Egypt 17 years before his death in 1689 B.C.# (see 1 & Gen.47:28). This event likely occurred within weeks of Jacob's entry into the land of Egypt, likely in 1706 B.C.? (see 2).
Supporting Evidence
1. **Death of Jacob** (at age 147) [p.181] also see "Genesis Genealogical Chart"
2. **Joseph's Family Enters Egypt** – [p.174]
Probable age of contemporaries
Jacob 130 – Judah 42 – Joseph 39
Shelah 19

Joseph Provides for Jacob's Journey –   [1706 B.C.?]
      Gen.45:21-28 – ²¹ And the children of Israel did so: and Joseph gave
them wagons, according to the commandment of Pharaoh, and gave them
provision for the way. ²² To all of them he gave each man changes of
raiment; but to Benjamin he gave three hundred *pieces* of silver, and five
changes of raiment. ²³ And to his father he sent after this *manner*; ten asses
laden with the good things of Egypt, and ten she asses laden with corn and
bread and meat for his father by the way. ²⁴ So he sent his brethren away,
and they departed: and he said unto them, See that ye fall not out by the
way.
      ²⁵ And they went up out of Egypt, and came into the land of Canaan
unto Jacob their father, ²⁶ And told him, saying, Joseph *is* yet alive, and he
is governor over all the land of Egypt. And Jacob's heart fainted, for he
believed them not. ²⁷ And they told him all the words of Joseph, which he
had said unto them: and when he saw the wagons which Joseph had sent
to carry him, the spirit of Jacob their father revived: ²⁸ And Israel said, *It is*
enough; Joseph my son *is* yet alive: I will go and see him before I die.

Jacob Journeys to Beersheba
- see Map 6(10) p.216 -

Jacob Offers Sacrifices at Beersheba –   [1706 B.C.?]
      Gen.46:1-4 – ¹ And Israel took his journey with all that he had, and
came to Beersheba, and offered sacrifices unto the God of his father Isaac. ²
And God spake unto Israel in the visions of the night, and said, Jacob,
Jacob. And he said, Here *am* I. ³ And he said, I *am* God, the God of thy
father: fear not to go down into Egypt; for I will there make of thee a great
nation: ⁴ I will go down with thee into Egypt; and I will also surely bring
thee up *again*: and Joseph shall put his hand upon thine eyes.

Jacob Journeys to Egypt
- see Map 6(11) p.216 -

Joseph's Family Enters Egypt –   [1706 B.C.?]
      Gen.46:5-28 – ⁵ And Jacob rose up from Beersheba: and the sons of Israel
carried Jacob their father, and their little ones, and their wives, in the
wagons which Pharaoh had sent to carry him. ⁶ And they took their cattle,
and their goods, which they had gotten in the land of Canaan, and came
into Egypt, Jacob, and all his seed with him: ⁷ His sons, and his sons' sons
with him, his daughters, and his sons' daughters, and all his seed brought

he with him into Egypt. 8 And these *are* the names of the children of Israel, which came into Egypt, Jacob and his sons: Reuben, Jacob's firstborn. 9 And the sons of Reuben; Hanoch, and Phallu, and Hezron, and Carmi. 10 And the sons of Simeon; Jemuel, and Jamin, and Ohad, and Jachin, and Zohar, and Shaul the son of a Canaanitish woman. 11 And the sons of Levi; Gershon, Kohath, and Merari. 12 And the sons of Judah; Er, and Onan, and Shelah, and Pharez, and Zerah: but Er and Onan died in the land of Canaan. And the sons of Pharez were Hezron and Hamul. 13 And the sons of Issachar; Tola, and Phuvah, and Job, and Shimron. 14 And the sons of Zebulun; Sered, and Elon, and Jahleel. 15 These *be* the sons of Leah, which she bare unto Jacob in Padanaram, with his daughter Dinah: all the souls of his sons and his daughters *were* thirty and three. 16 And the sons of Gad; Ziphion, and Haggi, Shuni, and Ezbon, Eri, and Arodi, and Areli. 17 And the sons of Asher; Jimnah, and Ishuah, and Isui, and Beriah, and Serah their sister: and the sons of Beriah; Heber, and Malchiel. 18 These *are* the sons of Zilpah, whom Laban gave to Leah his daughter, and these she bare unto Jacob, *even* sixteen souls. 19 The sons of Rachel Jacob's wife; Joseph, and Benjamin. 20 And unto Joseph in the land of Egypt were born Manasseh and Ephraim, which Asenath the daughter of Potipherah priest of On bare unto him. 21 And the sons of Benjamin *were* Belah, and Becher, and Ashbel, Gera, and Naaman, Ehi, and Rosh, Muppim, and Huppim, and Ard. 22 These *are* the sons of Rachel, which were born to Jacob: all the souls *were* fourteen. 23 And the sons of Dan; Hushim. 24 And the sons of Naphtali; Jahzeel, and Guni, and Jezer, and Shillem. 25 These *are* the sons of Bilhah, which Laban gave unto Rachel his daughter, and she bare these unto Jacob: all the souls *were* seven. 26 All the souls that came with Jacob into Egypt, which came out of his loins, besides Jacob's sons' wives, all the souls *were* threescore and six; 27 And the sons of Joseph, which were born him in Egypt, *were* two souls: all the souls of the house of Jacob, which came into Egypt, *were* threescore and ten.

28 And he sent Judah before him unto Joseph, to direct his face unto Goshen; and they came into the land of Goshen.

Probability Scenario

Jacob is destined to live in Egypt 17 years before his death in 1689 B.C.# (see 1 & Gen.47:28). This journey likely occurred within weeks of Jacob being reunited with Joseph in Egypt, likely in 1706 B.C.? (see 2).

Supporting Evidence

1. **Death of Jacob** (at age 147) [p.181] also see "Genesis Genealogical Chart"
2. **Jacob Reunited with Joseph** – [p.176]

Note

It would seem that Pharez could only be a few months old at this point in time. In this case, the son's of Pharez, Hezron and Hamul (v.12), likely are

---

> counted as entering Egypt while still in the loins of Pharez (see Heb.7:9-10).
> **Probable age of contemporaries**
> Jacob 130 – Leah 113 – Zilpah 80 – Bilhah 70 – Ruben 45 – Simeon 44 – Levi 43
> Dan 43 – Judah 42 Naphtali 42 – Gad 41 – Issachar 41 – Asher 40 – Zebulun 40
> Joseph 39 – Dinah 39 – Benjamin 23
> Shelah 19 – Pharez (months)

Jacob Reunited with Joseph – [1706 B.C.?]

Gen.46:29-34 – 29 And Joseph made ready his chariot, and went up to meet Israel his father, to Goshen, and presented himself unto him; and he fell on his neck, and wept on his neck a good while. 30 And Israel said unto the men *are* shepherds, for their trade hath been to feed cattle; and they have brought their flocks, and their herds, and all that they have. 33 And it shall come to pass, when Pharaoh shall call you, and shall say, What *is* your occupation? 34 That ye shall say, Thy servants' trade hath been about cattle from our youth even until now, both we, *and* also our fathers: that ye may dwell in the land of Goshen; for every shepherd *is* an abomination unto the Egyptians.

Jacob Meets Pharaoh (at age 130) [1706 B.C.#]

Gen.47:1-10 – 1 Then Joseph came and told Pharaoh, and said, My father and my brethren, and their flocks, and their herds, and all that they have, are come out of the land of Canaan; and, behold, they *are* in the land of Goshen. 2 And he took some of his brethren, *even* five men, and presented them unto Pharaoh. 3 And Pharaoh said unto his brethren, What *is* your occupation? And they said unto Pharaoh, Thy servants *are* shepherds, both we, *and* also our fathers. 4 They said moreover unto Pharaoh, For to sojourn in the land are we come; for thy servants have no pasture for their flocks; for the famine *is* sore in the land of Canaan: now therefore, we pray thee, let thy servants dwell in the land of Goshen. 5 And Pharaoh spake unto Joseph, saying, Thy father and thy brethren are come unto thee: 6 The land of Egypt *is* before thee; in the best of the land make thy father and brethren to dwell; in the land of Goshen let them dwell: and if thou knowest *any* men of activity among them, then make them rulers over my cattle. 7 And Joseph brought in Jacob his father, and set him before Pharaoh: and Jacob blessed Pharaoh. 8 And Pharaoh said unto Jacob, How old *art* thou? 9 And Jacob said unto Pharaoh, The days of the years of my pilgrimage *are* an hundred and thirty years: few and evil have the days of the years of my life been, and have not attained unto the days of the years of the life of my fathers in the days of their pilgrimage. 10 And Jacob blessed Pharaoh, and went out from before Pharaoh.

Joseph Provides for Jacob and His Brothers –   [1706 B.C.?]
    Gen.47:11-12 – ¹¹ And Joseph placed his father and his brethren, and gave them a possession in the land of Egypt, in the best of the land, in the land of Rameses, as Pharaoh had commanded. ¹² And Joseph nourished his father, and his brethren, and all his father's household, with bread, according to *their* families.

Joseph Returns to Governing Over Egypt –   [1706 B.C.?]
    Gen.47:13-27 – ¹³ And *there was* no bread in all the land; for the famine *was* very sore, so that the land of Egypt and *all* the land of Canaan fainted by reason of the famine. ¹⁴ And Joseph gathered up all the money that was found in the land of Egypt, and in the land of Canaan, for the corn which they bought: and Joseph brought the money into Pharaoh's house. ¹⁵ And when money failed in the land of Egypt, and in the land of Canaan, all the Egyptians came unto Joseph, and said, Give us bread: for why should we die in thy presence? for the money faileth. ¹⁶ And Joseph said, Give your cattle; and I will give you for your cattle, if money fail. ¹⁷ And they brought their cattle unto Joseph: and Joseph gave them bread *in exchange* for horses, and for the flocks, and for the cattle of the herds, and for the asses: and he fed them with bread for all their cattle for that year. ¹⁸ When that year was ended, they came unto him the second year, and said unto him, We will not hide *it* from my lord, how that our money is spent; my lord also hath our herds of cattle; there is not ought left in the sight of my lord, but our bodies, and our lands: ¹⁹ Wherefore shall we die before thine eyes, both we and our land? buy us and our land for bread, and we and our land will be servants unto Pharaoh: and give *us* seed, that we may live, and not die, that the land be not desolate. ²⁰ And Joseph bought all the land of Egypt for Pharaoh; for the Egyptians sold every man his field, because the famine prevailed over them: so the land became Pharaoh's. ²¹ And as for the people, he removed them to cities from *one* end of the borders of Egypt even to the *other* end thereof. ²² Only the land of the priests bought he not; for the priests had a portion *assigned them* of Pharaoh, and did eat their portion which Pharaoh gave them: wherefore they sold not their lands. ²³ Then Joseph said unto the people, Behold, I have bought you this day and your land for Pharaoh: lo, *here is* seed for you, and ye shall sow the land. ²⁴ And it shall come to pass in the increase, that ye shall give the fifth *part* unto Pharaoh, and four parts shall be your own, for seed of the field, and for your food, and for them of your households, and for food for your little ones. ²⁵ And they said, Thou hast saved our lives: let us find grace in the sight of my lord, and we will be Pharaoh's servants. ²⁶ And Joseph made it a law over the land of Egypt unto this day, *that* Pharaoh should have the fifth *part*; except the land of the priests only, *which* became not Pharaoh's.

27 And Israel dwelt in the land of Egypt, in the country of Goshen; and they had possessions therein, and grew, and multiplied exceedingly.

Joseph Vows to Bury Jacob in Canaan –   [1689 B.C.?]
    Gen.47:29-31 – 29 And the time drew nigh that Israel must die: and he called his son Joseph, and said unto him, If now I have found grace in thy sight, put, I pray thee, thy hand under my thigh, and deal kindly and truly with me; bury me not, I pray thee, in Egypt: 30 But I will lie with my fathers, and thou shalt carry me out of Egypt, and bury me in their buryingplace. And he said, I will do as thou hast said. 31 And he said, Swear unto me. And he sware unto him. And Israel bowed himself upon the bed's head.

Probability Scenario
It is probable that this event occurred within a few weeks, or possibly days, of Jacob's death in 1689 B.C.? (see 1).
Supporting Evidence
1. **Death of Jacob** (at age 147) [p.181] also see "Genesis Genealogical Chart"
Probable age of contemporaries
Jacob 147 – Zilpah 97 – Bilhah 87 – Ruben 62 – Simeon 61 – Levi 60 – Dan 60
Judah 59 – Naphtali 59 – Gad 58 – Issachar 58 – Asher 57 – Zebulun 57
Joseph 56 – Dinah 56 – Benjamin 40
Shelah 36 – Pharez 17

Joseph is Told His Father is Sick –   [1689 B.C.?]
    Gen.48:1-7 – 1 And it came to pass after these things, that *one* told Joseph, Behold, thy father *is* sick: and he took with him his two sons, Manasseh and Ephraim. 2 And *one* told Jacob, and said, Behold, thy son Joseph cometh unto thee: and Israel strengthened himself, and sat upon the bed. 3 And Jacob said unto Joseph, God Almighty appeared unto me at Luz in the land of Canaan, and blessed me, 4 And said unto me, Behold, I will make thee fruitful, and multiply thee, and I will make of thee a multitude of people; and will give this land to thy seed after thee *for* an everlasting possession. 5 And now thy two sons, Ephraim and Manasseh, which were born unto thee in the land of Egypt before I came unto thee into Egypt, *are* mine; as Reuben and Simeon, they shall be mine. 6 And thy issue, which thou begettest after them, shall be thine, *and* shall be called after the name of their brethren in their inheritance. 7 And as for me, when I came from Padan, Rachel died by me in the land of Canaan in the way, when yet *there was* but a little way to come unto Ephrath: and I buried her there in the way of Ephrath; the same *is* Bethlehem.

Jacob Blesses Joseph's Sons –   [1689 B.C.?]

Gen.48:8-22 – ⁸ And Israel beheld Joseph's sons, and said, Who *are* these? ⁹ And Joseph said unto his father, They *are* my sons, whom God hath given me in this *place*. And he said, Bring them, I pray thee, unto me, and I will bless them. ¹⁰ Now the eyes of Israel were dim for age, *so that* he could not see. And he brought them near unto him; and he kissed them, and embraced them. ¹¹ And Israel said unto Joseph, I had not thought to see thy face: and, lo, God hath shewed me also thy seed. ¹² And Joseph brought them out from between his knees, and he bowed himself with his face to the earth. ¹³ And Joseph took them both, Ephraim in his right hand toward Israel's left hand, and Manasseh in his left hand toward Israel's right hand, and brought *them* near unto him. ¹⁴ And Israel stretched out his right hand, and laid *it* upon Ephraim's head, who *was* the younger, and his left hand upon Manasseh's head, guiding his hands wittingly; for Manasseh *was* the firstborn. ¹⁵ And he blessed Joseph, and said, God, before whom my fathers Abraham and Isaac did walk, the God which fed me all my life long unto this day, ¹⁶ The Angel which redeemed me from all evil, bless the lads; and let my name be named on them, and the name of my fathers Abraham and Isaac; and let them grow into a multitude in the midst of the earth. ¹⁷ And when Joseph saw that his father laid his right hand upon the head of Ephraim, it displeased him: and he held up his father's hand, to remove it from Ephraim's head unto Manasseh's head. ¹⁸ And Joseph said unto his father, Not so, my father: for this *is* the firstborn; put thy right hand upon his head. ¹⁹ And his father refused, and said, I know *it*, my son, I know *it*: he also shall become a people, and he also shall be great: but truly his younger brother shall be greater than he, and his seed shall become a multitude of nations. ²⁰ And he blessed them that day, saying, In thee shall Israel bless, saying, God make thee as Ephraim and as Manasseh: and he set Ephraim before Manasseh. ²¹ And Israel said unto Joseph, Behold, I die: but God shall be with you, and bring you again unto the land of your fathers. ²² Moreover I have given to thee one portion above thy brethren, which I took out of the hand of the Amorite with my sword and with my bow.

Jacob Blesses His Sons and Declares Their Future –   [1689 B.C.?]

Gen.49:1-32 – ¹ And Jacob called unto his sons, and said, Gather yourselves together, that I may tell you *that* which shall befall you in the last days. ² Gather yourselves together, and hear, ye sons of Jacob; and hearken unto Israel your father. ³ Reuben, thou *art* my firstborn, my might, and the beginning of my strength, the excellency of dignity, and the excellency of power: ⁴ Unstable as water, thou shalt not excel; because thou wentest up to thy father's bed; then defiledst thou *it*: he went up to my couch.

5 Simeon and Levi *are* brethren; instruments of cruelty *are in* their habitations. 6 O my soul, come not thou into their secret; unto their assembly, mine honour, be not thou united: for in their anger they slew a man, and in their selfwill they digged down a wall. 7 Cursed *be* their anger, for *it was* fierce; and their wrath, for it was cruel: I will divide them in Jacob, and scatter them in Israel.

8 Judah, thou *art he* whom thy brethren shall praise: thy hand *shall be* in the neck of thine enemies; thy father's children shall bow down before thee. 9 Judah *is* a lion's whelp: from the prey, my son, thou art gone up: he stooped down, he couched as a lion, and as an old lion; who shall rouse him up? 10 The sceptre shall not depart from Judah, nor a lawgiver from between his feet, until Shiloh come; and unto him *shall* the gathering of the people *be*. 11 Binding his foal unto the vine, and his ass's colt unto the choice vine; he washed his garments in wine, and his clothes in the blood of grapes: 12 His eyes *shall be* red with wine, and his teeth white with milk.

13 Zebulun shall dwell at the haven of the sea; and he *shall be* for an haven of ships; and his border *shall be* unto Zidon. 14 Issachar *is* a strong ass couching down between two burdens: 15 And he saw that rest *was* good, and the land that *it was* pleasant; and bowed his shoulder to bear, and became a servant unto tribute. 16 Dan shall judge his people, as one of the tribes of Israel. 17 Dan shall be a serpent by the way, an adder in the path, that biteth the horse heels, so that his rider shall fall backward. 18 I have waited for thy salvation, O LORD. 19 Gad, a troop shall overcome him: but he shall overcome at the last. 20 Out of Asher his bread *shall be* fat, and he shall yield royal dainties. 21 Naphtali *is* a hind let loose: he giveth goodly words.

22 Joseph *is* a fruitful bough, *even* a fruitful bough by a well; *whose* branches run over the wall: 23 The archers have sorely grieved him, and shot *at him*, and hated him: 24 But his bow abode in strength, and the arms of his hands were made strong by the hands of the mighty *God* of Jacob; (from thence *is* the shepherd, the stone of Israel:) 25 *Even* by the God of thy father, who shall help thee; and by the Almighty, who shall bless thee with blessings of heaven above, blessings of the deep that lieth under, blessings of the breasts, and of the womb: 26 The blessings of thy father have prevailed above the blessings of my progenitors unto the utmost bound of the everlasting hills: they shall be on the head of Joseph, and on the crown of the head of him that was separate from his brethren. 27 Benjamin shall ravin *as* a wolf: in the morning he shall devour the prey, and at night he shall divide the spoil.

28 All these *are* the twelve tribes of Israel: and this *is it* that their father spake unto them, and blessed them; every one according to his blessing he

blessed them. ²⁹ And he charged them, and said unto them, I am to be gathered unto my people: bury me with my fathers in the cave that *is* in the field of Ephron the Hittite, ³⁰ In the cave that *is* in the field of Machpelah, which *is* before Mamre, in the land of Canaan, which Abraham bought with the field of Ephron the Hittite for a possession of a buryingplace. ³¹ There they buried Abraham and Sarah his wife; there they buried Isaac and Rebekah his wife; and there I buried Leah. ³² The purchase of the field and of the cave that *is* therein *was* from the children of Heth.

Death of Jacob (at age 147)   [1689 B.C.#]

Gen.49:33 – ³³ And when Jacob had made an end of commanding his sons, he gathered up his feet into the bed, and yielded up the ghost, and was gathered unto his people.

Gen.47:28 – ²⁸ And Jacob lived in the land of Egypt seventeen years: so the whole age of Jacob was an hundred forty and seven years.

Years are Calculated from Scripture References
see "Genesis Genealogical Chart"
Probable age of contemporaries
Zilpah 97 – Bilhah 87 – Ruben 62 – Simeon 61 – Levi 60 – Dan 60 – Judah 59
Naphtali 59 – Gad 58 – Issachar 58 – Asher 57 – Zebulun 57 – Joseph 56
Dinah 56 – Benjamin 40 – Shelah 36 – Pharez 17

Jacob's Burial –   [1689 B.C.?]

Gen.50:1-13 – ¹ And Joseph fell upon his father's face, and wept upon him, and kissed him. ² And Joseph commanded his servants the physicians to embalm his father: and the physicians embalmed Israel. ³ And forty days were fulfilled for him; for so are fulfilled the days of those which are embalmed: and the Egyptians mourned for him threescore and ten days. ⁴ And when the days of his mourning were past, Joseph spake unto the house of Pharaoh, saying, If now I have found grace in your eyes, speak, I pray you, in the ears of Pharaoh, saying, ⁵ My father made me swear, saying, Lo, I die: in my grave which I have digged for me in the land of Canaan, there shalt thou bury me. Now therefore let me go up, I pray thee, and bury my father, and I will come again. ⁶ And Pharaoh said, Go up, and bury thy father, according as he made thee swear.

⁷ And Joseph went up to bury his father: and with him went up all the servants of Pharaoh, the elders of his house, and all the elders of the land of Egypt, ⁸ And all the house of Joseph, and his brethren, and his father's house: only their little ones, and their flocks, and their herds, they left in the land of Goshen. ⁹ And there went up with him both chariots and horsemen: and it was a very great company. ¹⁰ And they came to the

threshingfloor of Atad, which *is* beyond Jordan, and there they mourned with a great and very sore lamentation: and he made a mourning for his father seven days. ¹¹ And when the inhabitants of the land, the Canaanites, saw the mourning in the floor of Atad, they said, This *is* a grievous mourning to the Egyptians: wherefore the name of it was called Abelmizraim, which *is* beyond Jordan. ¹² And his sons did unto him according as he commanded them: ¹³ For his sons carried him into the land of Canaan, and buried him in the cave of the field of Machpelah, which Abraham bought with the field for a possession of a buryingplace of Ephron the Hittite, before Mamre.

Joseph's Brothers Fearful – reassured by Joseph   [1689 B.C.?]
        Gen.50:14-22 – ¹⁴ And Joseph returned into Egypt, he, and his brethren, and all that went up with him to bury his father, after he had buried his father.

        ¹⁵ And when Joseph's brethren saw that their father was dead, they said, Joseph will peradventure hate us, and will certainly requite us all the evil which we did unto him. ¹⁶ And they sent a messenger unto Joseph, saying, Thy father did command before he died, saying, ¹⁷ So shall ye say unto Joseph, Forgive, I pray thee now, the trespass of thy brethren, and their sin; for they did unto thee evil: and now, we pray thee, forgive the trespass of the servants of the God of thy father. And Joseph wept when they spake unto him. ¹⁸ And his brethren also went and fell down before his face; and they said, Behold, we *be* thy servants. ¹⁹ And Joseph said unto them, Fear not: for *am* I in the place of God? ²⁰ But as for you, ye thought evil against me; *but* God meant it unto good, to bring to pass, as *it is* this day, to save much people alive. ²¹ Now therefore fear ye not: I will nourish you, and your little ones. And he comforted them, and spake kindly unto them.

        ²² And Joseph dwelt in Egypt, he, and his father's house: …

Death of Joseph (at age 110)   [1635 B.C.#]
        Gen.50:22-26 – ²² … and Joseph lived an hundred and ten years. ²³ And Joseph saw Ephraim's children of the third *generation*: the children also of Machir the son of Manasseh were brought up upon Joseph's knees. ²⁴ And Joseph said unto his brethren, I die: and God will surely visit you, and bring you out of this land unto the land which he sware to Abraham, to Isaac, and to Jacob. ²⁵ And Joseph took an oath of the children of Israel, saying, God will surely visit you, and ye shall carry up my bones from hence. ²⁶ So Joseph died, *being* an hundred and ten years old: and they embalmed him, and he was put in a coffin in Egypt.

Years are Calculated from Scripture References
see "Genesis Genealogical Chart"

Death of Levi (at age 137)   [1612 B.C.#]

Ex.6:16 – [16] And these *are* the names of the sons of Levi according to their generations; Gershon, and Kohath, and Merari: and the years of the life of Levi *were* an hundred thirty and seven years.

Ex.1:6 – [6] And Joseph died, and all his brethren, and all that generation.

Death of Job (at age 210)   [1585 B.C.?]
Job 42:16-17

Probability Scenario
It seems that Job may have lived approximately 70 years before satan challenged his loyalty to God (see 1). After Job's encounter with satan, "... *Job lived an hundred and forty years, and saw his sons, and his sons' sons, even four generations*" (Job 42:16).
Supporting Evidence
1. **Job's Loyalty to God Disputed by satan** [p.154]
Factors involved in calculating the year
x = 1795 B.C.? – Birth of Job
y1 =   70 ? – age of Job when loyalty to God challenged by satan
y2 =   140 ? – years Job lived after being challenged by satan
z = 1585 B.C.? – year of Job's death
Formula
$(x) + (y1 + y2) = z$
(1795 B.C.?) - (70 + 140) = 1585 B.C.?
(1795 B.C.?) - (210) = 1585 B.C.?

Chapter 1

Eternity Past

Chapter 2

Creation

Chapter 3

Fall of Man

Page #	Event	Date B.C.
11	Deception of Humankind -	4004
12	Fall of Humankind -	"
"	Consequence - (guilty conscience)	"
13	Confession - (Adam & Eve pass the blame)	"
"	Judgment & Curse - (serpent/Eve/ground)	"
14	Adam Names His Wife Eve - ("... mother of all living")	"
"	God Bestows Mercy - (atonement/animal sacrificed)	"
15	Expulsion from Eden -	"
"	God Bestows Grace - (prevents eternal suffering)	"

Chapter 4

The First Society

Pg. #	Event	Date B.C.
17	The Generations of Adam -	-
"	**Cain and Able**	-
"	Birth of Cain - son of Adam	4003
18	Birth of Abel - son of Adam	4002
"	Offerings to the LORD - (Abel's accepted/Cain's rejected)	3875
19	God Offers Grace - (Cain offered repentance/warning)	"
"	**Cain murders Abel**	-
"	Cain's Anger Escalates -	3875
"	Cain Judged and Cursed -	"
20	Cain Appeals to God -	"
"	God Bestows Grace - (Cain is marked/sign of God's protection)	"

Chapter 4

The First Society
(Continued)

* * * * * * * * * * * * * * BEGIN PARALLEL NATIONS * * * * * * * * * * * * * *

Page #	Event	Date B.C.	Event	Date B.C.
21	**GODLY LINE OF SETH**	-	**UNGODLY LINE OF CAIN**	-
"	Birth of Seth – son of Adam	3874	Birth of Enoch – son of Cain	3874
"			Birth of Irad – son of Enoch	?
"	Birth of Enos – son of Seth	3769	Birth of Mehujael – son of Irad	?
"			Birth of Methusael – son of Mehujael	?
22	Birth of Cainan - son of Enos	3679	Birth of Lamech – son of Methusael	?
"			Birth of Jabal and Jubal – sons of Lamech and Adah	?
"	Birth of Mahalaleel – son of Cainan	3609	Birth of Tubalcain, Naamah - children of Lamech and Zillah	?
"			Lamech Acts in Self Defense -	?
"	Birth of Jared – son of Mahalaleel	3544		
"	Birth of Enoch - son of Jared	3382		
23	Birth of Methuselah – son of Enoch	3317		
"	Enoch Walks with God -	"		
24	Birth of Lamech – son of Methuselah	3130		
"	Death of Adam - (at age 930)	3074		
"	Enoch Taken by God - (at age 365)	3017		
25	Death of Seth - (at age 912)	2962		
"	Birth of Noah - son of Lamech	2948		
26	Death of Enos - (at age 905)	2864		
"	Death of Cainan - (at age 910)	2769		
"	Death of Mahalaleel - (at age 895)	2714		
27	Death of Jared - (at age 962)	2582		

* * * * * * * * * * * * * PAUSE PARALLEL NATIONS * * * * * * * * * * * * *

Chapter 4

The First Society
(Continued)

Chapter 5

Flood to Patriarchs

Chapter 5

Flood to Patriarchs
(Continued)

Page #	Event	Date B.C.
47	**Tower of Babel**	–
"	Man Seeks to Enthrone Self and Dethrone God–	–
"	God Observes Man's Disobedience -	2165
48	God Passes Judgment and Administers Justice -	"

* * * * * * * * * * BEGINNING OF NATIONS * * * * * * * * * *

Page #	Event	Date B.C.
48	**Godly Line of Seth**	
	(continued through Nahor I)	–
"	Birth of Nahor I - son of Serug	2155
49	Birth of Terah - son of Nahor I	2126
"	**Formation of the Patriarchal Period** – Map 1(1)	–
"	Terah Began Having Children – (in Ur of the Chaldees)	2056
"	Birth of Haran - son of Terah	"
50	Death of Nimrod - (at age 274 ?)	2021
"	Death of Peleg - (at age 239)	2008
"	Death of Nahor I - (at age 148)	2007
51	Birth of Nahor II - son of Terah	2005
"	Birth of Lot - son of Haran & nephew of Abram	"
52	Birth of Milcah - daughter of Haran (Abram's brother)	2002
"	Birth of Iscah - daughter of Haran (Abram's brother)	1999
53	Death of Noah - (at age 950)	1998
"	**Godly Line of Seth**	
	(continued through Abram)	–
"	Birth of Abram / Abraham – son of Terah	1996

Chapter 6

Abraham to Isaac

Chapter 6

Abraham to Isaac
(Continued)

Chapter 6

Abraham to Isaac
(Continued)

Chapter 6

Abraham to Isaac
(Continued)

Chapter 7

Isaac to Jacob

Chapter 7

Isaac to Jacob
(Continued)

Chapter 8

Jacob to Joseph

Page #	Event	Date B.C.
105	Isaac Becomes Abraham's Heir -	1826
"	Abraham Sends Keturah's Children Away -	"
106	Death of Abraham (at age 175)	1821
"	Abraham's Sons Bury Him (Isaac and Ishmael)	"
"	God Blesses Isaac -	"
"	Birth of Leah - daughter of Laban/Abraham's kinsman	1819
107	Death of Eber (at age 464)	1817
"	**Jacob Acquires Esau's Birthright**	-
"	Esau Becomes an Outdoors Man & Jacob a Homebody -	1811
108	Isaac Loved Esau & Rebekah Loved Jacob -	"
"	Birth of Rachel - daughter of Laban/Abraham's kinsman	1799
"	Esau Sells His Birthright -	1796
109	Esau Marries Foreign Wives - Isaac and Rebekah grieved	"

* * * * * * BEGIN PARALLEL ACCOUNTS OF ELIPHAZ AND JOB * * * * * *

Page #	Event	Date B.C.	Event	Date B.C.
110	EVENTS ASSOCIATED WITH ELIPHAZ (son of Esau)	-	EVENTS ASSOCIATED WITH JOB (friend of Eliphaz)	-
"	Birth of Eliphaz (the Teamanite?)	1795	Birth of Job -	1795
"			Job's Early Adult/Married Life- (reference only)	1765 to 1745
111	Birth of Teman – son of Eliphaz	1764		
"			Job's Loyalty to God Disputed - (reference only)	1725
"			God Confronts Job & Friends - (reference only)	"
"			Job Blessed by God – (reference only)	"
"			Death of Job – (a future event)	1585

* * * * * * END PARALLEL ACCOUNTS OF ELIPHAZ AND JOB * * * * * *

Chapter 8

Jacob to Joseph
(continued)

Chapter 8

Jacob to Joseph
(continued)

* * * * * BEGIN PARALLEL ACCOUNTS OF LEAH AND RACHEL * * * * *

* * * * * PAUSE PARALLEL ACCOUNTS OF LEAH AND RACHEL * * * * *

Chapter 8

Jacob to Joseph
(continued)

Page #	Event	Date B.C.
129	Leah and Rachel Barter Over Mandrakes –	Jul. 1748

* * * * RESUME PARALLEL ACCOUNTS OF LEAH AND RACHEL * * * *

Page #	Event	Date B.C.	Event	Date B.C.
129	**Children of Jacob and Leah** (and Leah's handmaid – Zilpah)	-	**Children of Jacob and Rachel** (and Rachel's handmaid – Bilhah)	-
"	Birth of Gad – son of Jacob/Zilpah	Apr. 1747		
130	Birth of Issachar – son of Jacob/Leah	May 1747		
"	Birth of Asher – son of Jacob/Zilpah	Mar. 1746		
131	Birth of Zebulun – son of Jacob/Leah	May 1746		
"	Birth of Dinah – daughter of Jacob/Leah	Apr. 1745		
"			Birth of Joseph – son of Jacob/Rachel	May 1745

* * * * * END PARALLEL ACCOUNTS OF LEAH AND RACHEL * * * * *

Chapter 9

Joseph

Chapter 9

Joseph
(continued)

Chapter 9

Joseph
(continued)

Page #	Event	Date B.C.	Event	Date B.C.
155	**Events Associated with Joseph** (continued)	-	**Events Associated with Judah / Job** (continued)	-
"			Job's Loyalty to God Disputed - by his friends	1725
"			Job Confronted - by God	"
"			Job's Friends Confronted – by God	"
"			Job Blessed - by God	"

* * * PAUSE PARALLEL ACCOUNTS OF JOSEPH AND JUDAH / JOB * * *

Page #	Event	Date B.C.
155	**God Prepares Joseph to Save Israel**	-
"	Joseph Accused of Improper Conduct -	1719
156	Joseph Thrown in Prison - the LORD continues to bless	"
157	Joseph Interprets Dreams of Pharaoh's Servants -	1717
158	Death of Isaac (at age 180)	1716
"	Joseph Interprets Dreams of Pharaoh -	1715
160	Joseph Elevated to Governor in Egypt (at age30)	"
161	Joseph Fulfills Asenath's Week -	"
"	Bountiful Harvests Begin -	"
"	Birth of Manasseh (son of Joseph)	1714
162	Birth of Ephraim (son of Joseph)	1712

Chronological Index

Chapter 9

Joseph
(continued)

* * * * RESUME PARALLEL ACCOUNTS OF JOSEPH AND JUDAH * * * *

Page #	Event	Date B.C.	Event	Date B.C.
162	**Events Associated with Joseph** (continued)	-	**Events Associated with Judah** (continued)	-
"	Bountiful Harvests End -	1708	Judah's Eldest Marries Tamar-	1708
163	Seven Years of Famine Begin -	"	Judah's Two Sons Die -	"
164			Judah Tricked by Tamar –	1707
165			Judah Returns to Jacob – in Hebron	"
166	Joseph's Brothers go to Egypt-	1706	Birth of Pharez & Zarah – sons of Judah/Tamar	1706

* * * * * * END PARALLEL ACCOUNTS OF JOSEPH AND JUDAH * * * * * *

Page #	Event	Date B.C.
167	Joseph Speaks Harshly to His Brothers - accuses them of spying	1706
168	Joseph Demands His Brothers Prove Their Integrity -	"
"	Joseph Puts Simeon in Custody -	"
"	Joseph's Brothers Return to Jacob in Canaan -	"
169	Joseph's Brothers Return and Prove Their Integrity -	"
171	Joseph Tests His Brothers -	"
"	Judah Volunteers to Protect Benjamin -	"
172	Joseph Reveals His Identity -	"
173	Joseph Sends for Jacob -	"
174	Joseph Provides for Jacob's Journey -	"
"	**Jacob Journeys to Beersheba** – Map 6(10)	"
"	Jacob Offers Sacrifices at Beersheba -	"
"	**Jacob Journeys to Egypt** – Map 6(11)	"
"	Joseph's Family Enters Egypt -	"
176	Jacob Reunited with Joseph -	"
"	Jacob Meets Pharaoh (at age 130)	"
177	Joseph Provides for Jacob and His Brothers -	"

202

Chapter 9

Joseph
(continued)

Points to Ponder

Points to Ponder
(continued)

18   Noah – How long was he and his family on the Ark?
19   Noah – Which son fathered the first grand-son after the flood?
20   Does "after the flood" mean after the flood began or ended?
21   Noah - Did he curse his grandson Canaan, for something his son Ham did?
22   Nimrod – About when might he have been born?
23   Nimrod – About when might he have died?
24   Nimrod – About when might the Tower of Babel been built?
25   Did God confuse the language of the Godly line?
26   Abraham - Was he Terah's eldest son – he is almost always named first?
27   Abraham - When was his year of birth?
28   Lot – About when might he have been born?
29   Sarah - When was her year of birth?
30   Abraham – About when did God call him?
31   Haran - About when might he have died? (Abraham's eldest brother)
32   Abraham – About when did he marry his half-sister Sarah?
33   Abraham - What might have caused him to move from his homeland?
34   Lot – Did he marry his sister, Iscah?
35   Lot – When did he begin fathering children?
36   King Chedorlaomer – When did he begin to Rule Southern Canaan

Points to Ponder
(continued)

Points to Ponder
(continued)

88   Judah - About how old was his son Er when he died?

Judah's Two Sons Die - Probability Scenario - p.163

89   Judah – What caused Tamar to trick him?

Judah Tricked by Tamar - Probability Scenario - p.163

90   Judah – Was he both a father and a grandfather to the same child? (careful)

Birth of Pharez and Zerah - Probability Scenario - p.166

91   Joseph – How old was he when the famine began?

Seven Years of Famine Begin - Probability Scenario - p.163

92   Joseph – Did his eleven brothers make obeisance to him?

Joseph's Brothers Return and Prove Their Integrity - Gen.43:28 – p.169

93   Jacob – Did his great-grand sons, Hezron and Hamul, actually enter Egypt?

Joseph's Family Enters Egypt – Note – p.174

94   Jacob – How old was he when he entered Egypt?

Jacob Meets Pharaoh – Scripture text – p.176

95   Jacob – How many years did he live in Egypt?

Death of Jacob – Scripture text – p.181

96   Jacob – Which of his sons carried on the Godly line?

Jacob Blesses His Sons and Declares Their Future – Gen.49:10 – p.179

97   Jacob – Which of his sons received the highest praise?

Jacob Blesses His Sons and Declares Their Future – Gen.49:22-26 – p.179

98   Which of his sons lived the longest?

Ex.1:6 & 6:16 – p.183

99   Which person born in the Patriarchal period lived the longest? (careful)

See p.183 (last entry)

100 How old was he when he died?

See bottom of next page

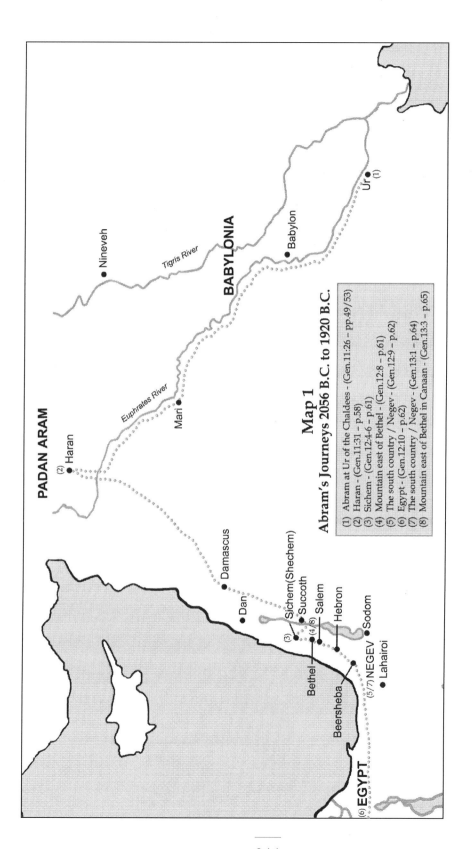

Map 1
Abram's Journeys 2056 B.C. to 1920 B.C.

(1) Abram at Ur of the Chaldees - (Gen.11:26 - pp.49/53)
(2) Haran - (Gen.11:31 - p.58)
(3) Sichem - (Gen.12:4-6 - p.61)
(4) Mountain east of Bethel - (Gen.12:8 - p.61)
(5) The south country / Negev - (Gen.12:9 - p.62)
(6) Egypt - (Gen.12:10 - p.62)
(7) The south country / Negev - (Gen.13:1 - p.64)
(8) Mountain east of Bethel in Canaan - (Gen.13:3 - p.65)

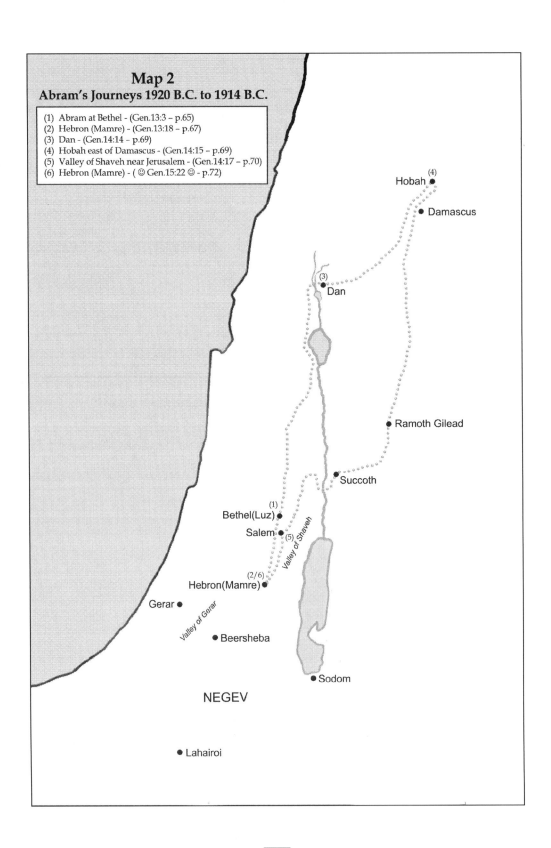

Map 2
Abram's Journeys 1920 B.C. to 1914 B.C.

(1) Abram at Bethel - (Gen.13:3 – p.65)
(2) Hebron (Mamre) - (Gen.13:18 – p.67)
(3) Dan - (Gen.14:14 – p.69)
(4) Hobah east of Damascus - (Gen.14:15 – p.69)
(5) Valley of Shaveh near Jerusalem - (Gen.14:17 – p.70)
(6) Hebron (Mamre) - (☺ Gen.15:22 ☺ - p.72)

Hobah (4)

Damascus

(3) Dan

Ramoth Gilead

Succoth

Bethel(Luz) (1)

Salem (5)

Valley of Shaveh

Hebron(Mamre) (2/6)

Gerar

Valley of Gerar

Beersheba

Sodom

NEGEV

Lahairoi

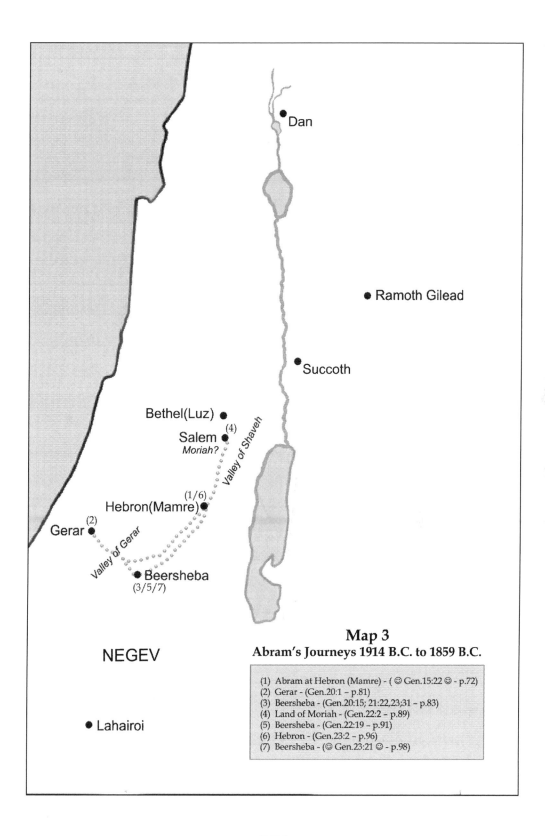

Dan

Ramoth Gilead

Succoth

Bethel(Luz)

Salem (4)
Moriah?

Valley of Shaveh

Hebron(Mamre) (1/6)

Gerar (2)

Valley of Gerar

Beersheba
(3/5/7)

NEGEV

Lahairoi

Map 3
Abram's Journeys 1914 B.C. to 1859 B.C.

(1) Abram at Hebron (Mamre) - (☺ Gen.15:22 ☺ - p.72)
(2) Gerar - (Gen.20:1 – p.81)
(3) Beersheba - (Gen.20:15; 21:22,23;31 – p.83)
(4) Land of Moriah - (Gen.22:2 – p.89)
(5) Beersheba - (Gen.22:19 – p.91)
(6) Hebron - (Gen.23:2 – p.96)
(7) Beersheba - (☺ Gen.23:21 ☺ - p.98)

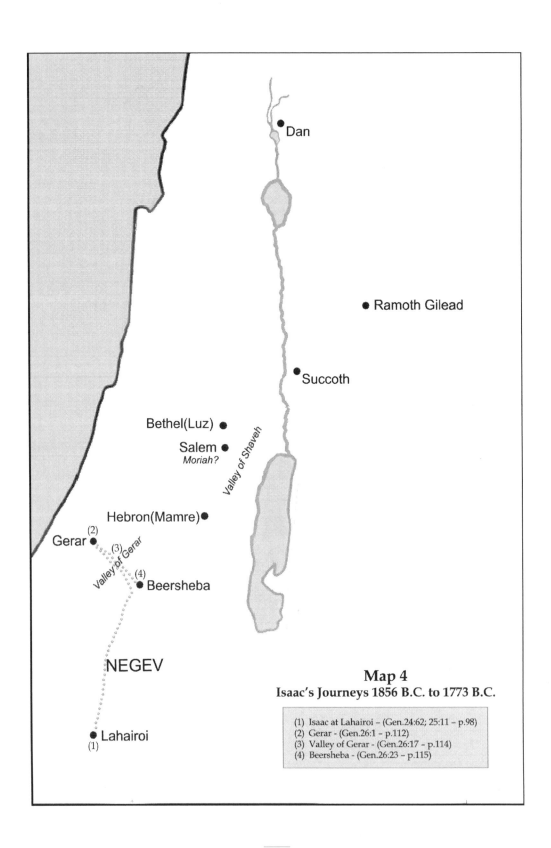

Dan

Ramoth Gilead

Succoth

Bethel(Luz)

Salem
Moriah?

Valley of Shaveh

Hebron(Mamre)

Gerar (2)

(3)
Valley of Gerar

(4) Beersheba

NEGEV

Map 4
Isaac's Journeys 1856 B.C. to 1773 B.C.

(1) Isaac at Lahairoi – (Gen.24:62; 25:11 – p.98)
(2) Gerar - (Gen.26:1 – p.112)
(3) Valley of Gerar - (Gen.26:17 – p.114)
(4) Beersheba - (Gen.26:23 – p.115)

Lahairoi
(1)

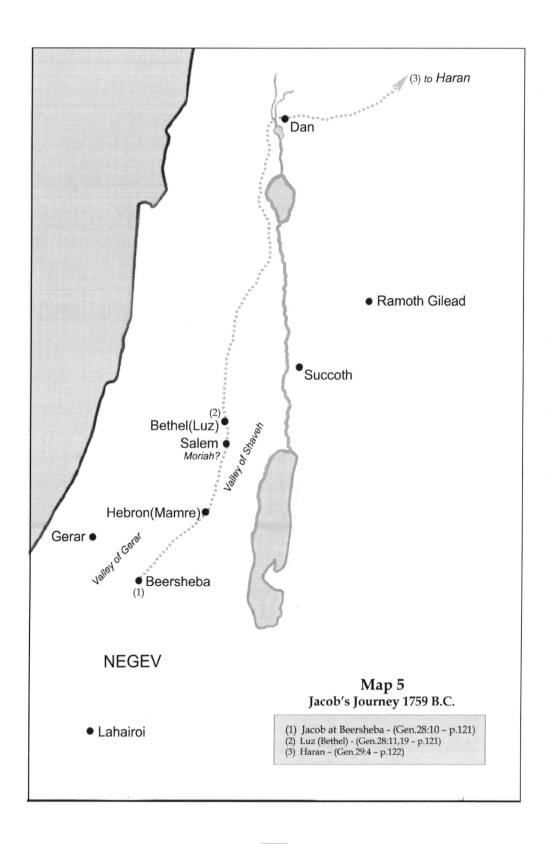

(3) *to Haran*

Dan

● Ramoth Gilead

● Succoth

(2)
Bethel(Luz) ●
Salem ●
Moriah?

Valley of Shaveh

Hebron(Mamre) ●

Gerar ●

Valley of Gerar

● Beersheba
(1)

NEGEV

Map 5
Jacob's Journey 1759 B.C.

(1) Jacob at Beersheba - (Gen.28:10 – p.121)
(2) Luz (Bethel) - (Gen.28:11,19 – p.121)
(3) Haran – (Gen.29:4 – p.122)

● Lahairoi

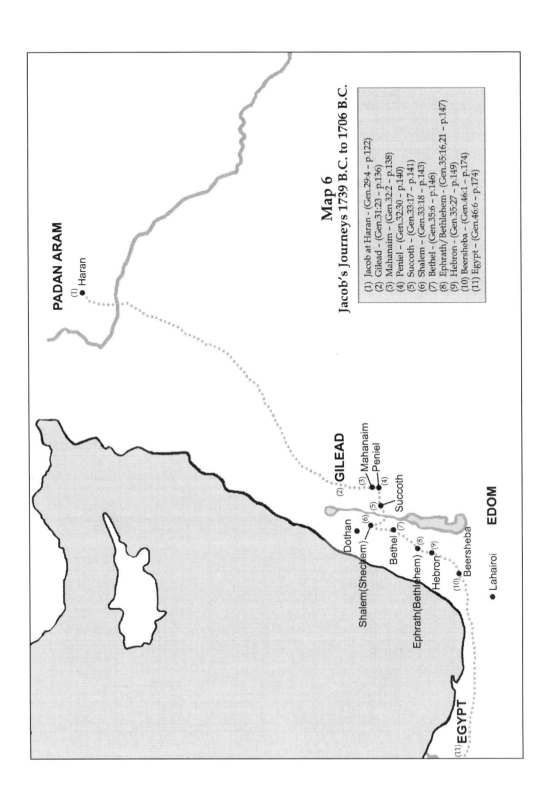

Map 6
Jacob's Journeys 1739 B.C. to 1706 B.C.

(1) Jacob at Haran - (Gen.29:4 - p.122)
(2) Gilead - (Gen.31:23 - p.136)
(3) Mahanaim - (Gen.32:2 - p.138)
(4) Peniel - (Gen.32:30 - p.140)
(5) Succoth - (Gen.33:17 - p.141)
(6) Shalem - (Gen.33:18 - p.143)
(7) Bethel - (Gen.35:6 - p.146)
(8) Ephrath/Bethlehem - (Gen.35:16,21 - p.147)
(9) Hebron - (Gen.35:27 - p.149)
(10) Beersheba - (Gen.46:1 - p.174)
(11) Egypt - (Gen.46:6 - p.174)

PADAN ARAM

(1) Haran

GILEAD

(2)

(3) Mahanaim
Peniel (4)

(5) Succoth

Dothan

Shalem(Shechem) (6)

Bethel (7)

Ephrath(Bethlehem) (8)

Hebron (9)

(10) Beersheba

EDOM

• Lahairoi

EGYPT

(11)

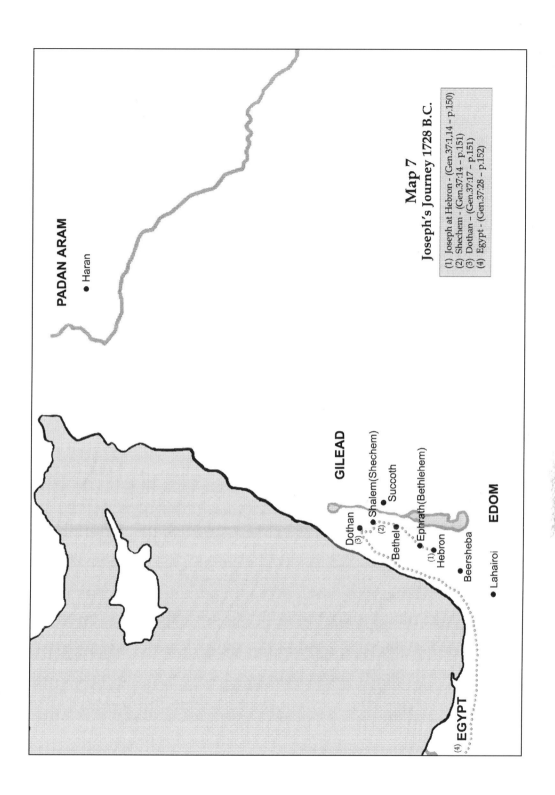

PADAN ARAM

• Haran

GILEAD

Shalem(Shechem)
• Succoth
Dothan •
(3)
(2)
Bethel •
Ephrath(Bethlehem)
•
(1)
Hebron
• Beersheba

EDOM

• Lahairoi

EGYPT
(4)

Map 7
Joseph's Journey 1728 B.C.

(1) Joseph at Hebron - (Gen.37:1,14 - p.150)
(2) Shechem - (Gen.37:14 - p.151)
(3) Dothan - (Gen.37:17 - p.151)
(4) Egypt - (Gen.37:28 - p.152)

Genesis Genea

Born Date BC (Before Christ)	Born Date AC (After Creation)	Age Begot	Age Lived on	Age Died	Died Date AC (After Creation)	Died Date BC (Before Christ)	4000	3900	3800	3700	3600	3500
4004	0	130	800	930	930	3074	ADAM x———					
see Gen.	1:27	5:3	5:4	5:5			4004 - - - - - - - - -					
3874	130	105	807	912	1042	2962		SETH x—				
see Gen.	5:3	5:6	5:7	5:8				3874 - - - - - -				
3769	235	90	815	905	1140	2864		ENOSH x—				
see Gen.	5:6	5:9	5:10	5:11				3769 - - - - -				
3679	325	70	840	910	1235	2769			CAINAN x—			
see Gen.	5:9	5:12	5:13	5:14					3679 - - - -			
3609	395	65	830	895	1290	2714			MAHALALEL x—			
see Gen.	5:12	5:15	5:16	5:17					3609 - - - -			
3544	460	162	800	962	1422	2582				JARED x—		
see Gen.	5:15	5:18	5:19	5:20						3544 - - -		
3382	622	65	300	365	987	3017						ENOCH
see Gen.	5:18	5:21	5:22	5:23								
3317	687	187	782	969	1656	2348						METHUSELAH
see Gen.	5:21	5:25	5:26	5:27								
3130	874	182	595	777	1651	2353						
see Gen.	5:25	5:28	5:30	5:31								
2948	1056	502	448	950	2006	1998						
see Gen.	5:28	05:32	No Ref	9:29								
2446	1558	100	500	600	2158	1846						
see Gen.	5:32	11:10	11:11	No Ref								
2346	1658	35	403	438	2096	1908						
see Gen.	11:10	11:12	11:13	No Ref								
2311	1693	30	403	433	2126	1878						
see Gen.	11:12	11:14	11:15	No Ref								
2281	1723	34	430	464	2187	1817						
see Gen.	11:14	11:16	11:17	No Ref								
2247	1757	30	209	239	1996	2008						
see Gen.	11:16	11:18	11:19	No Ref								
2217	1787	32	207	239	2026	1978						
see Gen.	11:18	11:20	11:21	No Ref								
2185	1819	30	200	230	2049	1955						
see Gen.	11:20	11:22	11:23	No Ref								
2155	1849	29	119	148	1997	2007						
see Gen.	11:22	11:24	11:25	No Ref								
2126	1878	130	75	205	2083	1921						
see Gen.	11:24	11:32-12:4	No Ref	11:32								
1996	2008	100	75	175	2183	1821						
see Gen.	11:26	21:5	No Ref	25:7								
1896	2108	60	120	180	2288	1716						
see Gen.	21:5	25:26	No Ref	35:28								
1836	2168	91	56	147	2315	1689						
see Gen.	25:26	No Ref	No Ref	47:28								
1745	2259	Unknown	110	110	2369	1635						
see Gen.	No Ref	No Ref	50:26	50:26								

logical Chart

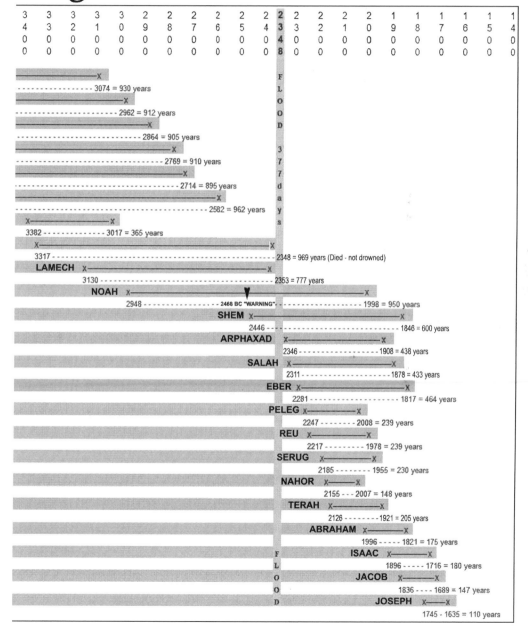

3 4 0 0	3 3 0 0	3 2 0 0	3 1 0 0	3 0 0 0	2 9 0 0	2 8 0 0	2 7 0 0	2 6 0 0	2 5 0 0	2 4 0 0	2 3 4 8	2 3 0 0	2 2 0 0	2 1 0 0	2 0 0 0	1 9 0 0	1 8 0 0	1 7 0 0	1 6 0 0	1 5 0 0	1 4 0 0

x
-------------- 3074 = 930 years
x
------------------ 2962 = 912 years
x
------------------- 2864 = 905 years
x
-------------------- 2769 = 910 years
x
---------------------- 2714 = 895 years
x
------------------------ 2582 = 962 years

x————————x
3382 ------------- 3017 = 365 years

x ——————————————————————————— x
3317 - 2348 = 969 years (Died - not drowned)

LAMECH x—————————————————x
3130 - 2353 = 777 years

NOAH x————————————▼————————————x
2948 - - - - - - - - - - - - - - **2468 BC "WARNING"** - - - - - - - - - - - - - - - - 1998 = 950 years

SHEM x——————————————————x
2446 - 1846 = 600 years

ARPHAXAD x————————————x
2346 - - - - - - - - - - - - - - - - - - - 1908 = 438 years

SALAH x————————————x
2311 - - - - - - - - - - - - - - - - - - - 1878 = 433 years

EBER x————————————————x
2281 - - - - - - - - - - - - - - - - - - - 1817 = 464 years

PELEG x—————————x
2247 - - - - - - - - 2008 = 239 years

REU x—————————x
2217 - - - - - - - - 1978 = 239 years

SERUG x—————————x
2185 - - - - - - - 1955 = 230 years

NAHOR x———————x
2155 - - - 2007 = 148 years

TERAH x————————x
2126 - - - - - - - 1921 = 205 years

ABRAHAM x————————x
1996 - - - - - 1821 = 175 years

ISAAC x————————x
1896 - - - - - 1716 = 180 years

JACOB x————————x
1836 - - - - 1689 = 147 years

JOSEPH x———————x
1745 - 1635 = 110 years

FLOOD 377 days

FLOOD

219

Made in the USA
Lexington, KY
17 May 2014